The *Turkish Embassy Letters* were written by **Lady Mary Wortley Montagu** after her return to England as an edited version of her actual correspondence and provide an intriguing example of authorial selectivity. In the letters Montagu treats the political, historical and social mores of the German, Austrian and Turkish courts, interweaving her narrative with observations on her reading of classical and contemporary writers. She became a great admirer of Turkish culture, documenting in detail the position of women within it, and came to the startling conclusion that the veil provided women with a freedom undreamed of in the West.

Friendships with poets such as Pope, Congreve and Addison, and her connection with Whig politicians through her father and husband, gave Lady Mary access to the worlds of literature and politics. Her confidence and education claimed for her letters, essays and poems an authority rare in a society that debarred women from public life.

Anita Desai is the renowned author of *Clear Light of Day*, *In Custody* and *Baumgartner's Bombay*, amongst other novels. Born and educated in India, she now lives in Delhi, in the USA, where she teaches English at Mount Holyoke College, and in Britain, where she is a Fellow of Girton College, Cambridge.

Malcolm Jack is an independent scholar living in London. A specialist in eighteenth-century English and French literature, his doctoral thesis was on Mandeville. He is the author of *Corruption and Progress: The Eighteenth-Century Debate*; *William Beckford: An English Fidalgo* and the editor of *Vathek and Other Stories: a William Beckford Reader* and *The Episodes of Vatheli*.

LADY MARY WORTLEY MONTAGU

THE

TURKISH EMBASSY

LETTERS

Introduction by

ANITA DESAI

Text edited and annotated by

MALCOLM JACK

Virago

A *Virago* Book

Published by Virago Press 1994

Reprinted 1995, 1996, 1998, 2000, 2001, 2003

This edition first published in Great Britain by Pikkering & Chatto
in the Pikkering Women's Classics Series, edited by Janet Todd 1993

Introduction copyright © Anita Desai 1993
Textual note copyright © Malcolm Jack 1993

The moral right of the author has been asserted.

A CIP catalogue record for this book
is available from the British Library.

ISBN 1 85381 679 5

Printed and bound in Great Britain by Clays Ltd, St Ives plc

Virago Press
An imprint of
Time Warner Books UK
Brettenham House
Lancaster Place
London WC2E 7EN

www.virago.co.uk

CONTENTS

INTRODUCTION

At a gathering, in 1697, of eminent Whigs with literary and political ambitions at the Kit-Kat Club, Lord Kingston nominated his daughter Mary as their toast for the year. When the others objected that they had never set eyes on the candidate, he had her finely dressed and brought to the tavern. She had her health drunk by all present and was passed from lap to lap of the poets and statesmen gathered there. Her granddaughter, Lady Louisa Stuart, was often to describe this heady experience of being 'feasted with sweetmeats, overwhelmed with caresses', but went on to say, 'and ... what pleased her better than either, heard her wit and beauty loudly extolled on every side. Pleasure, she said, was too poor a word to express her sensations; they amounted to ecstasy.'[1]

Perhaps this was the experience that Lady Mary tried to match for the rest of her life, for she remarked later: 'I came young into the hurry of the world.'[2] Not that recognition and adulation were handed to her on a silver salver. Although her birth, in 1689, seemed auspicious enough, her father, Evelyn Pierrepont, being elected to Parliament for East Retford in Nottinghamshire that same year, and destined to inherit his mother Elizabeth Pierrepont's estate and his father the Earl of Kingston's title, her childhood was not entirely happy. Her mother, Lady Mary Fielding, the daughter of the Earl of Denbigh, bore four children in three and a half years, and died in 1693, a tragedy that her daughter Mary described, in an autobiographical novel, in heart-rending terms: 'The death of a noble Mother, whose virtue and good sense might have supported and instructed her youth, which was left to a young Father who, tho' naturally an honest man, was abandoned to his

pleasures, and (like most of his quality) did not think himself
obliged to be very attentive to his child's education.'[3] In fact, he
handed over his three daughters and one son to his mother,
Elizabeth Pierrepont, at West Dean, near Salisbury, so that Lady
Mary spent the first eight years of her life in a solid, square
Jacobean manor set in groves of elm trees and surrounded by
terraces, parks, water channels and deer. It was clearly in the
most fortunate part of England that she found herself, one that
protected such property by acts of Parliament like the Inclosure
Act and the Black Act of 1723, conceived to keep land, timber,
corn and game in the hands of the wealthy and privileged and as
far from the poor and the desperate as the art of Gainsborough
and Reynolds is from that of Hogarth and Rowlandson. Although
it was evidently a lovely and comfortable home for the children,
Lady Mary seldom referred to the place later, and seemed to
retain only one memory of it, that of her 'childish desire of
catching the setting sun, which I can remember running very
hard to do: a fine thing truly if it could be caught; but experience soon shows it to be impossible' (as she wrote later to her
daughter, Lady Bute).[4] If childhood experiences and desires do
affect the course of later life, then this was surely symbolic.

The sun she chased soon manifested itself in literary terms.
When Elizabeth Pierrepont died, in 1698 – leaving a fortune of
£12,000 to her youngest granddaughter Evelyn, £1,000 to
Frances, and nothing at all to Lady Mary, an omission for which
no explanation has been discovered and which seemed to lead to
no ill-will or resentment either – Lady Mary began to divide her
time between her father's country seat, Thoresby, and his
London house which was a splendid Palladian mansion. What
delighted the child was not the architecture but the libraries
these houses contained, and that supplied her with whatever
education she can be said to have had, her formal teaching
having been 'one of the worst in the world.'[5] Escaping from the
superstitions and false notions'[6] that were all that lady had to
give her, Lady Mary took refuge amongst her father's books and,
by the age of fourteen, had read Dryden, Fletcher, Congreve,
Molière and Corneille, as well as a large number of French and

English romances with richly redolent titles like *Grand Cyrus,
Pharimond, Almahide* and *Parthenissa*. Clearly under their influence,
she wrote poems that she copied into an album entitled 'Poems,
Songs & c. Dedicated to the Fair Hands of the Beauteous
Hermensilde by her most obedient Strephon', and to which she
supplied a preface:

> I Question not but here is very manny faults but if any reason-
> able Person considers 3 things they would forgive them
> 1   I am a Woman
> 2   without any advantage of Education
> 3   all these was writ at the age of 14.[7]

The verses inscribed within reveal the usual juvenile need to
imitate, in varying degrees of clumsiness and success, as well as
stilted adult reflections on love, life and death.

Another volume, *The Entire Works of Clarinda*, written a year or
two later, showed growing self-confidence and imagination as
she described Strephon's quest for true love: finding himself in a
castle called Marriage, he encountered Discord, Strife and
Uneasiness, and learnt that 'Love and marriage are irreconcil-
able enemies.'[8] (One can hardly refrain from thinking of Lady
Mary as having been a child prophetess.)

Next she developed such a passion for Ovid's *Metamorphoses*
that she resolved to learn Latin 'with the help of an uncommon
memory and indefatigable labour.'[9] Hiding from her governess,
with a Latin dictionary and grammar, she pursued this secret
passion for as long as ten hours a day, if she is to be believed,
later receiving kindly encouragement from Dr Burnet, the
Bishop of Salisbury, who helped her with her translation of
Epictetus's *Enchiridion*.

Clearly she had launched her own career as a proverbial
'bluestocking' (a term that actually came into use half a century
later, but was famously applied to a relation of hers by marriage,
Elizabeth Montagu), but when she was seventeen years old,
her father became the Marquess of Dorchester and a full-
blooded representative of a class of parliamentarians who
thought of politics as a means to acquiring a fortune as well as

power and influence in Church and State. The notion of the divine right of kings had been revoked in 1689 and in 1714 the Protestant Hanoverians had triumphed over the Catholic Stuarts. The social ambitions of men like her father rose with their political and financial status. The daughter was permitted tuition in such aristocratic indulgences as drawing and Italian, but also, more seriously, in the art of carving. Lady Mary took lessons in it three times a week from 'a carving master'[10] so that she could preside over her father's dinner table. At parties she had to dine alone beforehand so that she could apply herself to the arduous task of slicing the mutton and serving the guests who would have been offended if not shown such service (the master being employed in passing the bottle).

This was surely a dire fate for a young woman capable of writing in imitation of Ovid's Epistles and Virgil's Eclogues, but her role of hostess did bring her in touch with some of the library luminaries of the Augustan Age such as Joseph Addison, Richard Steele and William Congreve, for it was a time when politics and letters knew no division but lived off each other, creating an urbane, sophisticated, anti-romantic and even cynical literature that delighted in witticism, satire and innuendo. A less confident or ambitious girl might have found such company overwhelming but clearly Lady Mary found herself a match for it.

A life of letters was not that of a recluse in such circumstances, and Lady Mary participated in the social whirl of the winter season along with other young débutantes and heiresses. Amongst them was one Anne Wortley whose brother was Edward Wortley Montagu, a grandson of the first Earl of Sandwich, and known for his political aspirations as well as his friendships with such literary figures of the day as Steele and Addison. As a wealthy young man who had gone to Westminster School and Trinity College, Cambridge, then to the Middle Temple where he was called to the bar at twenty-one, and in 1705 elected to Parliament from Huntingdon, he had a bright future. Lady Mary would have been equally impressed by the fact that Addison had dedicated a volume of *The Tatler* to him. He appears to have been charmed by her wit and beauty and sent her gifts and flattering letters, with his sister Anne acting as the intermediary till she died, suddenly, in 1709.

The friendship continued, and the correspondence grew to voluminous proportions. What is striking is how dominant is the element of argument in it: the two seem scarcely ever to have agreed, whether discussing their mutual friends or the relative merits of town and country. Perhaps it was what made their relationship interesting to them, and so did the fact that it had to be kept a secret from Lord Pierrepont who had his own plans for his daughter. When Wortley finally made a formal proposal, the father insisted on two conditions being met – that he was to maintain a house in London, and that his estate be entailed to the first son born to him. The negotiations were conducted purely on points of finance, and the discussions were precise but interminable, and came to nothing: neither would give way and Wortley was dismissed as a suitor. The indignant young man contributed an essay to *The Tatler* in which he denounced the system of mercenary marital arrangements. His point of view was not, however, feminist, since his sympathies lay chiefly with the male suitor of the woman put at auction: 'Her first lover has ten to one against him. The very hour after he has opened his heart and his rent rolls he is made no other use of but to raise her price ...'[11]

Although Lady Mary had a natural inclination to intrigue and appears to have been excited by the twists and turns of the negotiations, warning Wortley of other suitors being entertained by her father after he himself had departed on a tour of Europe, she seems also to have felt bitterly the indignity of her situation. When Wortley tried to find out, none too delicately, the size of her dowry, she replied: 'People in my way are sold like slaves; and I cannot tell what price my master will put on me.'[12] Many years later she wrote 'An Essay on the Mischief of Giving Fortunes with Women in Marriage', advising its abolition since it led to men choosing wives for their dowries rather than their qualities and doomed such marriages to disaster. When she guessed how serious was Wortley's interest in her dowry, she broke with him, writing: 'You say you are not determined; let me determine for you, and save you the trouble of writing again. Adieu forever! make no answer.'[13] Unfortunately, she tended to bid such dramatic farewells too often.

At this stage, the Whig government was replaced by a Tory parliament, but Wortley retained his seat and hurried back from Europe to take it in the Opposition where he put forward a bill forbidding a Member to accept a pension from the Ministry. This would have reduced corruption to a large degree, as the 'pension' was no less than a bribe, and for that very reason the bill was defeated in the House of Lords. During this time Lady Mary was ordered by her father to remain in the country but when she returned to London, she managed to meet Wortley again at dances, the theatre and the opera, as well as at private assignations in the homes of friends like the Steeles and Lady Jekyll. Still, Wortley resented her many other friendships and frequently voiced his jealousy of other young men he thought she favoured. Lady Mary's replies were both frank and realistic, and she wound up with the hint, 'If you can like me on my own terms, 'tis not to me you must make your proposals.'[14] The courtship was so involved as to resemble Richardson's novel *Clarissa*, as Lady Mary herself noticed when she read it thirty-five years later.

An example of the mercenary marriages contracted in those days: her brother William, still legally a child, was married to the sixteen-year-old Rachel Baynton, the illegitimate daughter of John Hall whose huge estate was settled on the young Lord Kingston, as also was Lord Dorchester's. Lady Mary prophesied no good would come of it, and when William was twenty he died of smallpox, leaving an eighteen-year-old widow with two small children. The young widow later lived with Lord Scarborough, expecting he would marry her, and when he refused, lost her power of speech and died. Lord Scarborough then became engaged to the Duchess of Manchester but committed suicide before his wedding day. Altogether, this string of lurid events should have caused Lord Dorchester pause for thought, but he would not give up meddling with his children's lives to his economic satisfaction and forbade Lady Mary to see Wortley again; he found as her new suitor one who might have been invented by P. G. Wodehouse – the Honourable Clotworthy Skeffington, son and heir to the Irish Viscount Massereene. He offered Lady Mary the town house her father demanded, as well as pin money and a settlement in the event of her widowhood. If she refused to marry him, Lord Dorchester told his daughter, she would have no more than £400 a year from him.

Lady Mary now proposed elopement to Wortley, romantically suggesting they settle in Naples. There is no evidence that Wortley encouraged this rosy dream – he had not only a political career to pursue but his family's immensely lucrative coal mines to manage – but it is to his credit that he agreed to elope with her, knowing he would forfeit her dowry if he did so. Arrangements were already underway for Lady Mary's wedding to Skeffington when a slight delay occurred – the marriage contract had to be sent back to Ireland for a signature and an amendment – and in this fortuitous gap of time, Lady Mary laid her cloak-and-dagger plans for elopement, as romantic as any in the French novels of her adolescence. The couple's talent for disagreement continued unabated, however, and while she waited on her balcony at the appointed hour, Wortley managed to be late, so that she was bundled into a coach and sent to West Dean, Wortley pursuing the coach on horseback. At one point, they spent the night at the same inn but without realizing it (restoration comedy was not so unlike life after all) and it is remarkable that they finally managed to meet, to escape, and to be married, at Salisbury, on 15 October 1712.

Had her life resembled one of the romances Lady Mary had loved as a girl, the story would now be ended with the sound of church bells, but in fact the romance came quickly and inexplicably to an end. Naples was never mentioned again, Wortley spent all his time away from his bride, attending to his political and business interests, and leaving her to move from the country home of one relation to another, till she finally rented one herself, in Middlethorpe, near York, with no help from him whatsoever. Even the birth of their son, Edward, in May 1713, did not bring Wortley closer to her. The letters she wrote him rang with bitter complaints of being neglected; Wortley rarely replied, and one can only speculate on the reasons for his absence of passion: probably it had existed only in her imagination. She had to content herself with her son and her life in the country about which she expressed her feelings in a semi-comic poem, 'The Bride in the Country', until the situation changed suddenly and dramatically.

On 1 August 1714 Queen Anne died and the Elector of Hanover was proclaimed king. With this proclamation the Tories went into decline and the Whigs into the ascendant. Lady Mary threw herself with enthusiasm into persuading Wortley to stand for election, choosing him a safe constituency, and even suggesting he 'buy some little Cornish borough.'[15] Her years as hostess in her father's house had prepared her and given her an appetite for just such dealings, and the lack of scruples she revealed so plainly was entirely in keeping with the times.

Wortley won the seat for the City of Westminster and Lady Mary arrived in London in January 1715 for the opening of Parliament. Her deeply resented exile in the country over, she set up house in Duke Street, close to St James's Palace, and ingratiated herself with the King (whom she privately called 'an honest blockhead')[16] and his court. George I was hardly glamorous – he spoke no English and brought with him two elderly German mistresses – but Lady Mary managed to find enjoyment in the social round of teas, cards, gossip, opera and the playhouse. She also befriended literary men such as the Abbé Conti, the poet John Gay and, most importantly, Alexander Pope. With Pope she collaborated, in the spirit of fun, in adapting Virgil's pastoral eclogues into satiric town eclogues in which the London belles and beaux replaced classical shepherds and shepherdesses. At this stage her literary ambitions seem to have been chiefly playful and did not include publication: she circulated her verses amongst friends, and advised Lord Cornbury that 'it was not the business of men of quality to turn author, and that he should confine himself to the applause of his friends and by no means venture on the press.'[17] (In this she also showed her critical acumen.) Caricature combined for her most delightfully with gossip.

At this juncture she was tragically struck by smallpox, the dread disease that had killed her brother. She was treated by the two most eminent physicians in London, Hans Sloane and Dr Garth, and recovered, but with her beauty marred: her eyelashes were gone, and her skin deeply pitted. This was not an age of compassion, and wits had it that 'she was very full [of pox] and yet not pitted [pitied].'[18] Lady Mary herself wound up the last of her town eclogues with 'Saturday, or the Small Pox', in which Flavia's beauty is ruined and she bids farewell to the world.

Once again she had displayed her prophetic gifts, for just then Wortley was appointed Ambassador Extraordinary to the Court of Turkey, to replace Sir Robert Sutton. He was also to represent the Levant Company which held the charter for trade in the Near East; the latter provided him with £500 for expenses. Lady Mary, who retained her essentially romantic spirit under the lacquered veneer of the society lady and wit, was charmed by the prospect of travel in the East; the fact that appointments were made for five years at a time and could extend to ten or fifteen did not deter her: it meant only that the preparations had to be lengthy and monumental. She had to engage servants, a maid for her child, a chaplain and a surgeon, as well as see to provisions: there was much discussion of the cost of livery, with or without lace. Her friends gave her several small commissions and farewells were made; Pope's was magnificently emotional and for a present he copied out the five town eclogues they had written together into an album bound in red leather.

The Montagus left for Turkey on 2 August 1716 on board a yacht bound for Holland, Lady Mary wearing 'a full-bottomed black wig'[19] for the occasion.

Wortley had been entrusted with a diplomatic task to which he

proved sadly inadequate. Turkey was at war with the Venetian
Republic; Austria was committed by treaty to come to the aid of
Venice. England needed to prevent Austria from becoming
embroiled as its support was required to offset Spanish power in
the Mediterranean. Wortley was given a letter to the Emperor
Charles VI with the proposal that England might mediate and
bring about a truce. This required the Montagus to travel
through Holland to Austria, Lady Mary appreciating the clean-
liness and orderliness of the Dutch towns she passed through on
the way. When they reached Vienna, the Imperial Army under
Prince Eugene of Savoy had already defeated a Turkish army
twice its size at Peterwardein and driven it as far back as
Belgrade. It was thought the Turks could be driven further
without Belgrade having to be captured. Wortley was to try and
bring about a peace treaty. He spent two months in Vienna for
the purpose, and Lady Mary had the opportunity to observe the
court of Vienna and compare it with the English court.
Curiously, there is no mention in her letters of Wortley's
negotiations and she seems to have taken no part in his official
activities, withholding the advice she had given freely earlier.
She was either distracted by the novelty of the scene, or she was
being diplomatically discreet. She made friends at court, and her
wit and vivacity appear to have captivated the King, making her
a great favourite. They spent the carnival season in Vienna, then
set off across the plains of Hungary for Peterwardein, the
Turkish Sultan Ahmed III having expressed his willingness to
allow the English to mediate. Travel by boat down the Danube
was not possible since it was frozen, so their coaches were
attached to sleighs and the journey proved faster and easier than
they had expected. They reached Buda and found it devastated
by the war between Turkey and Austria, and travelled on to
Peterwardein where they were given an Imperial escort of 100
musketeers, 50 grenadiers and 50 hussars and met by a Turkish
guard of 130 horsemen as escort to Belgrade. Their host here
was the learned and cultivated *effendi* Ahmed Bey who charmed
Lady Mary with his knowledgable talk of the literature and
culture of his land. At the same time there were brutal scenes to

be witnessed in the city which was controlled not so much by the pasha as by the barbaric janissaries who looted the country and terrorized the population. Travelling through a land both physically and metaphorically 'plagued', they reached Adrianople, the Sultan having transferred the court to the more salubrious surroundings of gardens and villas along the river.

Lady Mary settled down in a palace and quickly made friends with the French ambassador's wife and went sightseeing, studied Arabic and read Arabic poetry. Meanwhile Wortley negotiated with the Grand Vizier and obtained the terms of the truce: the Turks would stop fighting if Temeshwar were restored to them. He sent the terms to Vienna, confident of their acceptance. In Vienna, they were considered absurd – he had been sent to Turkey to urge them to sign a truce, not plead on Turkey's behalf. Wortley had returned to Constantinople and rented a palace in Pera, on a hill overlooking the Golden Horn, unaware that Abraham Stanyan, the English ambassador to Vienna, was conniving to have him removed from his post for incompetence. Stanyan was able to convince Lord Sunderland that the terms Wortley had negotiated were unacceptable, and offered his own services 'in case Mr Wortley be recalled.'[20] In September 1717, Addison, by then Secretary of State, informed the Levant Company that Wortley was recalled and Stanyan appointed ambassador. Addison also wrote to Wortley, trying to console him with the post of Auditor of the Imprest, saying this would bring him closer to the King. By the time Wortley received the news, the Admiralty had already ordered a ship to carry him home with his family. Wortley showed his naïvety by appealing to Prince Eugene to intercede with the King on his behalf and naturally met with an icy rebuff.

In some distress, the Montagus – now four in number, a daughter having been born five months earlier – sailed on board the *Preston*, Lady Mary telling Wortley: 'I hope 'tis less shocking to you than to me, who have really suffered in my health by the uneasiness it has given me, tho' I take care to conceal it.'[21] Still, her gift for being amused by all she saw and experienced helped her to enjoy the voyage across the Aegean Sea and especially their visits to the ruins of Troy and Carthage which she was able to connect with her early reading of Latin classics. From the port of Leghorn they proceeded to Paris overland, via the Alpine passes, and thence to Calais and the English Channel.

Wortley never again held a post of any importance, nor took an active part in politics. According to the *Dictionary of National Biography*, he 'devoted himself chiefly to saving money' which included endless wrangling with the Levant Company for reimbursement of his embassy expenses. By opposing the Peerage Bill he antagonized Lord Sunderland, and by refusing to support Sir Robert Walpole he brought an end to his political career. (Addison had died shortly after his return.) Lady Mary, who had shown so much ambition on his behalf earlier, appeared to lose interest in him as well. Instead, she involved herself in making known the Turkish method of inoculation against smallpox that she had learnt during her sojourn in Turkey. This provoked a fierce debate in which physicians, surgeons and the Royal Society took part. Lady Mary, who had had her son inoculated in Turkey, now had her daughter inoculated before witnesses. The Princess Caroline followed her example with her two children, in 1722, scandalizing many of her subjects who called it an 'Experiment practised only by a few ignorant Women amongst an illiterate and unthinking people.'[22] Lady Mary remained convinced that it would 'do good to mankind'[23] and was applauded by Steele in *The Plain Dealer*. After her death, a cenotaph commemorating her introduction of inoculation to England was erected in Lichfield Cathedral. In a way, it can also be said to commemorate her brief domicile in Turkey and all that captivated her there.

This was by no means the end of her activities or the full extent of them. Although she and her husband bought a house in the Piazza, Covent Garden, and she resumed court life, managing adroitly to make herself welcome at both St James's Palace and the estranged Prince of Wales's court at Leicester House, she was not destined to end her life a society lady, playing cards and going to the opera. Possibly because Wortley's career was not likely to proceed without the patronage of Sir

Robert Walpole that he had spurned, and possibly because of a fright she received when she was blackmailed by Nicholas François Remond de Saint-Mard for whom she invested and lost money in the South Sea Company, she withdrew to Twickenham and bought a house near Pope's on the bank of the Thames. She claimed to be entirely content with its river view, gardens and grottoes, and declared, 'After having seen part of Asia and Africa, and almost made the tour of Europe, I think the honest English squire more happy, who verily believes the Greek wines less delicious than March beer; that the African fruits have not so fine a flavour as golden pippins . . .'[24]

Far from leading a bucolic existence, however, Lady Mary became the centre of a social whirl that included Pope. It was said in July that year that 'She and Pope keep so close yonder that they are the talk of the whole town.'[25] Pope seemed infatuated with her, commissioning Kneller to paint a portrait of her in Turkish dress, a portrait that he hung in 'his best room fronting the Thames, and there it remained for the rest of his life.'[26]

The friendship proved less steadfast, and by September had degenerated into a vituperative battle. Lady Mary hinted that Pope had made her a passionate declaration of love at which she had laughed, infuriating him. In 'The Lady's Resolve' she wrote, 'Too near he has approached, who is denied.' It is also suggested that Pope grew jealous of the attention paid her by the Duke of Wharton, while some named Lord Hervey as coming between them. It was the custom in their circle to circulate squibs, epigrams and lampoons, and these took an ugly turn when Pope and Lady Mary used them as vehicles for vilification. In a ballad 'The Capon's Tale' Pope made an obscene and libellous attack on her, and in 'The Use of Riches' called Wortley 'Worldly' and Lady Mary 'Lewd Lesbia', thereby making insinuations about her close friendship with Maria Skerrit, first mistress and later second wife of Sir Robert Walpole. In 1733, in 'In Imitation of the First Satire of the Second Book of Horace', he called her 'furious Sappho' and Lord Hervey 'Lord Fanny'. The two retaliated in 'Verses Addressed to the Imitator of Horace, by a Lady', published in *The Daily Post*:

And with the emblem of thy crooked mind
Marked on thy back, like Cain, by God's sure hand,
Wander like him, accursed through the land.

Pope's rejoinder was equally cruel:

How oft from Sappho have I fear'd that fate:
P-x'd by her love or poison'd by her hate.[27]

His scurrilities had their effect and Lady Mary began to
acquire a scandalous reputation. Lady Irwin wrote of her that
'her principles are as corrupt as her wit is entertaining',[28] and
even Lord Chesterfield seemed to share this view when he
called her 'eminent for her parts and her vices'.[29] She did have
staunch friends as well – the early feminist Mary Astell found
her admirable and begged her to publish her Turkish letters,
Edward Young singled her out for praise in his ode 'On
Women', and Voltaire did her the singular honour of giving her
in manuscript his essay on epic poetry for comment. But the
stress of her difficult relationships showed; she admitted to
being frightened of 'the damn'd damn'd quality of growing older
and older every day.'[30] The death of her father moved her, she
worried about her sister Lady Mar who was seriously ill with
depression and her daughter who planned to marry the Earl of
Bute who had no fortune, and her son caused her much pain
and anxiety by repeatedly running away and falling into debt.
He was placed in the care of a tutor and sent to Holland to
avoid scandal. Wortley spent his time in the north, managing his
estate and his fortune, and it was obvious that their marriage
had failed and was unlikely to recover.

At this stage of her life, active but not fulfilling, there stepped a
deus ex machina, a young Italian, Francesco Algarotti, who had
acquired a reputation at the University of Bologna for his record
in natural science, and came to England to reduce Newton's
Optics to a set of dialogues based on Fontenelle's. Voltaire
introduced him to Lord Hervey who in turn introduced him to
Lady Mary. Both of them fell head over heels in love with the

androgynous young man with the full pouting lips and the heavy-lidded dark eyes we see in a portrait by Richardson. He was ambitious, pleased by all the attention he was receiving from the English aristocracy, but he was also fickle and he returned to Italy. Both Lady Mary and Lord Hervey wrote him passionate letters, Lady Mary comparing herself with other love-lorn heroines – Sappho, Dido, Penelope – and Lord Hervey ending his letters with the sigh 'Adio, Carrissmo.'[31] Lady Mary suggested, at first delicately and then more openly, that she join him in Italy (shades of her early desire to live with Wortley in Naples), and appears to have persuaded her husband that her health required a change of air, to which he readily acquiesced. In July 1739, she left for Italy, destined never to see Wortley again and to return to England only to die.

Lord Hervey, who alone knew of her romance with Algarotti, much to his credit kept it a secret, and it was revealed only when Lord Byron came upon some letters of hers in Venice and sent them to his publisher, John Murray, in 1818. Not that there was much to reveal for the romance turned out to be largely a figment of Lady Mary's imagination. Algarotti had found himself a patron – and possibly a lover – in the Crown Prince Frederick of Prussia – who addressed him as 'The Swan of Padua'[32] – and she did not see him till March 1741 when they spent two months together in Turin. He then returned to Prussia and they met only once more, in 1756, when Lady Mary was sixty-seven, and Algarotti ill. In 1758 she wrote a short lyrical poem, 'A Hymn to the Moon', and sent it to him; he published it in a volume of his works, acknowledging it gracefully, and they carried on a literary correspondence in French, but no more was said of a life together.

Algarotti is unlikely, however, to have been her sole reason for departing from England. There was little to keep her there any longer – her marriage an empty charade, her son a source of shame and scandal, many of her friendships ruined by spite and malice; and her early travels, that had provided her with so much delight, seemed to have opened her eyes to the possibilities of a freed personality and a new life unencumbered by her past and her society. In any event, Lady Mary left England without regret, saying 'people were grown so stupid, she could not endure their company, all England was infected with dulness.'[33]

Arrived in Venice, she appears to have been relieved that 'Here it is so much the established fashion for anybody to live their own way that nothing is more ridiculous than censuring the action of another ... We have a clear bright sun, and fogs and factions are things unheard of in this climate.'[34]

Still, like any expatriate, she kept the company of her countrymen in whatever strange part she found herself. Some of them became her close and dear friends, others came merely to look at her because of her reputation. The young Horace Walpole, for instance, who could not forget that she was a friend of his hated stepmother, wrote after seeing her in Florence:

> She is laughed at by the whole town. Her dress, her avarice, and her impudence must amaze any one that never heard her name. She wears a foul mob that does not cover her greasy black locks that hang loose, never combed or curled; an old mazarine blue wrapper that gapes open, and discovers a canvas petticoat. Her face swelled violently to one side ... partly covered with a plaster, and partly with white paint which, for cheapness, she has bought so coarse that you would not use it to wash a chimney.[35]

He called her 'Moll Worthless'[36] and addressed a crude imitation of an ode of Horace to the postchaise in which she travelled:

> Oh Chaise, who art condemn'd to carry
> The rotten hide of Lady Mary,
> To Italy's last corner drive;
> And prithee set her down alive;
> Nor jumble off with jolts and blows,
> The half she yet retains of nose.[37]

Pope heard rumours of her notoriety and wrote to Hugh Bethel

'I wish you had just told me if her character be more avaricious or amatory, and which passion has got the better at last.'[38]

To leave behind such rotten remnants of her disputatious existence, Lady Mary was obliged to travel to Geneva, to Cahambery, and to Avignon where she settled for a while. News came from England of the death of her friend Lord Hervey, and of Pope. More distressing were the many reports of her son's adventures, all of a scandalous nature. She discussed these at length with her husband to whom she continued to write regularly and dutifully and to which he replied with decreasing frequency so that she once ended a letter with the words, 'I beg you would write soon. When you are long silent, I am so uneasy on the account of your health that it affects mine',[39] recalling her early correspondence with him, but, although he visited France three times, no meeting was suggested or arranged. Her chief contact with England during those years was with her daughter, Lady Bute, to whom she addressed all her tenderness and affection, as well as her loneliness. Lady Bute sent her boxes of books to read, for which Lady Mary continued to have a passion, and Lady Mary sent her long letters on the upbringing of her grandchildren. She was particularly keen that her grand-daughters have a good education and this was certainly not heeded by her daughter or son-in-law; the one daughter, Louisa, who showed an inclination to read and study, was laughed at and derided by her family.

Lady Mary continued to move about restlessly, travelling to Brescia, then Gottolengo where she bought a house and laid out an extensive garden with a dairy and poultry with which she busied herself happily, and when she was ill to Lovere where she took the waters on the bank of the Lago d'Iseo. In these years she seems to have become entangled with a strange and hysteri-cal Count Ugolino Palazzi who managed to defraud her of a good many of her possessions, including jewels and money, but to whom she remained grateful for escorting her on her travels and finding her homes to live in even if they were ruins that she first had to restore. She mentioned none of this in her letters home. She was sometimes very ill indeed.

When Wortley died, on 21 January 1761, he left her only £1,200 a year, leaving the bulk of his estate to his daughter and her second son who was to take the name of Wortley. Lady Mary's share can be seen as insulting when one considers the size of the estate he left – £800,000 in money and £17,000 a year in land, mines, and so on, leading Elizabeth Montagu to remark that she hoped it would 'make his heirs as happy and illustrious as the getting it made him anxious and odious.' The will must have dealt Lady Mary a blow but she behaved with all the decorum of a widow and decided to return to England, setting off in September that year. When she reached Rotterdam, she was held up first by the illness of her maid and then by storms. While she waited for calmer weather to sail, she lodged with the Reverend Benjamin Sowden, and gave him a copy of her Turkish letters, inscribing on the cover: 'These two volumes are given to the Rev. Benjamin Sowden, minister at Rotterdam, to be disposed of as he thinks proper. This is the will and design of M. Wortley Montagu.'[40] Once again, she had shown her uncanny ability to foresee the course of events – and also a sober and realistic appraisal of her family. Then, on 15 Janurary 1762, she returned to England after an absence of twenty-three years.

Her daughter, Lady Bute, took a house for her in St George Street, and many of her old friends and acquaintances visited her, some out of mere curiosity, it seems, and Walpole found her 'woefully tedious in her narratives'.[41] Her return seems to have caused her daughter little but unease and apprehension. She feared a flaring up of scandals around her mother again, but Lady Mary was gravely ill with cancer, and lived less than a year, dying on 21 August 1762. During that time she voiced her restlessness and desire to return to Italy. Characteristically, Walpole noted that she left her son £1 in her will, neglecting to mention that he was to inherit her share of her husband's estate; it was typical of the malice of that age. It was not malice, however, but censure that led her daughter to throw the diaries and journals her mother had kept since her marriage onto a fire, consigning to the flames what was surely the most important, intimate and interesting of her mother's writing.

It is highly ironic that out of her long and colourful life, the years best known are the ones she recorded in the *Embassy Letters*, written over a brief period that was lived in foreign parts, far removed from the society and milieu of which she was such a brilliant and celebrated representative. It is not entirely accidental either, because she worked at these letters, evidently intending them for publication, making copies, editing, polishing and weaving in extracts from her journal (which was itself sacrificed to philistinism). At the time, she drew back from publication, seeing the material as unsuitable for the aristocracy, but she apprears to have changed her mind when she handed over the manuscript to the Reverend Sowden, perhaps foreseeing her imminent demise. Her daughter and son-in-law would not hear of publication and bought the manuscript from the Reverend Sowden for £500, but to their shock and horror it found its way into print in 1763 when it appeared in *The London Chronicle*. According to Sowden, a pair of young Englishmen had borrowed the letters for a night and evidently copied them out and smuggled them into a printer's hands. Lady Mary would most likely have approved, as she would of the title page that stated the letters were addressed to 'Persons of Distinction, Men of Letters &c.' The letters reveal a great anxiety to stress that the society Lady Mary moved in was 'of the first quality', the houses she visited belonged to 'people of quality', even the nuns she met were 'all of quality'. She repeatedly pointed out that previous travellers had not come in contact with such society and therefore remained ignorant of its superior civilization, basing their accounts on encounters with the common people. The customs, culture, dress and art she praised so highly were the attributes only of the upper class and not revealed to those whose contact was confined to the poor and the negligible with whom she was not concerned.

At the same time, Lady Mary proved a traveller of 'a very diligent curiosity',[42] and the reason why the *Embassy Letters* have survived the years may be that in travelling to the East she was able to break away from the rigid confinements – mental and intellectual as much as physical – of her own society, and showed herself exceptionally open to new impressions and points of view. This gives her letters an immediacy and vivacity that remain as fresh as the mosaics on the ancient monuments she saw and the eastern gardens that gave her such delight.

To begin with, she tended to compare all she saw with what she had left behind in England, and she could be scathing of foreign ways: Viennese housing shocked her, the apartments of the nobility 'divided but by a partition from that of a taylor or a shoemaker' and 'the great stairs ... as common and dirty as the streets';[43] Austrian women's fashion was 'monstrous, and contrary to all reason and commonsense' including 'fabrics of gauze on their heads, about a yard high, consisting of three or four stories ... exactly of the same shape and kind, but about four times as big as those rolls our prudent milk-maids make use of to fix their pails upon';[44] and Hanoverian morality was extraordinary since 'getting a lover is so far from losing, that 'tis properly getting reputation, ladies being much more respected in regard to the rank of their lovers, than that of their husbands.'[45] Travelling 'in these popish countries'[46] made her acutely aware of her Protestant attitudes, and what she saw of Catholic churches with their 'profusion of pearls, diamonds and rubies bestowed on the adornment of rotten teeth, and dirty rags (relics)'[47] made her deride religious superstition and human gullibility. Still, she enjoyed herself in the European courts and gave praise where praise was due – to the heating provided by the excellent stoves, and the hothouses that furnished the tables with 'ananas' in the dead of winter, both luxuries that she intended to introduce if possible to England.

She was not inclined to exaggerate, and did not colour her accounts with dramatic effects: travelling through the Hungarian plains in winter proved not so arduous, she confessed, when provided with furs to keep one warm and the hospitality of the peasantry that kept the travellers supplied with fowl and venison. The sight of such peasants being harassed and looted by the soldiery – not paid servants of the state but freebooters – aroused in her one of her rare moments of compassion, even if it did not cause her to lose her head: what was the point of giving them money, she reasoned, if the 'bassa' were instantly to relieve them of it. She could even take a plague in her stride, commenting: 'there are many that escape it, nor is the air ever infected.'[48]

Curiously, it was Turkey and her first experience of a non-European, non-Christian civilization that provoked her most open and heart-felt admiration. There was certainly the charm of the new landscape, the splendid views of the Golden Horn from her palace in Pera, the gardens by the river in Adrianople that she likened to scenes from Horace and Theocritus, and the noble architecture of Constantinople – she found more to please her in Santa Sophia than in St Paul's – and she took to Turkish dress and furnishings ('These seats are so easy and convenient that I believe I shall never endure chairs as long as I live'),[49] but what interested her more than monuments or history was the people and their way of life. 'The ruins of Justinian's church ... did not afford me nearly so agreeable a prospect as I had left, being little more than a heap of stones'[50] and 'I took more pleasure in looking on Fatima than on the finest piece of sculpture.'[51]

Her first encounter with Turkish culture was a propitious one: in Belgrade, Ahmed Bey had read Arabic poetry to her that she found so exquisite she copied out verses to send Pope, likening them to the Song of Solomon. The 'sublime style' that Arabs employed for poetry she claimed was the language of the Scriptures. In fact, the dress and manners of the people brought to her mind classical poetry. Although she could not, as a woman, participate in court life, what she heard of it made her think that the manner in which the Sultan bestowed favours was not so different from that of an English court. The severity of Turkish law did not distress her: when she learnt that the punishment for lying was branding, she only remarked that, if it were practised in England, few men would be able to move about with their brows uncovered. In general, she ascribed to lying Greeks the Turkish reputation for harshness. The images of saints in the churches were not beheaded, she argued, but only ravaged by time. She insisted they treated their slaves humanely and that they traded no more in flesh than was done 'as publicly and infamously in all our Christian great cities.'[52] She found it reasonable that matters of family honour were dealt with by the family and not the state, and found it praiseworthy that adoption was undertaken by childless parents in preference to leaving estates to distant and unworthy relations as in England.

Her most heartfelt praise was reserved for Turkish women. She visited several in their homes and did not find their lives confined in any unpleasant way; she found their behaviour within their own company relaxed and natural, as would be that of men together in a coffee-house. Their apartments were beautifully furnished and surrounded by gardens and fountains where they sat embroidering or playing music and where they seemed to lack nothing. She was not in the least shocked by their custom of wearing the veil. In fact, she felt it gave them greater freedom since it allowed them to walk out in the streets without fear of being molested or recognized, and told her female correspondents that this disguise even permitted them to carry out secret assignations. 'I look upon Turkish women as the only free people in the empire.'[53] She herself wore the veil when she wanted to go sightseeing in the city of Constantinople and it helped her to slip undetected into the great mosque of Santa Sophia, an adventure she loved to recount later. She was particularly impressed by the stature accorded to women, the fact that they had money of their own – in some cases, much more than their husbands' – and that husbands were required to provide them with the richest garments and jewels. It was true that a Muslim could have four wives at a time, she allowed, but they rarely did so and would be regarded as rakes and libertines if they did; few women would agree to enter such an arrangement. What was demanded of women was that they bear as many children as possible – some boasted of having had as many as twenty or thirty. When a man died, the widow had to marry again immediately as an unmarried woman was looked upon with suspicion. Whether this was less or more divine than the Christian viewpoint that a virgin is most worthy of God, she left the reader to decide.

Apart from her ability to study an alien culture according to its own values, Lady Mary had a rare ability to see herself through the eyes of others, surely an indispensable talent for a traveller. On first entering a Turkish bath, she was struck by the great beauty of the women there, and by the fact that it was combined with such grace, 'not the least wanton smile or immodest gesture amongst them' or 'those disdainful smiles, and satirical whispers that never fail in our assemblies.'[54] Thinking she must be hot and uncomfortable, they urged her to undress, and when she loosened her bodice, looked at her stays with horror and pity, believing that she was 'locked up in that machine, and that it was not in my power to open it, which contrivance they attributed to my husband.'[55]

Her attitude to Turkish women – her awareness of their superior beauty and particular powers, combined with the beneficent aspects of the veil – was extraordinary enough in her time, but continues to be so in ours; in which 'the veil' has such dark connotations for Western feminists and excites such a passion for 'reform'. She seems to have accepted naturally and instinctively the relativity of cultural and moral values, and defends her views by saying: 'I think it a virtue to admire without any mixture of envy or desire.'[56] She ended her stay in Constantinople by praising its pursuit of 'present pleasure' above that of knowledge or worldly achievement. 'I allow you to laugh at me,' she ends a letter, 'for the sensual declaration in saying that I had rather be a rich effendi, with all his ignorance, than Sir Isaac Newton with all his knowledge.'[57]

Perhaps it was such hedonism that frightened her daughter into trying to suppress the letters, although her alarm seems misplaced when one sees with what enthusiasm they were received. Voltaire declared them superior to Madame de Sévigné's (which had been her own honest opinion: 'very pretty they are, but I assert, without the least vanity, that mine will be full as entertaining forty years hence. I advise you, therefore to put none of them to the use of waste paper.')[58] Dr Johnson and Smollett praised them and Gibbon exclaimed: 'What fire, what ease, what knowledge of Europe and Asia!'[59] Lady Bute had to give up all hope of oblivion when the first edition was sold out, to be followed by others.

Dervla Murphy has said that Lady Mary was 'born too soon. Essentially she was a career woman, who needed the freedoms twentieth-century Englishwomen enjoy. Born 250 years later, she might have been a politician, a diplomat, an academic, a scientist, a writer (most probably the last). Born in 1689, she often had no choice but to go against her "instinctive conscience" and natural inclinations.'[60]

There are certainly tantalizing hints of all these possibilities – her extraordinary interest in the Turkish method of inoculation and her courage in experimenting with it, then her steadfast championing of it in England, being the most interesting of all for a female aristocrat in the eighteenth century – but it is finally as a writer that she is known and must be judged. Lady Mary wrote prolifically all her life; most of what she wrote was circulated privately, a little was published anonymously. The truth is that she was so much a creature of her times that she despised publication, considered it descending to 'trade',[61] and condemned Swift and Pope for being ungrateful to their patrons without whom 'these two superior beings were entitled by their birth and hereditary fortune to be only a couple of link-boys.'[62] She seems never to have realized how great a drawback were her aristocratic upbringing and the snobbishness it bred in her; the two are linked and together they erected a fence around her that proved her jail. The great success of the Turkish letters lies at least partially in the circumstance of her escaping for a year or two from her confining society and experiencing a new world without the prejudices with which she was born.

It is curious to find that Lady Mary who had participated so enthusiastically in the political machinations of the English court in her time, and had been largely responsible for her husband's election and appointment, as his consort in Turkey took no apparent interest in the politics of the place or period but contented herself with visits to the zenana, the mosques and pleasure gardens, and in reporting on these scenes with all the absorption in minutiae of a water colourist.

There are two possible explanations – one, that she later edited out of the letters all references to politics that might have been there originally, and two, that when on foreign soil she became – at least partially – a victim of what Sara Suleri has called 'the feminine picturesque'[63] that permitted English-women in the East no other role but that of an 'amateur ethnographer. They could sketch landscape and capture physiognomy as long as they remained immune to the sociological conclusions of their own data, entering the political domain in order to aestheticize rather than to analyze.'

This might be thought an uncharacteristically subaltern role for Lady Mary to assume; excluded from the political arena in which her husband acted, her role was to record the picturesque. She found herself then in much the same position as the ladies of the zenana. They did not seem to her so strange; on the contrary, they seemed entirely sympathetic, and her mind remained analytic enough to see that, in the context of their situation, they wielded power and influence of the kind she herself had known and understood.

It was in the later period of British imperialism that no English-woman, representing as she did the authority of Empire, could afford to make such an admission. In 1850, Fanny Parks wrote in her two-volume journal, *The Wanderings of a Pilgrim in Search of the Picturesque during Four and Twenty Years in the East, with Revelations of Life in the Zenana*, 'The perusal of Lady Mary Wortley Montagu's work has rendered me anxious to visit a zenana, and to become acquainted with ladies of the East.'[64] Like Lady Mary, Parks was so taken aback by what she found in the zenana – women living in comfort and luxury, and looking down upon the male world from their safe sanctuary through lattice screens without envy or rancour – that she needed to recover herself by describing their complexion as 'pale mahogany' and 'very dark colour, almost black'[65] in order to assert the superiority necessary to the imperial presence.

Lady Mary, in an earlier age, was not called upon to establish colonial power and did not suffer from any threat to her self-confidence. She was able, in Turkey, to give full rein to the romanticism and sensuality in which she revelled. Of these one has only rare glimpses in her 'English' days, such as the prescription she gave to her sister, Lady Mar, who suffered from severe depression: 'galloping all day, and a modest glass of champagne at night in good company.'[66] In another letter to her, she emphasized the need to enjoy 'the golden now'.[67]

That talent to enjoy was poisoned and distorted by the society in which she moved, what Dervla Murphy calls not the Age of Reason but the Age of Savagery. The attacks made on her by Pope would have dragged him into a court of law for libel nowadays, and Horace Walpole's insinuation that she suffered from venereal disease ('the half she yet retains of nose') would have got him a ruinous fine. In the eighteenth century these jibes were permissible, and Lady Mary's record as an adversary in the field is not negligible. Her caricature of the hunchbacked Pope could only be considered acceptable amongst hardened cynics. On hearing of the birth of a still-born child to Lord Sandwich's daughter-in-law, she wrote: 'Lady Hinchinbroke has a dead daughter – it were unchristian not to be sorry for my cousin's misfortune; but if she has no live son, Mr Wortley is heir – so there's comfort for a Christian.'[68] Clearly it was an age that could take the shock of such blunt speech, and fine feelings for others did not exist. Travelling in north Africa, Lady Mary wrote of the women she saw that 'they differ so little from their own country people, the baboons, 'tis hard to fancy them a distinct race, and I could not help thinking there had been some ancient alliance between them.'[69]

What can be redeemed from such bigotry is only the quality of honesty in blunt speech, and it becomes most appealing when she turns it on herself, as she very often does. She noted: 'I am in perfect health and hear it said I look better than I ever did in my life, which is one of those lies one is always glad to hear'[70]

and 'I love flattery so well, I would fain have some circumstances of probability added so that I might swallow it with
comfort.'[71] She claimed she took care 'to improve as much as
possible that stock of vanity and credulity that Heaven in its
mercy furnished me with; being sensible that to have these two
qualities, simple as they appear, all the pleasures of life are
owing.'[72]

While her comments on people are too highly coloured by
her desire to amuse and her bigotry, her writing on issues is
original and bold. Some of it is eccentric – as when she
suggested that Parliament should be abolished and England
governed by its virtuous king – but that on feminist issues
remains interesting and relevant today. In 1726, a two-volume
Miscellanea published by Curll included an anonymous essay 'On
the Mischief of Giving Fortunes With Women in Marriage' that
advised the abolition of the practice of giving dowries, and,
more radically still, a septennial bill that would give married
people the liberty every seven years of choosing whether to
continue with their married state. This essay is often attributed
to Lady Mary since it contains her ideas and a style recognizably
hers. It is certainly known that she contributed articles to a
short-lived journal, *The Nonsense of Common Sense*, that was
printed from 1737 to 1738 to refute the views of the political
opposition published in a journal called *Common Sense*. The sixth
of them dealt with 'Feminism': 'I have some thoughts of exhibit-
ing a Set of Pictures of some meritorious Ladies, where I shall
say nothing of the Fire of their Eyes, or the Pureness of their
Complexions; but give them such Praises as befits a rational
sensible Being: Virtues of Choice, and not Beauties by
Accident.'[73] She advised those 'Ladies' who read it to begin 'by
paying those Authors with Scorn and Contempt, who, with a
Sneer of Affected Admiration would throw you below the
Dignity of the human Species,'[74] a project that is still being
tackled today.

In a more personal vein, she undertook to advise her daughter on the education of her granddaughters. Absolute honesty
was imperative in the relationship, she declared, as well as a

frank appraisal of their qualities and failings. (One recalls that she described her son as an excellent linguist and a thorough liar, so weak-willed as to be capable of turning 'monk one day and a Turk three days after'[75] and 'It happens very luckily ... that the sobriety and discretion are on my daughter's side. I am sorry the ugliness is so too, for my son grows extremely handsome.')[76] Urging a wide-ranging education for the children, Lady Mary wrote 'Every branch of knowledge is entertaining',[77] but when Lady Bute mentioned one daughter's proficiency in arithmetic, Lady Mary advised an emphasis on languages, history, geography and philosophy rather than a course that was unlikely to be a portion of her life. She also advised her granddaughters to hide their learning as they might a physical deformity – which illustrates her bleak and uncompromising sense of realism. She clearly referred to her own experience when she advised against matrimony and suggested that the girls be prepared for spinsterhood instead. This must have displeased the very conventional Lady Bute, for Lady Mary had to retreat, conceding that 'everyone has the right to educate their children after their own way, and I shall speak no more on that subject.'[78] Without the inconvenient constraints of the family, how much more Lady Mary would have had to say!

Yet it is difficult to cast her as the twentieth-century career woman: her character had too many idiosyncrasies to make such a transformation simple. Her class prejudices would not carry over, for instance, and the wild romanticism that made her find in Turkey a more congenial climate and pursue in Italy what her life in England lacked belongs to Rousseau's age. These contradictions were perhaps best summarized by the young Joseph Spence who met her in Rome and wrote to his mother: 'Lady Mary is one of the most extraordinary shining characters in the world; but she shines like a comet; she is all irregular and always wandering. She is the most wise, most imprudent; loveliest, disagreeablest; best natured, cruellest woman in the world.'[79]

Cambridge, 1991   ANITA DESAI

NOTES

Halsband's *Letters* are the principal source of reference for letters but those referenced by place and date only are contained in the present edition.

[1] *Letters of Lady Louisa Stuart to Miss Louisa Clinton*, ed. James A. Holme (1901), 1:254.
[2] To Wortley, 9 April 1711, 1:99.
[3] Harrowby MS, Sandon Hall, Stafford (owned by the Duke of Portland), vols 74–81 (Wortley MSS I–VIII); mostly published in George Paston [Emily Morse Symonds] (London, 1907), 2nd ed. pp. 4ff.
[4] To Lady Bute, 7 July 1757, 3:132.
[5] To Lady Bute, 6 March, 1753, 3:25.
[6] Robert Halsband, *The Life of Lady Mary Wortley Montagu* (Oxford, 1956), p. 5.
[7] Wortley MSS (Harrowby MS, vol. 250).
[8] Ibid., vol. 251.
[9] Paston, p. 4.
[10] Halsband, p. 7.
[11] *The Tatler*, 18 July 1710.
[12] Quoted by Halsband, p. 16.
[13] To Wortley, November 1710, 1:66.
[14] To Wortley, 25 April 1710, 1:31.
[15] To Wortley, October 1714, 1:232; Paston, p. 189.
[16] Lady Mary's 'Account of the Court of George the First at his Accession', I, 123. *Letters and Works of Lady Mary Wortley Montagu*, ed. Lord Wharncliffe, 3rd ed. (rev.) W. Moy Thomas (London, 1861) 1:126.
[17] To Lord Cornbury, quoted by Dervla Murphy, Introduction to Lady Mary Wortley Montagu, *Embassy to Constantinople*, ed. and compiled by Christopher Pick (London, 1988).
[18] Lady Loudon, 22 December 1715, MS in the Henry E. Huntingdon Library, San Marino, California.
[19] Alexander Pope to Lady Mary, 10 November 1716, *Correspondence*, ed. George Sherburn, 5 vols (Oxford, 1956), 1:368.
[20] 21 August 1717, State Papers, Public Record Office.

[21] To Wortley, 9 April 1717; Paston, p. 276.

[22] William Wagstaffe, in a pamphlet quoted by Halsband, p. 111.

[23] Quoted by Murphy, p. 27.

[24] Paston, p. 285.

[25] MS owned by the Earl of Haddington, 14 July 1722.

[26] Halsband, p. 99.

[27] MS in Berg Collection, New York Public Library.

[28] Lady Irwin in a letter to her father, Lord Carlisle, 8 April 1730. Quoted by Paston, p. 357.

[29] Chesterfield. Quoted by Lewis Gibbs in *The Admirable Lady Mary* (London, 1949), p. 182.

[30] To Lady Mar, December 1724, 2:44.

[31] 17/28 September 1737; quoted in *Lord Hervey and his Friends*, ed. the Earl of Ilchester (London, 1950), p. 273.

[32] Halsband. p. 184.

[33] Quoted by Halsband, p. 179.

[34] 10 October, 6 November 1739, 2:159.

[35] Horace Walpole, *Correspondence*, ed. W. S. Lewis and others, 48 vols (Yale, 1937–83), 1:84–5.

[36] 2 October 1740; ibid., 13:233.

[37] Ibid., XIV, 247.

[38] Pope, to Hugh Bethel. Quoted by Paston, p. 389.

[39] To Wortley, 15 November 1741; Wortley MSS, 2:36–7.

[40] 11 December 1761; facsimile in *The Works of Lady Mary Wortley Montagu*, ed. I. Dallaway, 5 vols (London, 1803), 1:30.

[41] Walpole to Horace Mann, 22 March 1762; *Correspondence*, 5:190.

[42] Vienna, 10 October 1716.

[43] Vienna, 8 September 1716.

[44] Vienna, 14 September 1716.

[45] Vienna, 20 September 1716.

[46] Vienna, 14 September 1716.

[47] Ibid.

[48] Adrianople, 1 April 1717.

[49] Ibid.

[50] Halsband, p. 128.

[51] Adrianople, 18 April 1717.

[52] To the Countess of BEM, undated.

[53] Adrianople, 1 April 1717.

[54] Ibid.

[55] Ibid.

[56] Adrianople, 18 April 1717.

[57] Constantinople, 19 May 1718.

[58] To Lady Mar, 1726; quoted by Murphy, p. 37.

[59] Edward Gibbon, 17 February 1764; quoted by Halsband, p. 289.

[60] Murphy, p. 28.

[61] Quoted by Halsband, p. 255.

[62] To Lady Bute, 23 June 1754, 3:57.

[63] Sara Suleri, *The Rhetoric of English India* (The University of Chicago Press), p. 75.

[64] Quoted by Sara Suleri in *The Rhetoric of English India*, p. 93.

[65] Ibid; p. 94.

[66] To Lady Mar, May 1727, 2:76.

[67] To Lady Mar, May 1726, 2:65.

[68] Lady Louisa Stuart, 'Introductory Anecdotes' in MWM's *Letters and Works*, 1:65.

[69] Tunis, 31 July 1718.

[70] Halsband, p. 128.

[71] To Lady Mar, June 1725, 2:52.

[72] To Lady Mar, January 1725, 2:44–5.

[73] 24 January 1738, *Letters and Works of Lady Mary Wortley Montagu* ed. Lord Wharncliffe, 3rd ed. (rev.) W. Moy Thomas (London, 1861) 2:418.

[74] Ibid.

[75] Substance of her letter to Wortley, 10 June 1742, quoted by Paston, pp. 403–4.

[76] Paston, p. 331.

[77] Quoted by Murphy, p. 7.

[78] To Lady Bute, 3 June 1753, 3:31.

[79] Joseph Spence, 'Anecdotes', MS in the Henry E. Huntington Library, San Marino, California.

A NOTE ON EDITORIAL POLICY

This edition of the Turkish Embassy Letters and two additional letters originally written in French (to the Abbé Conti in February 1718 and to Madame de Bonnac in April 1718) is based upon the authoritative text established by Robert Halsband in his three-volume edition of *The Complete Letters of Lady Mary Wortley Montagu*, Oxford, 1965. Halsband's translations of the two additional letters have also been used.

To facilitate the modern reader, some modernization of spelling (including place names) and punctuation has been imposed on Halsband's text; however 'tis' has been left in where the rhythm of the sentence requires it.

A set of end-notes has been provided to explain foreign or archaic words and to give historical and biographical references. Some of the details in the notes have been taken from Halsband.

London, January 1993

MALCOLM JACK

CHRONOLOGY

1689 – Birth of Mary Pierrepont.

1690 – Her father, Evelyn Pierrepont, made Earl of Kingston. His daughter Mary henceforth called Lady Mary Pierrepont. Birth of Frances Pierrepont.

1692 – Birth of her brother, William.

1693 – Death of her mother, Lady Mary Fielding.

1699 – Death of her paternal grandmother, Elizabeth Pierrepont.

1706 – Her father becomes the Marquis of Dorchester.

1712 – Elopes and marries Edward Wortley Montagu.

1713 – Birth of the Montagu's son, Edward Wortley Montagu. Her brother dies from smallpox.

1714 – Death of Queen Anne. The Elector of Hanover proclaimed King George I.
Edward Wortley Montagu elected to Parliament from Westminster. Appointed Junior Commissioner by Lord Halifax.

1715 – Lady Mary takes up residence in London.
Lady Mary struck by smallpox.

1716 – *Town Eclogues* (with Pope and Gay) and *Court Poems by a Lady of Quality* published.
Wortley Montagu appointed ambassador to the court of Turkey.

1717 – Arrival in Constantinople.

1718 – Birth of the Montagus' daughter Mary.
Wortley Montagu recalled to England.

1719 – Lady Mary takes up residence in Twickenham.

1720 – *Verses Written in the Chiosk of the British Palace* published.

1721 – Lady Mary has her daughter inoculated publicly against smallpox.

1722 – *A Plain Account of the Innoculating of the Small Pox by a Turkey Merchant* (in the Flying Post) published.

1726 – Her essay 'On the Mischief of Giving Fortunes with Women in Marriage' published anonymously in Curll's *Miscellanea*.

1728 – Attacked by Pope in verse.

1729 – Lady Mary becomes guardian to her sister, the Countess of Mar on seeing *A Portrait of Sir Robert Walpole* published.

1733 – Publication of *Verses addressed to the Imitator of the First Satire of the Second Book of Horace*.

1736 – Meets Francesco Algarotti.
Lady Mary's daughter marries the Earl of Bute.

1737–38 – Publishes six anonymous essays as *The Nonsense of Common-Sense*.

1739 – Follows Algarotti to Italy and takes up residence in Venice.

1740 – Visits Florence, Rome, Naples, Leghorn, Turin, Genoa, Geneva, Chambéry, Lyons, Avignon.

1742–46 – Lives in Avignon.

1746 – Travels to Brescia, resides in Gottolengo and visits Lovere.

1747 – *Town Eclogues*, reissued by Horace Walpole.

1755 – *Letters to Margaret of Navarre*.

1756 – Returns to Venice and Padua.

1758 – Writes *A Hymn to the Moon*, which is published by Algarotti in a volume of his work.

1761 – Death of Edward Wortley Montagu.
Lady Mary leaves Italy for Germany and Holland.

1762 – Returns to England.

1762 – Death of Lady Mary.

SELECT BIBLIOGRAPHY

PRIMARY SOURCES

Town Eclogues and *Court Poems by a Lady of Quality.* London: Edmund Curll, 1716. *Court Eclogues written in the year 1716.* New York: New York Public Library, c. 1977.

The Genuine Copy of a Letter written from Constantinople by an English Lady . . . To a Venetian Nobleman. London: J. Roberts and A. Dodd, 1719.

'On the Mischief of Giving Fortunes with Women in Marriage', published anonymously in *Miscellanea.* 2 vols. London: Edmund Curll, 1726.

Verses addressed to the Imitator of the First Satire of the Second Book of Horace [i.e. Alexander Pope] *By a Lady* [i.e. Lady Mary and Lord Hervey]. London: A. Dodd, 1733.

A proper reply to a lady, occasioned by her verses addressed to the imitator of the first satire of the second book of Horace. By a gentleman. London: T. Osborne, 1733.

An Elegy to a Young Lady, in the manner of Ovid . . . With an Answer. By a Lady, author of the Verses to the Imitator of Horace. London: 1733.

The Nonsense of Common-Sense. London: 1737–38. (including the essay 'An Expedient to put a stop to the Spreading Vice of Corruption'), ed. with an introduction and notes by Robert Halsband. Evanston: Northwestern University, 1947.

Woman not inferior to man, or, A short and modest vindication of the natural right of the fair-sex to a perfect equality of power, dignity and esteem with the men; by Sophia, a person of quality [attributed to Lady Mary Wortley Montagu]. London: John Hawkins, 1739. London: Brentham Press (facsimile repr.), 1975.

Letters of the Right Honourable Lady M[ar]y W[ortle]y M[ontag]e, written, during her travels in Europe, Asia and Africa to persons of distinction (with a preface by Mary Astell). London: T. Becket and P. A. de Hondt, 1763.

The Works of the Right Honourable Lady Mary Wortley Montagu, published, by permission, from her genuine papers, ed. with a memoir of the author, by I. Dallaway. 5 vols. London: R. Phillips, 1803.

Original Letters from the Right Honourable Lady Mary Wortley Montagu to Sir James and Lady Frances Stewart ... ed. John Dunlop. Greenock: Robert Donaldson, 1818.

The Letters and Works of Lady Mary Wortley Montagu, ed. by her great grandson Lord Wharncliffe. 3 vols. London: R. Bentley, 1837. Third ed. with additions and corrections derived from the original manuscript, illustrative notes and a new memoir by W. Moy Thomas (introductory anecdotes by Lady L. Stuart). 2 vols. London, 1861.

The Complete Letters of Lady Mary Wortley Montagu, ed. Robert Halsband. 3 vols. Oxford: Clarendon Press, 1965–7.

Essays and Poems; and, Simplicity: a comedy, ed. Robert Halsband and Isobel Grundy. 3 vols. Oxford: Clarendon Press, 1977.

Embassy to Constantinople: the Travels of Lady Mary Wortley Montagu, introduced by Dervla Murphy, ed. and compiled by Christopher Pick. London: Century, 1988.

Mary Wortley Montagu, Letters, introduced by Clare Brant, London: Everyman, 1992.

SECONDARY SOURCES

Paston, George [Emily Morse Symonds]. *Lady Mary Wortley Montagu and her Times.* London: Methuen, 1907.

Melville, Lewis. *Lady Mary Wortley Montagu: her Life and Letters, 1689–1762,* etc. London: Hutchinson, 1925.

Barry, Iris. *Portrait of Lady Mary Wortley Montagu.* London: Ernest Benn, 1928.

Gibbs, Lewis. *The Admirable Lady Mary. The Life and Times of Lady Mary Wortley Montagu, 1689–1762.* London: Dent, 1949.

Curling, Jonathon. *Edward Wortley Montagu 1713–1776.* London: Andrew Melrose, 1954.

Halsband, Robert. *The Life of Lady Mary Wortley Montagu.* Oxford: Clarendon Press, 1956.

Dixon, Cyril William. *Mary and Caroline and the lay contribution to preventive medicine* ... *An inaugural lecture,* etc. [on the efforts of Lady Mary and Caroline, Princess of Wales, to introduce inoculation for smallpox into England]. Dunedin: University of Otago Press, 1961.

Rumbold, Valerie. *Women's Place in Pope's World.* Cambridge University Press, 1989.

Shaw, S. *History of the Ottoman Empire and Modern Turkey,* 2 vols. Cambridge, 1976.

Turkish Embassy Letters

LETTER I[1]

To Lady Mar,[2]   *Rotterdam, 3 August 1716*

I flatter myself, dear sister, that I shall give you some pleasure in letting you know that I am safely past the sea, though we had the ill fortune of a storm. We were persuaded by the captain of our yacht to set out in a calm, and he pretended that there was nothing so easy as to tide it over; but, after two days slowly moving, the wind blew so hard that none of the sailors could keep their feet and we were all Sunday night tossed very handsomely. I never saw a man more frighted than the captain. For my part I have been so lucky neither to suffer from fear or sea-sickness, though I confess I was so impatient to see myself once more upon dry land that I would not stay till the yacht could get to Rotterdam, but went in the long boat to Helvoets-luys, where we hired voitures[3] to carry us to the Briel. I was charmed with the neatness of this little town, but my arrival in Rotterdam presented me a new scene of pleasure. All the streets are paved with broad stones, and before the meanest artificers' doors seats of various coloured marbles, and so neatly kept that, I'll assure you, I walked almost all over the town yesterday, incognito, in my slippers, without receiving one spot of dirt, and you may see the Dutch maids washing the pavement of the street with more application than ours do our bedchambers. The town seems so full of people, with such busy faces, all in motion, that I can hardly fancy that it is not some celebrated fair, but I see it is every day the same. 'Tis certain no town can be more advantageously situated for commerce. Here are seven large canals, on which the merchant ships come up to the very doors of their houses. The shops and warehouses are of a surprising neatness and magnificence, filled with an incredible quantity of fine merchandise, and so much cheaper than what we see in England I have much ado to persuade myself I am still so near it. Here is neither dirt nor beggary to be seen. One is not shocked with those loathsome cripples so common in London, nor teased with the importunities of idle fellows and wenches that choose to be nasty and lazy. The common servants and the little shop women here are more nicely clean than most of our ladies, and the great variety of neat dresses (every woman dressing her head after her own fashion) is an additional pleasure in seeing the town.[4]

You see, hitherto, dear sister, I make no complaints, and if I continue to like travelling as well as I do at present, I shall not repent my project. It will go a great way in making me satisfied with it, if it affords me opportunities of entertaining you. But it is not from Holland that you must expect a disinterested offer. I can write enough in the style of Rotterdam to tell you plainly, in one word, that I expect returns of all the London news. You see I have already learnt to make a good bargain, and that it is not for nothing I will so much as tell you that I am your affectionate sister.

LETTER II

To Jane Smith,[5]   *The Hague, 5 August 1716*

I make haste to tell you, dear Madam, that after all the dreadful fatigues you threatened me with, I am hitherto very well pleased with my journey. We take care to make such short stages every day, I rather fancy myself upon parties of pleasure than upon the road, and sure nothing can be more agreeable than travelling in Holland. The whole country appears a large garden; the roads all well paved, shaded on each side with rows of trees, and bordered with large canals full of boats, passing and repassing. Every twenty paces gives you the prospect of some villa, and every four hours of a large town, so surprisingly neat I am sure you would be charmed with them. The place I am now at is certainly one of the finest villages in the world. Here are several squares finely built and (what I think a particular beauty), set with thick large trees. The Vourhout[6] is at the same time the Hyde Park and the Mall of the people of quality, for they take the air in it both on foot and in coaches. There are shops for wafers, cool liquors etc.. I have been to see several of the most celebrated gardens, but I will not tease you with their descriptions.

I dare swear you think my letter already long enough, but I must not conclude without begging your pardon for not obeying your commands in sending the lace you ordered me. Upon my word I can yet find none that is not dearer than you may buy it in London. If you want any Indian goods, here are great variety of pennyworths, and I shall follow your orders with great pleasure and exactness, being, dear madam, etc.

LETTER III

To Sarah Chiswell,[7]   *Nijmegen, 13 August 1716*

I am extremely sorry, my dear Sarah, that your fears of disobliging your relations, and their fears for your health and safety, has hindered me the happiness of your company, and you the pleasure of a diverting journey. I receive some degree of mortification from every agreeable novelty or pleasing prospect, by the reflection of your having so unluckily missed the same pleasure which I know it would have given you. If you were with me in this town you would be ready to expect to receive visits from your Nottingham friends. No two places were ever more resembling; one has but to give the Maese[8] the name of the Trent and there is no distinguishing the prospects; the houses, like those of Nottingham, built one above another and intermixed in the same manner with trees and gardens. The tower they call Julius Caesar's has the same situation with Nottingham castle, and I can't help fancying I see from it the Trent field, Adboulton, etc., places so well known to us. 'Tis true, the fortifications make a considerable difference. All the learned in the art of war bestow great commendations on them. For my part, that know nothing of the matter, I shall content myself with telling you 'tis a very pretty walk on the ramparts, on which there is a tower, very deservedly called the Belvedere, where people go to drink coffee, tea, etc., and enjoy one of the finest prospects in the world. The public walks have no great beauty but the thick shade of the trees. But I must not forget to take notice of the bridge, which appeared very surprising to me. It is large enough to hold hundreds of men with horses and carriages. They give the value of an English twopence to get upon it and then away they go, bridge and all, to the other side of the river, with so slow a motion one is hardly sensible of any at all.

I was yesterday at the French church, and stared very much at their manner of service. The parson claps on a broad-brimmed hat in the first place, which gave him entirely the air of what d'ye call him in *Bartholomew Fair*,[9] which he kept up by extraordinary antic gestures, and talking much such stuff as the other preached to the puppets. However, the congregation seemed to receive it with great devotion and I was informed by some of his flock that he is a person of particular fame among them.

I believe you are by this time, as much tired of my account of him as I was with his sermon, but I'm sure your brother[10] will excuse a digression in favour of the Church of England. You know, speaking disrespectfully of Calvinists is the same thing as speaking honourably of the Church.

Adieu, my dear Sarah. Always remember me, and be assured I can never forget you.

LETTER IV

To Lady – –,[11]   *Cologne, 16 August 1716*

If my Lady – – could have any notion of the fatigues that I have suffered this last two days, I am sure she would own it a great proof of regard that I now sit down to write to her.

We hired horses from Nijmegen hither, not having the conveniency of the post, and found but very indifferent accommodation at Reinberg, our first stage, but that was nothing to what I suffered yesterday. We were in hopes to reach Cologne. Our horses tired at Stamel, three hours from it, where I was forced to pass the night in my clothes in a room not at all better than a hovel. For though I have my own bed, I had no mind to undress, where the wind came in from a thousand places. We left this wretched lodging at daybreak and about six this morning came safe here, where I got immediately into bed and slept so well for three hours that I found myself perfectly recovered and have had spirits enough to go and see all that is curious in the town, that is to say, the churches, for there is nothing else worth seeing, though it is a very large town, but most part of it old built.

The Jesuits' church is the neatest, which was showed me, in a very complaisant manner, by a handsome young Jesuit, who, not knowing who I was, took a liberty in his compliments and railleries which very much diverted me. Having never before seen anything of that nature, I could not enough admire the magnificence of the altars, the rich images of the saints (all massy silver) and the *enchasures*[12] of the relics, though I could not help murmuring in my heart at that profusion of pearls, diamonds and rubies bestowed on the adornment of rotten teeth, dirty rags, etc. I own that I had wickedness enough to covet St Ursula's[13] pearl necklace, though perhaps it was no wickedness at all, an image not being certainly one's neighbour;

but I went yet farther and wished even she herself converted into dressing plate,[14] and a great St Christopher[15] I imagined would have looked very well in a cistern.[16] These were my pious reflections, though I was very well satisfied to see piled up to the honour of our nation the skulls of the eleven thousand virgins. I have seen some hundreds of relics here of no less consequence, but I will not imitate the common style of travellers so far as to give you a list of them, being persuaded that you have no manner of curiosity for the titles given to jaw bones and bits of worm-eaten wood.

Adieu, I am just going to supper, where I shall drink your health in an admirable sort of Lorraine wine, which I am sure is the same you call Burgundy in London.

LETTER V

To Lady Bristol,[17]   *Nuremberg, 22 August 1716*

After five days travelling post, I am sure I could sit down to write on no other occasion but to tell my dear Lady Bristol that I have not forgot her obliging command of sending her some account of my travels.

I have already passed a large part of Germany. I have seen all that is remarkable in Cologne, Frankfurt, Wurtzburg and this place, and 'tis impossible not to observe the difference between the free towns and those under the government of absolute princes, as all the little sovereigns of Germany are. In the first, there appears an air of commerce and plenty. The streets are well built and full of people, neatly and plainly dressed, the shops loaded with merchandise and the commonality clean and cheerful. In the other a sort of shabby finery, a number of dirty people of quality tawdered out, narrow nasty streets out of repair, wretchedly thin of inhabitants, and above half of the common sort asking alms. I can't help fancying one under the figure of a handsome clean Dutch citizen's wife, and the other like a poor town lady of pleasure, painted and ribboned out in her headdress, with tarnished silver-laced shoes and a ragged under-petticoat, a miserable mixture of vice and poverty.

They have sumptuary laws[18] in this town, which distinguish their rank by their dress and prevents that excess which ruins so many other cities and has a more agreeable effect to the eye of a stranger than our fashions. I think after the Archbishop of Cambrai having declared for them,[19] I need not be ashamed to own that I wish these laws were in force in other parts of the world. When one considers impartially the merit of a rich suit of clothes in most places, the respect and the smiles of favour it procures, not to speak of the envy and the sighs that it occasions (which is very often the principal charm to the wearer), one is forced to confess that there is need of an uncommon understanding to resist the temptation of pleasing friends and mortifying rivals, and that it is natural to young people to fall into a folly, which betrays them to that want of money which is the source of a thousand basenesses. What numbers of men have begun the world with generous inclinations that have afterwards been the instruments of bringing misery on a whole people, led by a vain expense into debts that they could clear no other way but by the forfeit of their honour, and which they would never have contracted if the respect the many pay to habits was fixed by law, only to a particular colour or cut of plain cloth! These reflections draw after them others that are too melancholy.

I will make haste to put them out of your head by the farce of relics with which I have been entertained in all Romish churches. The Lutherans are not quite free from these follies. I have seen here, in the principal church, a large piece of the cross set in jewels, and the point of the spear which they told me, very gravely was the same that pierced the side of our Saviour. But I was particularly diverted in a little Roman Catholic church, which is permitted here, where the professors of that religion are not very rich, and consequently cannot adorn their images in so rich a manner as their neighbours, but, not to be quite destitute of all finery, they have dressed up an image of our Saviour over the altar, in a fair full-bottomed wig, very well

powdered. I imagine I see your ladyship stare at this article, of
which you very much doubt the veracity; but, upon my word I
have not yet made use of the privilege of a traveller, and my
whole account is writ with the same plain sincerity of heart
with which I assure you that I am, dear madam, your Ladyship's
etc.

LETTER VI

To Anne Thistlethwayte,[20]   *Ratisbon,*[21] 30 August 1716

I had the pleasure of receiving yours but the day before I left
London. I give you a thousand thanks for your good wishes, and
have such an opinion of their efficacy I am persuaded that I owe
in part to them the good luck of having proceeded so far in my
long journey without any ill accident. For I do not reckon it any
being stopped a few days in this town by a cold, since it has not
only given me an opportunity of seeing all that is curious in it,
but of making some acquaintance with the ladies, who have all
been to see me, with great civility, particularly Madame von
Wrisberg, the wife of our king's envoy from Hanover.[22] She has
carried me to all the assemblies, and I have been magnificently
entertained at her house, which is one of the finest here. You
know that all the nobility of this place are envoys from different
states. Here are a great number of them, and they might pass
their time agreeably enough, if they were less delicate on the
point of ceremony. But instead of joining in the design of
making the town as pleasant to one another as they can, and
improving their little societies, they amuse themselves no other
way than with perpetual quarrels, which they take care to
eternize, by leaving them to their successors, and an envoy to
Ratisbon receives regularly half a dozen quarrels amongst the
perquisites of his employment.

You may be sure the ladies are not wanting on their side in
cherishing and improving these important piques, which divide

the town almost into as many parties as there are families, and they choose rather to suffer the mortification of sitting almost alone on their assembly nights, than to recede one jot from their pretensions. I have not been here above a week and yet I have heard from almost every one of them the whole history of their wrongs, and dreadful complaints of the injustice of their neighbours, in hopes to draw me to their party. But I think it very prudent to remain neuter, though if I was to stay amongst them there would be no possibility of continuing so, their quarrels running so high they will not be civil to those that visit their adversaries. The foundation of these everlasting disputes turns entirely upon place and the title of Excellency, which they all pretend to and, what is very hard, will give it to nobody. For my part I could not forbear advising them (for the public good) to give the title of Excellency to everybody, which would include the receiving it from everybody; but the very mention of such a dishonourable peace was received with as much indignation as Mrs Blackacre did the motion of a reference.[23] And I began to think myself ill-natured to offer to take from them, in a town where there are so few diversions, so entertaining an amusement. I know that my peaceable disposition already gives me a very ill figure, and that 'tis publicly whispered as a piece of impertinent pride in me, that I have hitherto been saucily civil to everybody, as if I thought nobody good enough to quarrel with. I should be obliged to change my behaviour if I did not intend to pursue my journey in a few days.

I have been to see the churches here, and had the permission of touching the relics, which was never suffered in places where I was not known. I had, by this privilege, the opportunity of making an observation, which I don't doubt might have been made in all the other churches, that the emeralds and rubies that they show round their relics and images are most of them false, though they tell you that many of the crosses and madonnas set round with these stones have been the gifts of emperors and other great princes, and I don't doubt but they were at first jewels of value, but the good fathers have found it convenient to apply them to other uses, and the people are just as well satisfied with bits of glass. Amongst these relics they showed me a prodigious claw set in gold, which they called the claw of a griffin, and I could not forbear asking the reverend priest that showed it whether the griffin was a saint. The question almost put him beside his gravity, but he answered they only kept it as a curiosity. But I was very much scandalized at a large silver image of the Trinity, where the Father is represented under the figure of a decrepit old man with a beard down to his knees and a triple crown on his head, holding in his arms the Son fixed on the cross and the Holy Ghost in the shape of a dove hovering over him.

Madame von Wrisberg is come this minute to call me to the assembly, and forces me to tell you, very abruptly, that I am ever yours.

LETTER VII

To Lady Mar,   *Vienna, 8 September 1716*

I am now, my dear sister, safely arrived at Vienna,[24] and I thank God, have not at all suffered in my health, nor (what is dearer to me) in that of my child, by all our fatigues. We travelled by water from Rastibon, a journey perfectly agreeable, down the Danube in one of those little vessels that they very properly call wooden houses, having in them all the conveniences of a palace, stoves in the chambers, kitchens etc.. They are rowed by twelve men each and move with such incredible swiftness that in the same day you have the pleasure of a vast variety of prospects, and within a few hours space of time one has the pleasure of seeing a populous city adorned with magnificent palaces and the most romantic solitudes, which appear distant from the commerce of mankind, the banks of the Danube being charmingly diversified with woods, rocks, mountains covered with vines, fields of corn, large cities and ruins of ancient castles. I saw the great towns of Passau and Lintz, famous for the retreat of the imperial court when Vienna was besieged.[25]

This town, which has the honour of being the Emperor's[26] residence, did not at all answer my ideas of it, being much less than I expected to find it. The streets are very close, and so narrow one cannot observe the fine fronts of the palaces, though many of them very well deserve observation, being truly magnificent, all built of fine white stone and excessive high. The town being so much too little for the number of the people that desire to live in it, the builders seem to have projected to repair that misfortune by clapping one town on the top of another, most of the houses being of five and some of them six, storeys. You may easily imagine that the streets being so narrow, the upper rooms are extreme dark and, what is an inconvenience much more intolerable in my opinion, there is no house that has so few as five or six families in it. The apartments of the greatest ladies and even of the ministers of state, are divided but by a partition, from that of a tailor or shoemaker, and I know nobody that has above two floors in any house, one for their own use and one higher for their servants. Those that have houses of their own let out the rest of them to whoever will take them, thus the great stairs (which are all of stone) are as common and as dirty as the street. 'Tis true, when you have once travelled through them, nothing can be more surprisingly magnificent than the apartments. They are commonly a suite of eight or ten large rooms, all inlaid, the doors and windows richly carved and gilt and the furniture such as is seldom seen in the palaces of sovereign princes in other countries: the hangings of the finest tapestry of Brussels, prodigious large looking glasses in silver frames, fine Japan tables, beds, chairs, canopies and window curtains of the richest Genoa damask or velvet, almost covered with gold lace or embroidery, the whole made gay by pictures, and vast jars of japan china, and almost in every room large lustres of rock crystal.

I have already had the honour of being invited to dinner by several of the first people of quality, and I must do them justice to say, the good taste and magnificence of their tables very well answers to that of their furniture. I have been more than once entertained with fifty dishes of meat, all served in silver, and well dressed; the desert proportionable, served in the finest china. But the variety and richness of their wines is what appears the most surprising. The constant way is to lay a list of their names upon the plates of the guests along with the napkins, and I have counted several times to the number of eighteen different sorts, all exquisite in their kinds.

I was yesterday at Count Schönborn's,[27] the vice-Chancellor's garden, where I was invited to dinner, and I must own that I never saw a place so perfectly delightful as the Fauxbourg of Vienna.[28] It is very large, and almost wholly composed of delicious palaces, and if the emperor found it proper to permit the gates of the town to be laid open, that the Fauxbourg might be joined to it, he would have one of the largest and best built cities in Europe. Count Schönborn's villa is one of the most magnificent; the furniture all rich brocades, so well fancied and fitted up, nothing can look more gay and splendid, not to speak of a gallery full of rarities of coral, mother of pearl etc., and throughout the whole house a profusion of gilding, carving, fine paintings, the most beautiful porcelain statues of alabaster and ivory, and vast orange and lemon trees in gilt pots. The dinner was perfectly fine and well ordered, and made still more agreeable by the good humour of the count. I have not yet been at court, being forced to stay for my gown, without which there is no waiting on the Empress,[29] though I am not without a great impatience to see a beauty that has been the admiration of so many different nations. When I have had that honour I will not fail to let you know my real thoughts, always taking a particular pleasure in communicating them to my dear sister.

LETTER VIII

To Alexander Pope,[30]   *Vienna, 14 September 1716*

Perhaps you'll laugh at me for thanking you very gravely for all the obliging concern you express for me. 'Tis certain that I may, if I please, take the fine things you say to me for wit and raillery, and it may be it would be taking them right. But I never, in my life, was half so well disposed to believe you in earnest and that distance which makes the continuation of your friendship improbable has very much increased my faith for it, and I find that I have (as well as the rest of my sex) whatever face I set on it, a strong disposition to believe in miracles. Don't fancy, however, that I am infected by the air of these popish countries though I have so far wandered from the discipline of the Church of England to have been last Sunday at the opera, which was performed in the garden of the Favorita and I was so much pleased with it I have not yet repented my seeing it. Nothing of that kind ever was more magnificent and I can easily believe what I am told, that the decorations and habits cost the Emperor £30,000 sterling. The stage was built over a very large canal and, at the beginning of the second act divided into two parts, discovering the water, on which there immediately came, from different parts, two fleets of little gilded vessels that gave the representation of a naval fight. It is not easy to imagine the beauty of this scene, which I took particular notice of, but all the rest were perfectly fine in their kind. The story of the opera is the enchantment of Alcina,[31] which gives opportunity for a great variety of machines and changes of the scenes, which are performed with a surprising swiftness. The theatre is so large that it is hard to carry the eye to the end of it, and the habits in the utmost magnificence to the number of 108. No house could hold such large decorations, but the ladies all sitting in the open air exposes them to great inconveniences, for there is but one canopy for the imperial family, and the first night it was represented, a shower of rain happening, the opera was broke off and the company crowded away in such confusion I was almost squeezed to death.

But if their operas are thus delightful, their comedies are in as high a degree ridiculous. They have but one playhouse, where I had the curiosity to go to a German comedy, and was very glad it happened to be the story of Amphitrion,[32] that subject having been already handled by a Latin, French and English poet, I was curious to see what an Austrian author would make of it. I understood enough of the language to comprehend the greatest part of it; and, besides, I took with me a lady that had the goodness to explain to me every word. The way is, to take a box which holds four, for yourself and company. The fixed price is a gold ducat. I thought the house very low and dark, but I confess, the comedy admirably recompensed that defect. I never laughed so much in my life. It began with Jupiter's falling in love out of a peephole in the clouds, and ended with the birth of Hercules. But what was most pleasant was the use Jupiter made of his metamorphoses, for you no sooner saw him under the figure of Amphitron but instead of flying to Alcmena, with the raptures Mr Dryden puts into his mouth, he sends to Amphitrion's tailor and cheats him of a laced coat, and his banker of a bag of money, a Jew of a diamond ring, and bespeaks a great supper in his name; and the greatest part of the comedy turns upon poor Amphitrion's being tormented by these people for their debts, and Mercury uses Sosia in the same manner. But I could not easily pardon the liberty the poet has taken of larding his play with, not only indecent expressions, but such gross words as I don't think our mob would suffer from a mountebank,[33] and the two Sosias very fairly let down their breeches in the direct view of the boxes, which were full of people of the first rank, that seemed very well pleased with their entertainment and they assured me this was a celebrated piece. I shall conclude my letter with this remarkable relation, very well worthy the serious consideration of Mr Collier.[34] I won't trouble you with farewell compliments, which I think generally as impertinent as courtesies at leaving the room when the visit has been too long already.

LETTER IX

To Lady Mar,   *Vienna, 14 September 1716*

Though I have so lately troubled you, dear sister, with a long letter, yet I will keep my promise in giving you an account of my first going to court. In order to that ceremony, I was squeezed up in a gown, and adorned with a gorget[35] and the other implements thereunto belonging; a dress very inconvenient, but which certainly shows the neck and shape to great advantage. I cannot forbear in this place giving you some description of the fashions here, which are more monstrous and contrary to all common sense and reason than 'tis possible for you to imagine. They build certain fabrics of gauze on their heads, about a yard high, consisting of three or four storeys, fortified with number-less yards of heavy ribbon. The foundation of this structure is a thing they call a bourlé, which is exactly of the same shape and kind, but about four times as big as those rolls our prudent milk-maids make use of to fix their pails upon. This machine they cover with their own hair, which they mix with a great deal of false, it being a particular beauty to have their heads too large to go into a moderate tub. Their hair is prodigiously powdered to conceal the mixture and set out with three or four rows of bodkins[36] (wonderfully large, that stick out two or three inches from their hair) made of diamonds, pearls, red, green and yellow stones, that it certainly requires as much art and experi-ence to carry the load upright as to dance upon May day with the garland. Their whalebone petticoats out-do ours by several yards' circumference and cover some acres of ground. You may easily suppose how much this extraordinary dress sets off and improves the natural ugliness with which God Almighty has been pleased to endow them all generally. Even the lovely

Empress herself is obliged to comply, in some degree, with these absurd fashions, which they would not quit for all the world.

I had a private audience, according to ceremony, of half an hour, and then all the other ladies were permitted to come make their court. I was perfectly charmed with the Empress; I cannot however tell you that her features are regular. Her eyes are not large, but have a lively look full of sweetness, her complexion the finest I ever saw, her nose and forehead well made but her mouth has ten thousand charms that touch the soul. When she smiles, 'tis with a beauty and sweetness that forces adoration. She has a vast quantity of fine fair hair; but then her person! One must speak of it poetically to do it rigid justice; all that the poets have said of the mein of Juno, the air of Venus, come not up to the truth. The Graces[37] move with her; the famous statue of Medicis[38] was not formed with more delicate proportions; nothing can be added to the beauty of her neck and hands. Till I saw them, I did not believe there were any in nature so perfect, and I was almost sorry that my rank here did not permit me to kiss them; but they are kissed sufficiently, for everybody that waits on her, pays that homage at their entrance and when they take leave. When the ladies were come in, she sat down to quinze.[39] I could not play at a game I had never seen before, and she ordered me a seat at her right hand, and had the goodness to talk to me very much, with that grace so natural to her. I expected every moment when the men were to come in to pay their court, but this drawing room is very different from that of England. No man enters it but the old grand master, who comes in to advertise the Empress of the approach of the Emperor. His imperial majesty did me the honour of speaking to me in a very obliging manner, but he never speaks to any of the other ladies and the whole passes with a gravity and air of ceremony that has something very formal in it. The empress Amelia, dowager of the late Emperor Joseph,[40] came this evening to wait on the reigning Empress, followed by the two Archduchesses her daughters, who are very agreeable young princesses. Their imperial majesties rise and go to meet her at the door of the room, after which she is seated in an armed chair next the Empress, and in the same manner at supper, and there the men have the permission of paying their court. The Archduchesses sit on chairs with backs without arms. The table is entirely served, and all the dishes set on by the Empress' maids of honour, which are twelve young ladies of the first quality. They have no salary but their chambers at court, where they live in a sort of confinement, not being suffered to go to the assemblies or public places in town, except in complement to the wedding of a sister maid, whom the empress always presents with her picture set in diamonds. The three first of them are called ladies of the key, and wear gold keys by their sides; but what I find most pleasant is the custom which obliges them as long as they live after they have left the Empress' service, to make her some present every year on the day of her feast. Her majesty is served by no married woman but the *grande maitresse*, who is generally a widow of the first quality, always very old, and is at the same time groom of the stole, and mother of the maids. The dressers are not at all in the figure they pretend to in England, being looked upon no otherwise than as downright chambermaids.

I had an audience the next day of the Empress Mother,[41] a princess of great virtue and goodness, but who piques herself so much on a violent devotion she is perpetually performing extraordinary acts of penance, without having ever done anything to deserve them. She has the same number of maids of honour, whom she suffers to go in colours, but she herself never quits mourning, and sure nothing can be more dismal than mournings here, even for a brother. There is not the least bit of linen to be seen; all black crepe instead of it; the neck, ears and side of the face covered with a plaited piece of the same stuff and the face that peeps out in the midst of it looks as if it were pilloried. The widows wear over and above, a crepe forehead-cloth, and in this solemn weed go to all the public places of diversion without scruple.

The next day I was to wait on the Empress Amelia, who is now at her palace of retirement, half a mile from the town. I had there the pleasure of seeing a diversion wholly new to me, but which is the common amusement of this court. The Empress herself was seated on a little throne at the end of the fine alley in the garden, and on each side of her ranged two parties of her ladies of honour with other young ladies of quality headed by the two young Archduchesses, all dressed in their hair, full of jewels, with fine light guns in their hands, and at proper distances were placed three oval pictures which were the marks to be shot at. The first was that of a cupid filling a bumper of Burgundy, and the motto, "Tis easy to be valiant here'; the second a fortune holding a garland in her hand, the motto 'For her whom Fortune favours'. The third was a sword with a laurel wreath on the point, the motto 'Here is no shame to the vanquished'. Near the Empress was a gilded trophy wreathed with flowers and made of little crooks, on which were hung rich Turkish handkerchiefs, tippets,[42] ribbons, laces etc. for the small prizes. The Empress gave the first with her own hand, which was a fine ruby ring set round with diamonds, in a gold snuff box. There was for the second a little cupid set with brilliants and besides these a set of fine china for a tea table, encased in gold, japan trunks, fans, and many gallantries of the same nature. All the men of quality at Vienna were spectators, but only the ladies had permission to shoot, and the Archduchess Amelia carried off the first prize. I was very well pleased with having seen this entertainment, and I don't know but it might make as good a figure as the prize shooting in the Aeneid, if I could write as well as Virgil.[43] This is the favourite pleasure of the Emperor, and there is rarely a week without some feast of this kind, which makes the young ladies skilful enough to defend a fort and they laughed very much to see me afraid to handle a gun.

My dear sister, you will easily pardon an abrupt conclusion. I believe by this time you are ready to fear I would never conclude at all.

LETTER X

To Lady Rich, *Vienna, 20 September 1716*

I am extremely pleased, but not at all surprised, at the long, delightful letter you have had the goodness to send me. I know that you can think of an absent friend even in the midst of a court, and that you love to oblige, where you can have no view of a return; and I expect from you that you should love me and think of me when you don't see me.

I have compassion for the mortifications that you tell me befall our little friend, and I pity her much more, since I know that they are only owing to the barbarous customs of our country. Upon my word if she was here she would have no other fault but being something too young for the fashion, and she has nothing to do but to transplant hither about seven years hence to be again a young and blooming beauty. I can assure you that wrinkles, or a small stoop in the shoulders, nay grey hair itself is no objection to the making new conquests. I know you cannot easily figure to yourself a young fellow of five and twenty ogling my Lady Suffolk with passion, or pressing to hand the Countess of Oxford[44] from an opera. But such are the sights I see every day, and I don't perceive anybody surprised at them but myself. A woman till five and thirty is only looked upon as a raw girl, and can possibly make no noise in the world till about forty. I don't know what your ladyship may think of this matter, but 'tis a considerable comfort to me to know there is upon earth such a paradise for old women, and I am content to be insignificant at present, in the design of returning when I am fit to appear no where else.

I cannot help lamenting on this occasion, the pitiful case of so many good English ladies, long since retired to prudery and ratafia[45] whom, if their stars had luckily conducted them hither, would shine in the first rank of beauties. And then, that perplexing word reputation has quite another meaning here than what you give it at London, and getting a lover is so far from losing, that 'tis properly getting reputation, ladies being much more respected in regard to the rank of their lovers than that of their husbands.

But what you'll think very odd, the two sects that divide our whole nation of petticoats are utterly unknown. Here are neither coquettes nor prudes. No woman dares appear coquette enough to encourage two lovers at a time, and I have not seen any such prudes as to pretend fidelity to their husbands, who are certainly the best natured set of people in the world, and look upon their wives' gallants as favourably as men do upon their deputies, that take the troublesome part of their business off of their hands, though they have not the less to do for they are generally deputies in another place themselves. In one word 'tis the established custom for every lady to have two husbands, one that bears the name and another that performs the duties, and these engagements are so well known that it would be a downright affront and publicly resented if you invited a woman of quality to dinner without at the same time inviting her two attendants of lover and husband, between whom she always sits in state with great gravity. The sub-marriages generally last twenty years together, and the lady often commands the poor lover's estate, even to the utter ruin of his family though they are as seldom begun by any passion as other matches. But a man makes but an ill figure that is not in some commerce of this nature, and a woman looks out for a lover as soon as she's married as part of her equipage, without which she could not be genteel; and the first article of the treaty is establishing the pension, which remains to the lady, though the gallant should prove inconstant and this chargeable point of honour I look upon as the real foundation of so many wonderful instances of constancy. I really know several women of the first quality whose pensions are as well known as their annual rents, and yet nobody esteems them the less. On the contrary, their discretion would be called in question if they should be suspected to be mistresses for nothing, and a great part of their emulation consists in trying who shall get most, and having no intrigue at all is so far a disgrace that, I'll assure you, a lady who is very much my friend here told me but yesterday how much I was obliged to her for justifying my conduct in a conversation on my subject, where it was publicly asserted that I could not possibly have common sense that had been about town above a fortnight and had made no steps towards commencing an amour. My friend pleaded for me that my stay was uncertain and she believed that was the cause of my seeming stupidity, and this was all she could find to say in my justification.

But one of the pleasantest adventures I ever met in my life was last night, and which will give you a just idea after what delicate manner the *belles passions* are managed in this country. I was at the assembly of the Countess of — and the young Count of — led me downstairs, asked he me how long I intended to stay here. I made answer that my stay depended on the emperor and it was not in my power to determine it. Well, madam, said he, whether your time here is to be long or short I think you ought to pass it agreeably, and to that end you must engage in a little affair in the heart. My heart, answered I gravely enough, does not engage very easily, and I have no design of parting with it. I see, madam, said he sighing, by the ill nature of that answer that I am not to hope for it, which is a great mortification to me that am charmed with you. But, however, I am still devoted to your service and since I am not worthy of entertaining you myself, do me the honour of letting me know who you like best amongst us, and I'll engage to manage the affair entirely to your satisfaction. You may judge in what manner I should have received this compliment in my own country, but I was well enough acquainted with the way of this, to know that he really intended me an obligation, and thanked him with a grave curtsey for his zeal to serve me, and only assured him that I had no occasion to make use of it.

Thus you see, my dear, gallantry and good breeding are as different in different climates as morality and religion. Who have the rightest notions of both we shall never know till the day of judgement; for which great day of *éclaircissement*[46] I own there is very little impatience in your, etc.

LETTER XI

To Mrs T—,[47]   *Vienna, 26 September 1716*

I never was more agreeably surprised than by your obliging letter. 'Tis a peculiar mark of my esteem, that I tell you so; and I can assure you, that if I loved you one grain less than I do, I should be very sorry to see it as diverting as it is. The mortal aversion I have to writing makes me tremble at the thoughts of a new correspondent and I believe I disobliged no less than a dozen of my London acquaintance by refusing to hear from them, though I did verily think they intended to send me very entertaining letters. But I had rather lose the pleasure of reading several witty things than be forced to write many stupid ones. Yet, in spite of these considerations, I am charmed with this proof of your friendship, and beg a continuation of the same goodness, though I fear the dullness of this will make you immediately repent of it.

It is not from Austria that one can write with vivacity, and I am already infected with the phlegm of the country. Even their amours and their quarrels are carried on with a surprising temper, and they are never lively but upon points of ceremony. There, I own, they show all their passions and 'tis not long since two coaches, meeting in a narrow street at night, the ladies in them not being able to adjust the ceremonial of which should go back, sat there with equal gallantry till two in the morning, and were both so fully determined to die upon the spot rather than yield in a point of that importance, that the street would never have been cleared till their deaths, if the emperor had not sent his guards to part them; and even then they refused to stir till the expedient was found out of taking them both out in chairs exactly at the same moment, after which it was with some difficulty the pass was decided between the two coachmen, no less tenacious of their rank than the ladies. Nay, this passion is so omnipotent in the breasts of the women, that even their husbands never die but they are ready to break their hearts, because that fatal hour puts an end to their rank, no widows having any place at Vienna.

The men are not much less touched with this point of honour, and they do not only scorn to marry, but even to make love to any woman of a family not as illustrious as their own, and the pedigree is much more considered by them than either the complexion or features of their mistresses. Happy are the shes that can number amongst their ancestors counts of the empire; they have neither occasion for beauty, money, or good conduct to get them lovers and husbands. 'Tis true, as to money, 'tis seldom any advantage to the man they marry; the laws of Austria confine a woman's portion not to exceed two thousand florins (about two hundred pounds English) and whatever they have beside remains in their own possession and disposal. Thus, here are many ladies much richer than their husbands, who are however obliged to allow them pin money agreeable to their quality, and I attribute to this considerable branch of prerogative the liberty that they take upon other occasions.

I am sure, you that know my laziness and extreme indifference on this subject will pity me, entangled amongst all these ceremonies which are wonderful burdensome to me, though I am the envy of the whole town, having, by their own customs, the pass before them all. But they revenge upon the poor envoys this great respect shown to ambassadors, using them with a contempt that with all my indifference, I should be very uneasy to suffer. Upon days of ceremony, they have no entrance at court, and on other days must content themselves with walking after every soul and being the very last taken notice of. But I must write a volume to let you know all the ceremonies, and I have already said too much on so dull a subject, which however employs the whole care of the people here. I need not, after this, tell you how agreeably the time slides away with me. You know as well as I do the taste of your, etc.

LETTER XII

To the Lady X—,   *Vienna, 1 October 1716*

You desire me, madam, to send you some account of the
customs here, and at the same time a description of Vienna. I
am always willing to obey your commands, but I must upon this
occasion desire you to take the will for the deed. If I should
undertake to tell you all the particulars in which the manner
here differ from ours, I must write a whole quire of the dullest
stuff that ever was read, or printed without being read.

Their dress agrees with the French or English in no one
article but wearing petticoats. They have many fashions peculiar
to themselves; as that 'tis indecent for a widow ever to wear
green or rose colour, but all the other gayest colours at her own
discretion. The assemblies here are the only regular diversion,
the operas being always at court and commonly on some
particular occasion. Madam Rabutin[48] has the assembly constantly every night at her house, and the other ladies, whenever
they have a fancy to display the magnificence of their apartments, or oblige a friend by complimenting them on the day of
their saint, they declare that on such a day the assembly shall be
at their house in honour of the feast of the count or countess
such-a-one. These days are called days of gala, and all the friends
or relations of the lady whose saint it is are obliged to appear in
their best clothes, and all their jewels. The mistress of the house
takes no particular notice of anybody, nor returns anybody's
visit; and, whoever pleases may go without the formality of
being presented. The company are entertained with ice in
several forms, winter and summer; afterwards they divide into
several parties of ombre, piquet[49] or conversation, all games of
hazard being forbid. I saw the other day the gala for Count
Althann,[50] the Emperor's favourite, and never in my life saw so
many fine clothes ill-fancied. They embroider the richest gold

stuffs and provided they can make their clothes expensive enough that is all the taste they show in them. On other days, the general dress is a scarf and what you please under it.

But now I am speaking of Vienna, I am sure you expect I should say something of the convents; they are of all sorts and sizes, but I am best pleased with that of St Lawrence,[51] where the ease and neatness they seem to live with appears to be much more edifying than those stricter orders where perpetual penance and nastiness must breed discontent and wretchedness. The nuns are all of quality. I think there is to the number of fifty. They have each of them a little cell perfectly clean, the walls covered with pictures more or less fine, according to their quality. A long white stone gallery runs by all of them, furnished with the pictures of exemplary sisters; the chapel extreme neat and richly adorned. But I could not forbear laughing at their showing me a wooden head of our Saviour, which they assured me spoke during the Siege of Vienna; and as a proof of it, bid me mark his mouth, which had been open ever since. Nothing can be more becoming than the dress of these nuns. It is a fine white camlet, the sleeves turned up with fine white calico, and their headdress of the same, only a small veil of black crepe that falls behind. They have a lower sort of serving nuns that wait on them as their chambermaids. They receive all visits of women and play at ombre in their chambers with permission of the abbess, which is very easy to be obtained. I never saw an old woman so good-natured; she is near fourscore and yet shows very little sign of decay, being still lively and cheerful. She caressed me as if I had been her daughter, giving me some pretty things of her own work and sweetmeats in abundance. The grate is not one of the most rigid; it is not very hard to put a head through, and I don't doubt but a man, a little more slender than ordinary, might squeeze in his whole person. The young Count of Salm[52] came to the grate while I was there and the abbess gave him her hand to kiss.

But I was surprised to find here the only beautiful young woman I have seen at Vienna and not only beautiful but genteel, witty and agreeable, of a great family and who had been the admiration of the town. I could not forbear showing my surprise at seeing a nun like her. She make me a thousand obliging compliments and desired me to come often. It will be an infinite pleasure to me, said she sighing, to see you but I avoid with the greatest care seeing any of my former acquaintance, and whenever they come to our convent I lock myself in my cell. I observed tears come into her eyes, which touched me extremely, and I began to talk to her in that strain of tender pity she inspired me with; but she would not own to me that she is not perfectly happy. I have since endeavoured to learn the real cause of her retirement, without being able to get any account, but that everybody was surprised at it, and nobody guessed the reason. I have been several times to see her, but it gives me too much melancholy to see so agreeable a young creature buried alive and I am not surprised that nuns have so often inspired violent passions; the pity one naturally feels for them, when they seem worthy of another destiny, making an easy way for yet more tender sentiments and I never in my life had so little charity for the Roman Catholic religion as since I see the misery it occasions so many poor unhappy women! And the gross superstition of the common people, who are some or other of them, day and night offering bits of candle to the wooden figures that are set up almost in every street. The processions I see very often are a pageantry as offensive and apparently contradictory to all common sense as the pagodas of China. God knows whether it be the womanly spirit of contradiction that works in me, but there never before was such zeal against popery in the heart of, dear madam, etc.

LETTER XIII

To Mr—,   *Vienna, 10 October 1716*

I deserve not all the reproaches you make me. If I have been some time without answering your letter it is not that I don't know how many thanks are due to you for it, or that I am stupid enough to prefer any amusements to the pleasure of hearing from you; but after the professions of esteem you have so obligingly made me, I cannot help delaying as long as I can, showing you that you are mistaken and if you are sincere when you say you expect to be extremely entertained by my letters I ought to be mortified at the disappointment that I am sure you will receive when you hear from me; though I have done my best endeavour to find out something worth writing to you.

I have seen everything that is to be seen with a very diligent curiosity. Here are some fine villas, particularly the late Prince of Liechtenstein's,[53] but the statues are all modern, and the pictures not of the first hands. 'Tis true, the Emperor has some of great value. I was yesterday to see that repository, which they call his treasure, where they seem to have been more diligent in amassing a great quantity of things than in the choice of them. I spend above five hours there, and yet there were very few things that stopped me long to consider them. But the number is prodigious, being a very long gallery filled on both sides, and five large rooms. There are a vast quantity of paintings, amongst which are many fine miniatures, but the most valuable pictures are a few of Corregio, those of Titian[54] being at the Favorita.

The cabinet of jewels did not appear to me so rich as I expected to see it. They showed me there a cup about the size of a tea dish of one entire emerald, which they had so particular a respect for only the Emperor has the privilege of touching it. There is a large cabinet full of curiosities of clockwork, only one of which I thought worth observing. That was a crawfish, with all the motions so natural it was hard to distinguish it from the life. The next cabinet was a large collection of agates, some of them extreme beautiful, and of an uncommon size, and several vases of lapis lazuli. I was surprised to see the cabinet of medals so poorly furnished; I did not remark one of any value, and they are kept in a most ridiculous disorder. As to the antiques, very few of them deserved that name. Upon my saying they were modern, I could not forbear laughing at the answer of the profound antiquary that showed them, that they were ancient enough; for, to his knowledge they had been there this forty year. But the next cabinet diverted me yet better, being nothing else but a parcel of wax babies and toys in ivory, very well worthy to be presented children of five year old. Two of the rooms were wholly filled with relics of all kinds, set in jewels, amongst which I was desired to observe a crucifix that they assured me had spoke very wisely to the Emperor Leopold. I won't trouble you with a catalogue of the rest of the lumber, but I must not forget to mention a small piece of loadstone[55] that held up an anchor of steel too heavy for me to lift. This is what I thought most curious in the whole treasure. There are some few heads of ancient statues, but several of them defaced by modern additions.

I foresee that you will be very little satisfied with this letter, and I dare hardly ask you to be good natured enough to charge the dullness of it on the barrenness of the subject and overlook the stupidity of your etc.

LETTER XIV

To Lady Mar,   *Prague, 17 November 1716*

I hope my dear sister wants no new proof of my sincere affection for her, but I am sure if you did, I could not give you a stronger than writing at this time, after three days or, more properly speaking, three nights and days hard post travelling. The kingdom of Bohemia is the most desert of any I have seen in Germany; the villages so poor and the post houses so miserable, that clean straw and fair water are blessings not always to be found, and better accommodation not to be hoped. Though I carried my own bed with me, I could not sometimes find a place to set it up in, and I rather chose to travel all night, as cold as it is, wrapped up in my furs, than to go into the common stoves, which are filled with a mixture of all sorts of ill scents.

This town was once the royal seat of the Bohemian kings, and is still the capital of the kingdom. There are yet some remains of its former splendour, being one of the largest towns in Germany, but for the most part old built and thinly inhabited, which makes the houses very cheap and those people of quality who cannot easily bear the expense of Vienna choose to reside here, where they have assemblies, music and all other diversions, those of a court excepted, at very moderate rates, all things being here in great abundance, especially the best wildfowl I ever tasted. I have already been visited by some of the most considerable ladies, whose relations I knew at Vienna. They are dressed after the fashions there, as people at Exeter imitate those of London; that is, their imitation is more excessive than the original and 'tis not easy to describe what extraordinary figures they make. The person is so much lost between headdress and petticoat, they have as much occasion to write upon their backs 'this is a woman' or the information of travellers, as ever signpost painter had to write 'this is a bear'.[56]

I will not forget to write to you again from Dresden and Leipzig, being much more solicitous to content your curiosity, than to indulge my own repose, I am etc.

LETTER XV

To Lady Mar,   *Leipzig,*[57] *21 November 1716*

I believe, dear sister, you will easily forgive my not writing to you from Dresden as I promised when I tell you that I never went out of my chaise from Prague to that place. You may imagine how heartily I was tired with twenty four hours' post travelling, without sleep or refreshment (for I can never sleep in coach, however fatigued). We passed by moonshine the frightful precipices that divide Bohemia from Saxony, at the bottom of which runs the river Elbe, but I cannot say I had reason to fear drowning in it, being perfectly convinced that, in case of a tumble, it was utterly impossible to come alive to the bottom. In many places the road is so narrow that I could not discern an inch of space between the wheels and the precipice. Yet I was so good a wife not to wake Mr Wortley, who was fast asleep by my side, to make him share in my fears, since the danger was unavoidable, till I perceived, by the bright light of the moon, our postilions nodding on horseback while the horses were on a full gallop, and I thought it very convenient to call out to desire them to look where they were going. My calling waked Mr Wortley, and he was much more surprised than myself at the situation we were in, and assured me that he had passed the Alps five times in different places without ever having done a road so dangerous. I have been told since 'tis common to find the bodies of travellers in the Elbe; but, thank God that was not our destiny, and we came safe to Dresden, so much tired with fear and fatigue, it was not possible for me to compose myself to write. After passing these dreadful rocks, Dresden appeared to me a wonderful agreeable situation, in a fine large plain on the banks of the Elbe. I was very glad to stay there a day to rest myself.

The town is the neatest I have seen in Germany; most of the houses are new built, the Elector's palace very handsome and his repository full of curiosities of different kinds, with a collection of medals very much esteemed. Sir Richard Vernon, our King's envoy, came to see me here, and Madam de Lorme, whom I knew in London, when her husband was minister to the King of Poland there.[58] She offered me all things in her power to entertain me and brought some ladies with her, whom she presented to me. The Saxon ladies resemble the Austrian no more than the Chinese do those of London. They are very genteelly dressed, after the French and English modes, and have generally pretty faces, but they are the most determined *minaudières*[59] in the whole world. They would think it a mortal sin against good breeding if they either spoke or moved in a natural manner. They all affect a little soft lisp, and a pretty pitty-pat step; which female frailties ought, however, to be forgiven them in favour of their civility and good nature to strangers, which I have a great deal of reason to praise.

The Countess of Cosel[60] is kept prisoner in a melancholy

castle some leagues from hence, and I cannot forbear telling you what I have heard of her, because it seems to me very extraordinary, though, I foresee I shall swell my letter to the size of a packet. She was mistress to the King of Poland (Elector of Saxony) with so absolute a dominion over him that never any lady had had so much power in that court. They tell a pleasant story of his majesty's first declaration of love, which he made in a visit to her, bringing in one hand a bag of a hundred thousand crowns, and in the other a horseshoe, which he snapped asunder before her face, leaving her to draw consequences from such remarkable proofs of strength and liberality. I know not which charmed her, but she consented to leave her husband and to give herself up to him entirely, being divorced publicly in such a manner as, by their law, permits either party to marry again. God knows whether it was at this time, or in some other fond fit, but 'tis certain, the king had the weakness to make her a formal contract of marriage, which, though it could signify nothing during the life of the Queen, pleased her so well that she could not be contented without telling all people she saw of it, and giving herself the airs of a queen.

Men endure everything while they are in love, but when the excess of passion was cooled by long possession his majesty began to reflect on the ill consequences of leaving such a paper in her hands and desired to have it restored to him. She rather chose to endure all the most violent effects of his anger than give it up; and though she is one of the richest and most avaricious ladies of her country, she has refused the offer of the continuation of a large pension and the security of a vast sum of money she has amassed and has at last provoked the King to confine her person, where she endures all the terrors of a strait imprisonment, and remains still inflexible, either to threats or promises though her violent passions have brought her into fits, which 'tis supposed will soon put an end to her life. I cannot forbear having some compassion for a woman that suffers for a point of honour, however mistaken, especially in a country where points of honour are not over scrupulously observed amongst ladies.

I could have wished Mr Wortley's business had permitted a longer stay at Dresden. Perhaps I am partial to a town where they profess the Protestant religion, but everything seemed to me with quite another air of politeness than I have found in other places. Leipzig, where I am at present, is a town very considerable for its trade, and I take this opportunity of buying pages' liveries, gold stuffs for myself, etc. all things of that kind being at least double the price at Vienna, partly because of the excessive customs and partly the want of genius and industry in the people, who make no one sort of thing there, and the ladies are obliged to send even for their shoes out of Saxony. The fair here is one of the most considerable in Germany, and the resort of all the people of quality, as well as the merchants. This is also a fortified town, but I avoid ever mentioning fortifications, being sensible that I know not how to speak of them. I am the more easy under my ignorance, when I reflect that I am sure you'll willingly forgive the omission; for if I made you the most exact description of all the ravelins[61] and bastions I see in my travels, I dare swear you would ask me, 'what is a ravelin?' and 'what is a bastion?'.

Adieu, my dear sister.

LETTER XVI

To the Countess of —,[62]   *Brunswick, 23 November 1716*

I am just come to Brunswick, a very old town, but which has the advantage of being the capital of the Duke of Wolfenbüttel's[63] dominions, a family, not to speak of its ancient honours, illustrious by having its younger branch on the throne of England, and having given two empresses to Germany.[64] I have not forgot to drink your health here in mum,[65] which I think very well deserves its reputation of being the best in the world.

This letter is the third I have writ to you during my journey, and I declare to you that if you do not send me immediately a full and true account of all the changes and chances amongst our London acquaintance, I will not write you any description of Hanover, where I hope to be tonight, though I know you have more curiosity to hear of that place than any other.

LETTER XVII

To Lady Bristol,   *Hanover, 25 November 1716*

I received your ladyship's but the day before I left Vienna, though, by the date I ought to have had it much sooner; but nothing was ever worse regulated than the post in most parts of Germany. I can assure you the packet at Prague was tied behind my chaise, and in that manner conveyed to Dresden. The secrets of half the country were at my mercy, if I had had any curiosity for them. I would not longer delay my thanks for yours, though the number of my acquaintance here, and my duty of attending at court leaves me hardly any time to dispose of. I am extremely pleased that I can tell you, without either flattery or partiality, that our young prince[66] has all the accomplishments that 'tis possible to have at his age, with an air of sprightliness and understanding, and something so very engaging and easy in his behaviour, that he needs not the advantage of his rank to appear charming. I had the honour of a long conversation with him last night, before the King came in. His governor retired on purpose (as he told me afterwards) that I might make some judgement of his genius, by hearing him speak without constraint and I was surprised at the quickness and politeness that appeared in everything he said, joined to a person perfectly agreeable, and the fine fair hair of the princess.

This town is neither large nor handsome, but the palace is capable of holding a greater court than that of St James's and the King has had the goodness to appoint us a lodging in one part of it, without which we should have been very ill accommodated, for the vast number of English crowds the town[67] so much 'tis very good luck to be able to get one sorry room in a miserable tavern. I dined today with the Portuguese Ambassador,[68] who thinks himself very happy to have two wretched parlours in an inn.

I have now made the tour of Germany and cannot help observing a considerable difference travelling here and in England. One sees none of those fine seats of noblemen, so common amongst us, nor anything like a country gentleman's house, though they have many situations perfectly fine. But the whole people are divided into absolute sovereignties, where all the riches and magnificence are at court, or communities of merchants, such as Nuremburg and Frankfurt, where they live always in town for the convenience of trade.

The King's company of French comedians play here every night. They are very well dressed, and some of them not ill actors. His majesty dines and sups constantly in public. The court is very numerous and his affability and goodness make it one of the most agreeable places in the world to, dear madam, your ladyship's etc.

LETTER XVIII

To Lady Rich,   *Hanover, 1 December 1716*

I am very glad, my dear Lady Rich, that you have been so well pleased as you tell me at the report of my returning to England; though, like other pleasures, I can assure you it has no real foundation. I hope you know me enough to take my word against any report concerning myself. 'Tis true, as to distance of place, I am much nearer London than I was some weeks ago, but as to the thoughts of a return, I never was farther off in my life. I own, I could with great joy indulge the pleasing hopes of seeing you, and the very few others that share my esteem, but while Mr Wortley is determined to proceed in his design, I am determined to follow him. I am running on upon my own affairs, that is to say, I am going to write very dully, as most people do when they write of themselves. I will make haste to change the disagreeable subject by telling you that I am now got into the region of beauty. All the women here have (literally) rosy cheeks, snowy foreheads and bosoms, jet eyebrows and scarlet lips, to which they generally add coal-black hair. These perfections never leave them, till the hour of their death, and have a very fine effect by candlelight; but I could wish they were handsome with a little more variety. They resemble one another as much as Mrs Salmon's court of Great Britain[69] and are in as much danger of melting away, by too near approaching the fire, which they for that reason carefully avoid, though 'tis now such excessive cold weather that I believe they suffer extremely by that piece of self-denial. The snow is already very deep, and the people begin to slide about in their traineaus. This is a favourite diversion all over Germany. They are little machines fixed upon a sledge that hold a lady and a gentleman, and drawn by one horse. The gentleman has the honour of driving, and they move with a prodigious swiftness. The lady, the horse and the traineau[70] are all as fine as they can be made, and when there are many of them together, 'tis a very agreeable show. At Vienna, where all pieces of magnificence are carried to excess, there are sometimes traineaus that cost five or six hundred pounds English. The Duke of Wolfenbüttel is now at this court; you know he is nearly related to our King, and uncle to the reigning Empress who is, I believe, the most beautiful queen upon earth. She is now with child, which is all the consolation of the imperial court for the loss of the Archduke.[71] I took my leave of her the day before I left Vienna and she began to speak to me with so much grief and tenderness of the death of that young prince, I had much ado to withhold my tears. You know that I am not at all partial to people for their titles, but I own that I love that charming princess, if I may use so familiar an expression, and if I did not, I should have been very much moved at the tragical end of an only son, born after being so long desired, and at length killed by want of good management, weaning him in the beginning of the winter.

Adieu, my dear Lady Rich. Continue to write to me and believe none of your goodness is lost upon your etc.

LETTER XIX

To Lady Mar,   *Blankenburg, 17 December 1716*

I received yours, dear sister, the very day I left Hanover. You may easily imagine I was then in too great a hurry to answer it, but you see I take the first opportunity of doing myself that pleasure. I came here the fifteenth, very late at night, after a terrible journey, in the worst roads and weather that ever poor traveller suffered. I have taken this little fatigue merely to oblige the reigning empress, and carry a message from her imperial majesty to the Duchess of Blankenburg,[72] her mother, who is a princess of great address and good breeding, and may be still called a fine woman. It was so late when I came to this town, I did not think it proper to disturb the Duke and Duchess with the news of my arrival and took up my quarters in a miserable inn; but as soon as I had sent my compliments to their highnesses they immediately sent me their own coach and six horses, which had however enough to do to draw us up the very high hill on which the castle is situated. The Duchess is extremely obliging to me, and this little court is not without its diversions. The Duke tallies at basset[73] every night, and the duchess tells me she is so well pleased with my company I should find it very difficult to steal time to write, if she was not now at church, where I cannot wait on her, not understanding the language enough to pay my devotions in it.

You will not forgive me if I do not say something of Hanover. I cannot tell you that the town is either large or magnificent. The opera house, which was built by the late elector, is much finer than that of Vienna.[74] I was very sorry the ill weather did not permit me to see Hernhausen[75] in all its beauty; but in spite of the snow, I thought the gardens very fine. I was particularly surprised at the vast number of orange trees, much larger than any I have ever seen in England, though this climate is certainly colder. But I had more reason to wonder that night at the King's table. There was brought to him from a gentleman of this country two large baskets full of ripe oranges and lemons of different sorts, many of which were quite new to me; and what I thought worth all the rest, two ripe ananasses,[76] which, to my taste, are a fruit perfectly delicious. You know they are naturally the growth of Brazil, and I could not imagine how they could come there but by enchantment. Upon enquiry I learnt that they have brought their stoves to such perfection, they lengthen the summer as long as they please, giving to every plant the degree of heat it would receive from the sun in its native soil. The effect is very near the same; I am surprised we do not practice in England so useful an invention. This reflection naturally leads me to consider our obstinacy in shaking with cold six months in the year rather than make use of stoves, which are certainly one of the greatest conveniences of life, and so far from spoiling the form of a room that they add very much to the magnificence of it, when they are painted and gilt, as they are at Vienna or at Dresden, where they are often in the shapes of china jars, statues or fine cabinets, so naturally represented they are not to be distinguished. If ever I return, in defiance to the fashion, you shall certainly see one in the chamber of, dear sister, etc.

I will write often, since you desire it, but I must beg you to be a little more particular in yours. You fancy me at forty miles distance, and forget that after so long an absence I can't understand hints.

LETTER XX

To Lady—,[77]   *Vienna, 1 January 1717*

I have just received here at Vienna you ladyship's compliment on my return to England, sent me from Hanover. You see, madam, all things that are asserted with confidence are not absolutely true, and that you have no sort of reason to complain of me for making my designed return a mystery to you when you say all the world are informed of it. You may tell all the world in my name, that they are never so well informed of my affairs as I am myself, and that I am very positive I am at this time at Vienna, where the carnival is begun, and all sort of diversions in perpetual practice, except that of masquing, which is never permitted during a war with the Turks. The balls are in public places, where the men pay a gold ducat at entrance, but the ladies nothing. I am told that these houses get sometimes a thousand ducats in a night. They are very magnificently furnished and the music good if they had not that detestable custom of mixing hunting horns with it, that almost deafen the company. But that noise is so agreeable here they never make a consort without them. The ball always concludes with English country dances to the number of thirty or forty couple, and so ill danced that there is very little pleasure in them. They know but half-a-dozen, and they have danced them over and over this fifty year. I would fain have taught them some new ones, but I found it would be some months labour to make them comprehend them.

Last night there was an Italian comedy acted at court. The scenes were pretty, but the comedy itself such intolerable low farce, without either wit or humour, that I was surprised how all the court could sit there attentively for four hours together. No women are suffered to act on the stage, and the men dressed like them were such awkward figures, they very much added to the ridicule of the spectacle. What completed the diversion was the excessive cold, which was so great I thought I should have died there. It is now the very extremity of the winter here; the Danube is entirely frozen, and the weather not to be supported without stoves and furs, but, however, the air so clear almost everybody is well, and colds not half so common as in England and I am persuaded there cannot be a purer air, nor more wholesome, than that of Vienna. The plenty and excellence of all sorts of provisions is greater here than in any place I was ever before, and 'tis not very expensive to keep a splendid table. 'Tis really a pleasure to pass through the markets and see the abundance of what we should think rarities of fowls and venisons that are daily bought in from Hungary and Bohemia. They want nothing but shellfish, and are so fond of oysters they have them sent from Venice, and eat them very greedily, stink or not stink.

Thus I obey your commands, madam, in giving you an account of Vienna, though I know you will not be satisfied with it. You chide me for my laziness, in not telling you a thousand agreeable and surprising things that you say you are sure I have seen and heard. Upon my word, madam, 'tis my regard to truth, and not laziness, that I do not entertain you with as many prodigies as other travellers use to divert their readers with. I might easily pick up wonders in every town I pass through, or tell you a long series of popish miracles, but I cannot fancy that there is anything new in letting you know that priests can lie, and the mob believe, all the world over. Then as for news, that you are so inquisitive about, how can it be entertaining to you, that don't know the people, that the Prince of — has forsaken the Countess of —, or that the prince such-a-one has an intrigue with the countess such-a-one? Would you have me write novels like the Countess of D'Aulnoy?[78] And is it not better to tell you a plain truth, that I am etc.

LETTER XXI

To Lady Mar, *Vienna, 16 January 1717*

I am now, dear sister, to take leave of you for a long time, and of Vienna for ever, designing tomorrow to begin my journey through Hungary, in spite of the excessive cold and deep snows, which are enough to damp a greater courage than I am mistress of, but my principle of passive obedience carries me through everything. I have had my audiences of leave of the Empresses.

His imperial majesty was pleased to be present when I waited on the reigning empress and after a very obliging conversation both their imperial majesties invited me to take Vienna in my road back, but I have no thoughts of enduring over again so great a fatigue.

I delivered a letter to the Empress from the Duchess of Blankenburg. I stayed but a few days at that court, though her highness pressed me very much to stay, and when I left her, engaged me to write to her. I writ you a long letter from thence, which I hope you have received, though you don't mention it; but I believe I forgot to tell you one curiosity in all the German courts which I cannot forbear taking notice of. All the princes keep favourite dwarfs. The Emperor and Empress have two of these little monsters, as ugly as devils, especially the female, but all bedaubed with diamonds and stands at her majesty's elbow in all public places. The Duke of Wolfenbüttel has one, and the Duchess of Blankenburg is not without hers, but indeed the most proportionable I ever saw. I am told the King of Denmark[79] has so far improved upon this fashion that his dwarf is his chief minister. I can assign no reason for their fondness for these pieces of deformity, but the opinion that all the absolute princes have, that it is below them to converse with the rest of mankind, and not to be quite alone they are forced to seek their companions amongst the refuse of human nature, these creatures being the only part of their court privileged to talk freely to them.

I am at present confined to my chamber by a sore throat, and am really glad of the excuse to avoid seeing people that I love well enough to be very much mortified when I think I am going to part with them for ever. 'Tis true, the Austrians are not commonly the most polite people in the world nor the most agreeable, but Vienna is inhabited by all nations, and I had formed to myself a little society of such as were perfectly to my own taste. And though the number was not very great, I could never pick up in any other place such a number of reasonable, agreeable people. We were almost always together, and you know I have ever been of opinion that a chosen conversation, composed of a few that one esteems, is the greatest happiness of life. Here are some Spaniards of both sexes that have all the vivacity and generosity of sentiments anciently ascribed to their nation, and could I believe that the whole kingdom were like them, I should wish nothing more than to end my days there.

The ladies of my acquaintance have so much goodness for me, they cry whenever they see me since I have determined to undertake this journey; and, indeed, I am not very easy when I reflect on what I am going to suffer. Almost everybody I see frights me with some new difficulty. Prince Eugene[80] has been so good as to say all the things he could to persuade me to stay till the Danube is thawed, that I may have the convenience of going by water, assuring me that the houses in Hungary are such as are no defence against the weather, and that I shall be obliged to travel three or four days between Buda and Essek without finding any house at all, through desert plains covered with snow, where the cold is so violent many have been killed by it. I own these terrors have made a very deep impression on my mind, because I believe he tells me things truly as they are, and nobody can be better informed of them.

Now I have named that great man, I am sure you expect I should say something particular of him, having the advantage of seeing him very often, but I am as unwilling to speak of him at Vienna as I should be to talk of Hercules in the court of Omphale,[81] if I had seen him there. I don't know what comfort other people find in considering the weaknesses of great men because, it brings them nearer to their own level but 'tis always a mortification to me to observe that there is no perfection in humanity. The young Prince of Portugal[82] is the admiration of the whole court. He is handsome and polite, with a great vivacity. All the officers tell wonders of his gallantry in the last campaign. He is lodged at court with all the honours due to his rank.

Adieu, dear sister; this is the last account you will have from me of Vienna. If I survive my journey you shall hear from me again. I can say with great truth, in the words of Moneses, I have long learnt to hold myself as nothing,[83] but when I think of the fatigue my poor infant must suffer, I have all a mother's fondness in my eyes, and all her tender passions in my heart.

P.S. I have writ a letter to my Lady—[84] that I believe she won't like, and upon cooler reflection I think I had done better to have let it alone, but I was downright peevish at all her questions, and her ridiculous imagination, that I have certainly seen abundance of wonders which I keep to myself out of mere malice. She is angry that I won't lie like other travellers. I verily believe she expects I should tell her of the anthropophagi,[85] and men whose heads grow below their shoulders. However, pray say something to pacify her.

LETTER XXII

To Alexander Pope, *Vienna, 16 January 1717*

I have not time to answer your letter, being in all the hurry of preparing for my journey, but I think I ought to bid adieu to my friends with the same solemnity as if I was going to mount a breach,[86] at least, if I am to believe the information of the people here, who denounce all sort of terrors to me; and indeed the weather is at present such as very few ever set out in. I am threatened at the same time with being froze to death, buried in the snow and taken by the Tartars, who ravage that part of Hungary I am to pass. 'Tis true we shall have a considerable escort[87] so that possibly I may be diverted with a new scene by finding myself in the midst of a battle. How my adventures will conclude I leave entirely to Providence; if comically, you shall hear of them.

Pray be so good as to tell Mr—[88] I have received his letter. Make him my adieus; if I live I will answer it. The same compliment to my Lady Rich.

LETTER XXIII

To Lady Mar,   *Peterwardein,*[89] *30 January 1717*

At length, dear sister, I am safely arrived, with all my family in good health, at Peterwardein, having suffered little from the rigour of the season (against which we were well provided by furs) and found everywhere, by the care of sending before, such tolerable accommodation that I can hardly forbear laughing when I recollect all the frightful ideas that were given me of this journey, which were wholly owing to the tenderness of my Vienna friends and their desire of keeping me with them for this winter. Perhaps it will not be disagreeable to give you a short journal of my journey, being through a country entirely unknown to you, and very little passed even by the Hungarians themselves, who generally choose to take the convenience of going down the Danube. We have had the blessing of being favoured with finer weather than is common at this time of the year, though the snow was so deep we were obliged to have our coaches fixed upon traineaus, which move so swift and so easily 'tis by far the most agreeable manner of travelling post.

We came to Raab the second day from Vienna, on the seventeenth instant, where Mr Wortley sending word of our arrival to the governor, we had the best house in the town provided for us, the garrison put under arms, a guard ordered at our door and all other honours paid to us; the governor and all other officers immediately waiting on Mr Wortley to know if there was anything to be done for his service. The Bishop of Temeswar[90] came to visit us, with great civility, earnestly pressing us to dine with him the next day, which, we refusing, as being resolved to pursue our journey, he sent us several baskets of winter fruit, and a great variety of Hungarian wines with a young hind just killed. This is a prelate of great power in this country, of the ancient family of Nádasdy[91] so considerable for many ages in this kingdom. He is a very polite, agreeable, cheerful old man, wearing the Hungarian habit with a venerable white beard down to his girdle.

Raab is a strong town, well garrisoned and fortified, and was a long time the frontier town between the Turkish and German empires. It has its name from the river Raab on which it is situated, just on its meeting with the Danube, in an open champaign country. It was first taken by the Turks under the command of the Pasha Sinan in the reign of Sultan Amurath III, in the year 1594.[92] The governor being supposed to have betrayed it, was afterwards beheaded by the emperor's command. The counts of Schwarzenberg and Palffy[93] retook it by surprise, 1598, since which time it has remained in the hands of the Germans, though the Turks once more attempted to gain it by stratagem, 1642.[94] The cathedral is large and well built, which is all that I saw remarkable in the town.

Leaving Comora on the other side the river we went the eighteenth to Nosmuhl, a small village where however, we made shift to find tolerable accommodation. We continued two days travelling between this place and Buda, through the finest plains in the world, as even as if they were paved, and extreme fruitful, but for the most part desert and uncultivated, laid waste by the long war between the Turk and the Emperor, and the more cruel civil war occasioned by the barbarous persecution of the Protestant religion by the emperor Leopold.[95] That prince has left behind him the character of an extraordinary piety, and was naturally of a mild merciful temper; but, putting his conscience into the hands of a Jesuit, he was more cruel and treacherous to his poor Hungarian subjects than ever the Turk has been to the Christians, breaking without scruple his coronation oath and his faith, solemnly given in many public treaties. Indeed, nothing can be more melancholy than travelling through Hungary, reflecting on the former flourishing state of that kingdom, and seeing such a noble spot of earth almost uninhabited.

This is also the present circumstances of Buda, where we arrived very early the twenty second, once the royal seat of the Hungarian kings, where their palace was reckoned one of the

most beautiful buildings of the age, now wholly destroyed, no
part of the town having been repaired since the last siege but
the fortifications and the castle, which is the present residence
of the governor, General Regal, an officer of great merit. He
came immediately to see us, and carried us in his coach to his
house, where I was received by his lady with all possible
civility, and magnificently entertained.[96] This city is situate
upon a little hill on the south side of the Danube, the castle
being much higher than the town, from whence the prospect is
very noble. Without the walls lie a vast number of little houses,
or rather huts, that they call the Rascian town, being altogether
inhabited by that people.[97] The governor assured me it would
furnish 12,000 fighting men. These towns look very odd; their
houses stand in rows, many thousands of them so close together
that they appear at a little distance like old fashioned thatched
tents. They consist, every one of them, of one hovel above and
another underground; these are their summer and winter apartments.

Buda was first taken by Süleiman the Magnificent in 1526,[98]
and lost the following year to Ferdinand I, King of Bohemia.
Süleiman regained it, 1529, by the treachery of the garrison, and
voluntarily gave it into the hand of King John of Hungary, after
whose death, his son being an infant, Ferdinand laid siege to it
and the Queen Mother was forced to call Süleiman to her aid,
who raised the siege, but left a Turkish garrison in the town and
commanded her to remove her court from thence, which she
was forced to submit to in 1541. It resisted afterwards the sieges
laid to it by the Marquis of Brandenburg, 1542; Count Schwarzenberg, 1598, General Russworm in 1602, and the Duke of
Lorrain, commander of the emperor's forces, in 1684, to whom
it yielded, 1686, after an obstinate defence, Abdul Pasha, the
governor, being killed fighting in the breach with a Roman
bravery.[99] The loss of this town was so important, and so much
resented by the Turks, that it occasioned the deposing of their
emperor Mehmed IV,[100] the year following.

We did not proceed on our journey till the twenty third,
passing through Adom and Fodwar, both considerable towns

when in the hands of the Turks. They are now quite ruined; only the remains of some Turkish towers show something of what they have been. This part of the country is very much overgrown with wood and so little frequented 'tis incredible what vast numbers of wildfowl we saw, who often live here to a good old age, and, undisturbed by guns, in quiet sleep.

We came the twenty fifth to Mohács,[101] and were showed the field near it where Louis, the young King of Hungary, lost his army and his life, being drowned in a ditch trying to fly from Balybeus, the general of Süleiman the Magnificent. This battle opened the first passage for the Turks into the heart of Hungary. I don't name to you the little villages, of which I can say nothing remarkable, but I'll assure you, I have always found a warm stove and great plenty, particularly of wild boar, venison and all kinds of *gibier*.[102] The few people that inhabit Hungary live easily enough. They have no money, but the woods and plains afford them provision in great abundance. They were ordered to give us all things necessary, even what horses we pleased to demand, gratis, but Mr Wortley would not oppress the poor country people by making use of this order, and always paid them to the full worth of what we had from them. They were so surprised at this unexpected generosity, which they are very little used to, they always pressed upon us at parting, a dozen of fat pheasants, or something of that sort, for a present. Their dress is very primitive, being only a plain sheep's skin without other dressing than being dried in the sun and a cap and boots of the same stuff. You may imagine this lasts them many winters, and thus they have very little occasion for money.

The twenty sixth we passed over the frozen Danube with all our equipage and carriages. We met on the other side General Veterani,[103] who invited us with great civility to pass the night at a little castle of his a few miles off, assuring us we should have a very hard day's journey to reach Essek, which we found but too true, the woods being scarce passable and very dangerous, from the vast quantity of wolves that herd in them. We came, however, safe, though late, to Essek, where we stayed a day to despatch a courier with letters to the Pasha of Belgrade, and I took that opportunity of seeing the town, which is not very large, but fair built and well fortified. This was a town of great trade, very rich and populous when in the hands of the Turks. It is situated on the Drave, which runs into the Danube. The bridge was esteemed one of the most extraordinary in the world, being 8000 paces long, and all built of oak, which was burnt, and the city laid in ashes by Count Leslie, 1685, but was again repaired and fortified by the Turks who, however, abandoned it, 1687, and General Dünnewalt[104] took possession of it for the Emperor, in whose hands it has remained ever since, and is esteemed one of the bulwarks of Hungary. The twenty eighth we went to Bocowar, a very large Rascian town, all built after the manner I have described to you. We were met out there by Colonel—, who would not suffer us to go anywhere but to his quarters, where I found his wife a very agreeable Hungarian lady, and his niece and daughter, two pretty young women, crowded into three or four Rascian houses cast into one and made as neat and convenient as those places were capable of being made. The Hungarian ladies are much handsomer than those of Austria. All the Vienna beauties are of that country; they are generally very fair and well-shaped. Their dress I think extreme becoming. This lady was in a gown of scarlet velvet, lined and faced with sables, made exact to her shape, and the skirt falling to her feet. The sleeves are strait to their arms and the stays buttoned before, with two rows of little buttons of gold, pearl or diamonds. On their heads they wear a cap embroidered with a tassel of gold that hangs low on one side, lined with sable, or some other fine fur. They gave us a handsome dinner, and I thought their conversation very polite and agreeable. They would accompany us part of our way.

The twenty ninth we arrived here, where we were met by the commandant at the head of all the officers of the garrison. We are lodged in the best apartment of the governor's house, and entertained in a very splendid manner by the emperor's order. We wait here till all points are adjusted concerning our reception on the Turkish frontiers. Mr Wortley's courier, which he sent from Essek, returned this morning with the Pasha's answer in a purse of scarlet satin, which the interpreter here has translated. 'Tis to promise him to be honourably received, and desires him to appoint where he would be met by the Turkish convoy. He has despatched the courier back, naming Betsko, a village in the mid-way between Peterwardein and Belgrade. We shall stay here till we receive the answer.

Thus, dear sister, I have given you a very particular and, I am afraid you'll think, a tedious account of this part of my travels. It was not an affectation of showing my reading that has made me tell you some little scraps of the history of the towns I have passed through. I have always avoided anything of that kind, when I spoke of places that I believe you knew the story of as well as myself, but Hungary being a part of the world which I believe quite new to you, I thought you might read with some pleasure an account of it, which I have been very solicitous to get from the best hands.[105] However, if you don't like it, 'tis in your power to forbear reading it. I am, dear sister, etc.

I am promised to have this letter carefully sent to Vienna.

LETTER XXIV

To Alexander Pope,   *Belgrade, 12 February 1717*

I did verily intend to write you a long letter from Peterwardein, where I expected to stay three or four days, but the Pasha here was in such haste to see us that he despatched our courier back which Mr Wortley had sent to know the time he would send the convoy to meet us, without suffering him to pull off his boots. My letters were not thought important enough to stop our journey and we left Peterwardein the next day, being waited on by the chief officers of the garrison and a considerable convoy of Germans and Rascians. The Emperor has several regiments of these people, but to say truth, they are rather plunderers than soldiers, having no pay and being obliged to furnish their own arms and horses. They rather look like vagabond gypsies or stout beggars than regular troops. I can't forbear speaking a word of this race of creatures who are very numerous all over Hungary. They have a patriarch of their own at Grand Cairo, and are really of the Greek church,[106] but their extreme ignorance gives their priests occasion to impose several new notions upon them. These fellows letting their hair and beards grow inviolate, make exactly the figure of the Indian Brahmins. They are heirs-general to all the money of the laity for which, in return, they give them formal passports signed and sealed for heaven, and the wives and children only inherit the houses and cattle. In most other points they follow the Greek rites.

This little digression has interrupted my telling you we passed over the fields of Karlowitz, where the last great victory was obtained by Prince Eugene over the Turks.[107] The marks of that glorious bloody day are yet recent, the field being strewed with the skulls and carcases of unburied men, horses and camels. I could not look without horror on such numbers of mangled human bodies, and reflect on the injustice of war that makes murder not only necessary but meritorious. Nothing seems to me a plainer proof of the irrationality of mankind, whatever fine claims we pretend to reason, than the rage with which they contest for a small spot of ground, when such vast parts of fruitful earth lie quite uninhabited. 'Tis true, custom has now made it unavoidable, but can there be a greater demonstration of want of reason than a custom being firmly established so plainly contrary to the interest of man in general? I am a good deal inclined to believe Mr Hobbes that the state of nature is a state of war,[108] but thence I conclude human nature not rational, if the word reason means common sense, as I suppose it does. I have a great many admirable arguments to support this reflection but I won't trouble you with them, but return in a plain style to the history of my travels.

We were met at Betsko, a village in the midway between Belgrade and Peterwardein, by an aga of the janissaries,[109] with a body of Turks, exceeding the Germans by one hundred men, though the Pasha had engaged to send exactly the same number. You may judge by this of their fears. I am really persuaded that they hardly thought the odds of one hundred men set them even with the Germans. However, I was very uneasy till they were parted, fearing some quarrel might arise, notwithstanding the parole given.

We came late to Belgrade, the deep snows making the ascent to it very difficult. It seems a strong city, fortified on the east side by the Danube and on the south by the river Save, and was formerly the barrier of Hungary. It was first taken by Süleiman the Magnificent and since, by the Emperor's forces, led by the Elector of Bavaria, who held it only two year, it being retaken by the Grand Vizier[110] and is now fortified with the utmost care and skill the Turks are capable of, and strengthened by a very numerous garrison of their bravest janissaries, commanded by a pasha seraskier (i.e. general). This last expression is not very just, for, to say truth, the seraskier is commanded by the janissaries who have an absolute authority here, not much unlike a rebellion which you may judge of by the following story which at the same time, will give you an idea of the admirable intelligence of the governor of Peterwardein, though so few hours distant.

We were told by him at Peterwardein that the garrison and inhabitants of Belgrade were so weary of the war they had killed their pasha about two months ago in a mutiny, because he had suffered himself to be prevailed upon by a bribe of five purses (five hundred pounds sterling) to give permission to the Tartars to ravage the German frontiers. We were very well pleased to hear of such favourable dispositions in the people, but when we came hither we found the governor had been ill informed, and this is the real truth of the story. The late pasha fell under the displeasure of his soldiers for no other reason but restraining their incursions on the Germans. They took it into their heads, from that mildness, that he was of intelligence with the enemy, and sent such information to the Grand Signor[111] at Adrianople; but redress not coming quick enough from thence, they assembled themselves in a tumultuous manner, and by force dragged their pasha before the cadi and mufti,[112] and there demanded justice in a mutinous way, one crying out why he protected the infidels? Another, why he squeezed them of their money? That easily guessing their purpose, he calmly replied to them that they asked him too many questions; he had but one life, which must answer for all. They immediately fell upon him with their scimitars, without waiting the sentence of their heads of the law, and in a few moments cut him in pieces. The present pasha has not dared to punish the murder; on the contrary, he affected to applaud the actors of it as brave fellows that knew how to do themselves justice. He takes all pretences of throwing money amongst the garrison, and suffers them to make little excursions into Hungary, where they burn some poor Rascian houses. You may imagine I cannot be very easy in a town which is really under the government of an insolent soldiery. We expected to be immediately dismissed after a night's lodging here, but the pasha detains us till he receives orders from Adrianople, which may possibly be a month a-coming.

In the meantime, we are lodged in one of the best houses, belonging to a very considerable man amongst them, and have a whole chamber of janissaries to guard us. My only diversion is the conversations of our host, Achmed Bey, a title something like that of count in Germany. His father was a great pasha, and he has been educated in the most polite eastern learning, being perfectly skilled in the Arabic and Persian languages, and is an extraordinary scribe, which they call *effendi*.[113] This accomplishment makes way to the greatest preferments, but he has had the good sense to prefer an easy, quiet, secure life to all the dangerous honours of the Porte.[114] He sups with us every night, and drinks wine very freely. You cannot imagine how much he is delighted with the liberty of conversing with me. He has explained to me many pieces of Arabian poetry which, I observed, are in numbers not unlike ours, generally alternate verse, and of a very musical sound. Their expressions of love are very passionate and lively. I am so much pleased with them, I really believe I should learn to read Arabic, if I was to stay here a few months. He has a very good library of their books of all kinds and, as he tells me, spends the greatest part of his life there. I pass for a great scholar with him, by relating to him some of the Persian tales,[115] which I find are genuine. At first he believed I understood Persian. I have frequent disputes with him concerning the difference of our customs, particularly the confinements of women. He assures me, there is nothing at all in it; only, says he, we have the advantage that when our wives cheat us nobody knows it. He has wit, and is more polite than many Christian men of quality. I am very much entertained with him. He has had the curiosity to make one of our servants set him an alphabet of our letters, and can already write a good Roman hand. But these amusements do not hinder my wishing heartily to be out of this place, though the weather is colder than I believe it ever was anywhere but in Greenland. We have a very large stove constantly kept hot, and yet the windows of the room are frozen on the inside.

God knows when I may have an opportunity of sending this letter, but I have written it for the discharge of my own conscience, and you cannot now reproach me that one of yours makes ten of mine.

LETTER XXV

To Frances Hewet,[116]   *Adrianople, 1 April 1717*

I dare say my dear Mrs Hewet thinks me the the most stupid thing alive to neglect so agreeable a correspondence, but it has hitherto been utterly out of my power to continue it. I have been hurried up and down, without intermission, these last eight months, wholly taken up either in going post or unavoidable court attendance. You know very well how little leisure it is possible to find on either of those employments. I like travelling extremely, and have had no reason to complain of having had too little of it, having now gone through all the Turkish dominions in Europe, not to reckon my journies through Hungary,

Bohemia and the whole tour of Germany. But those are trifles to this last. I cannot, however, thank God, complain of having suffered by fatigue, either in my own health or that of my family. My son never was better in his life. This country is certainly one of the finest in the world. Hitherto all I see is so new to me it is like a fresh scene of an opera every day. I will not tire you with descriptions of places or manner which perhaps you have no curiosity for; but only desire you would be so good as to let me hear as oft as you can (which can be no other than very seldom) what passes on your side of the globe. Before you can receive this you must consider all things as six months old which appear new to me. There will be a great field for you to write, if your charity extends so far, as it will be entirely disinterested and free from ostentation (it not being possible for me here to boast of your letters) and it will be very beneficial to your precious soul, which I pray heaven to put into your head to consider and practice accordingly.

LETTER XXVI

To Her Royal Highness the Princess of Wales,[117]   *Adrianople,*
1 April 1717

I have now, madam, passed a journey that has not been undertaken by any Christian since the time of the Greek emperors, and I shall not regret all the fatigues I have suffered in it if it gives me an opportunity of amusing your Royal Highness by an account of places utterly unknown amongst us, the emperor's ambassadors and those few English that have come hither always going on the Danube to Nicopolis. But that river was now frozen, and Mr Wortley so zealous for the service of his majesty he would not defer his journey to wait for the convenience of that passage. We crossed the deserts of Serbia, almost quite overgrown with wood, though a country naturally fertile and the inhabitants industrious. But the oppression of the peasants is so great, they are forced to abandon their houses and neglect their tillage, all they have being a prey to the janissaries, whenever they please to seize upon it. We had a guard of 500 of them, and I was almost in tears every day to see their insolencies in the poor villages through which we passed.

After seven days travelling through thick woods we came to Nissa, once the capital of Serbia, situate in a fine plain on the river Nissava, in a very good air and so fruitful a soil that the great plenty is hardly credible. I was certainly assured that the quantity of wine last vintage was so prodigious they were forced to dig holes in the earth to put it in, not having vessels enough in the town to hold it. The happiness of this plenty is scarce perceived by the oppressed people. I saw here a new occasion for my compassion. The wretches that had provided twenty waggons for our baggage from Belgrade hither for a certain hire, being all sent back without payment, some of their horses lamed and others killed, without any satisfaction made for them. The poor fellows came round the house weeping and tearing their hair and beards in the most pitiful manner, without getting anything but drubs from the insolent soldiers. I cannot express to your Royal Highness how much I was moved at this scene. I would have paid them the money out of my own pocket, with all my heart, but it would only have been giving so much to the aga who would have taken it from them without remorse.

After four days journey from this place over the mountains we came to Sofia, situated in a large beautiful plain on the river Isca, and surrounded with distant mountains. 'Tis hardly possible to see a more agreeable landscape. The city itself is very large and extremely populous. Here are hot baths, very famous for their medicinal virtues. Four days' journey from hence we arrived at Philippopolis,[118] after having passed the ridges between the mountains of Haemus and Rhodophe, which are always covered with snow. This town is situated on a rising ground near the river Hebrus and is almost wholly inhabited by Greeks. Here are still some ancient Christian churches. They have a bishop and several of the richest Greeks live here, but they are forced to conceal their wealth with great care, the appearance of poverty, which includes part of its inconveniences, being all their security against feeling it in earnest. The country from hence to Adrianople is the finest in the world. Vines grow wild on all the hills and the perpetual spring they enjoy makes everything look gay and flourishing. But this climate, as happy as it seems, can never be preferred to England with all its snows and frosts, while we are blessed with an easy government under a king who makes his own happiness consist in the liberty of his people and chooses rather to be looked upon as their father than their master.

This theme would carry me very far and I am sensible I have already tired out your Royal Highness' patience, but my letter is in your hands and you may make it as short as you please by throwing it into the fire when you are weary of reading it.

I am, madam, with the greatest respect etc.

LETTER XXVII

To Lady—,[119]   *Adrianople, 1 April 1717*

I am now got into a new world, where everything I see appears to me a change of scene, and I write to your ladyship with some content of mind, hoping at least that you will find the charm of novelty in my letters, and no longer reproach me that I tell you nothing extraordinary. I won't trouble you with a relation of our tedious journey, but I must not omit what I saw remarkable at Sofia, one of the most beautiful towns in the Turkish empire, and famous for its hot baths, that are resorted to both for diversion and health. I stopped here one day on purpose to see them. Designing to go incognito I hired a Turkish coach. These voitures are not at all like ours, but much more convenient for the country, the heat being so great that glasses would be very troublesome. They are made a good deal in the manner of the Dutch coaches, having wooden lattices painted and gilded, the inside being also painted with baskets and nosegays of flowers, intermixed commonly with little poetical mottos. They are covered all over with scarlet cloth, lined with silk, and very often richly embroidered and fringed. This covering entirely hides the persons in them, but may be thrown back at pleasure and the ladies peep through the lattices. They hold four people very conveniently, seated on cushions, but not raised.

In one of these covered waggons, I went to the bagnio[120] about ten o'clock. It was already full of women. It is built of stone in the shape of a dome, with no windows but in the roof, which gives light enough. There was five of these domes joined together, the outmost being less than the rest and serving only as a hall, where the portress stood at the door. Ladies of quality generally give this woman the value of a crown or ten shillings and I did not forget that ceremony. The next room is a very large one paved with marble, and all round it raised two sofas of marble one above another. There were four fountains of cold water in this room, falling first into marble basins, and then running on the floor in little channels made for that purpose, which carried the streams into the next room, something less than this, with the same sort of marble sofas, but so hot with steams of sulphur proceeding from the baths joining to it, 'twas impossible to stay there with one's clothes on. The two other domes were the hot baths, one of which had cocks of cold water turning into it to temper it to what degree of warmth the bathers have a mind to.

I was in my travelling habit, which is a riding dress, and certainly appeared very extraordinary to them. Yet there was not one of them that showed the least surprise or impertinent curiosity, but received me with all the obliging civility possible. I know no European court where the ladies would have behaved themselves in so polite a manner to a stranger. I believe, in the whole, there were two hundred women, and yet none of those disdainful smiles or satirical whispers that never fail in our assemblies when anybody appears that is not dressed exactly in fashion. They repeated over and over to me; 'Güzelle, pek güzelle', which is nothing but 'charming, very charming'. The first sofas were covered with cushions and rich carpets, on which sat the ladies, and on the second their slaves behind them, but without any distinction of rank by their dress, all being in the state of nature, that is, in plain English, stark naked, without any beauty or defect concealed. Yet there was not the least wanton smile or immodest gesture amongst them. They walked and moved with the same majestic grace which Milton describes of our general mother.[121] There were many amongst them as exactly proportioned as ever any goddess was drawn by the pencil of Guido[122] or Titian, and most of their skins shiningly white, only adorned by their beautiful hair divided into many tresses, hanging on their shoulders, braided either with pearl or ribbon, perfectly representing the figures of the Graces.

I was here convinced of the truth of a reflection I had often made, that if it was the fashion to go naked, the face would be hardly observed. I perceived that the ladies with finest skins and most delicate shapes had the greatest share of my admiration, though their faces were sometimes less beautiful than those of their companions. To tell you the truth, I had wickedness enough to wish secretly that Mr Gervase[123] could have been there invisible. I fancy it would have very much improved his art to see so many fine women naked, in different postures, some in conversation, some working, others drinking coffee or sherbet, and many negligently lying on their cushions while their slaves (generally pretty girls of seventeen or eighteen) were employed in braiding their hair in several pretty manners. In short, 'tis the women's coffee house, where all the news of the town is told, scandal invented etc. They generally take this diversion once a week, and stay there at least four or five hours, without getting cold by immediate coming out of the hot bath into the cool room, which was very surprising to me. The lady that seemed the most considerable amongst them entreated me to sit by her and would fain have undressed me for the bath. I excused myself with some difficulty, they being however all so earnest in persuading me, I was a last forced to open my shirt, and show them my stays, which satisfied them very well, for I saw they believed I was so locked up in that machine, that it was not in my own power to open it, which contrivance they attributed to my husband. I was charmed with their civility and beauty, and should have been very glad to pass more time with them, but Mr Wortley resolving to pursue his journey the next morning early I was in haste to see the ruins of Justinian's[124] church, which did not afford me so agreeable a prospect as I had left, being little more than a heap of stones.

Adieu, madam, I am sure I have now entertained you with an account of such a sight as you never saw in your life, and what no book of travels could inform you of, as 'tis no less than death for a man to be found in one of these places.

LETTER XXVIII

To the Abbé Conti,[125]   *Adrianople, 1 April 1717*

You see that I am very exact in keeping the promise you engaged me to make but I know not whether your curiosity will be satisfied with the accounts I shall give you, though I can assure you that the desire I have to oblige you to the utmost of my power has made me very diligent in my enquiries and observations. 'Tis certain we have but very imperfect relations of the manners and religion of these people, this part of the world being seldom visited but by merchants, who mind little but their own affairs, or travellers who make too short a stay to be able to report anything exactly of their own knowledge. The Turks are too proud to converse familiarly with merchants etc., who can only pick up some confused informations, which are generally false, and can give no better account of the ways here, than a French refugee lodging in a garret in Greek Street,[126] could write of the court of England. The journey we have made from Belgrade hither by land cannot possibly be passed by any out of a public character. The desert woods of Serbia are the common refuge of thieves who rob fifty in a company, that we had need of all our guards to secure us, and the villages so poor that only force could exort from them necessary provisions. Indeed the janissaries had no mercy on their poverty, killing all the poultry and sheep they could find without asking who they belonged to, while the wretched owners durst not put in their claim for fear of being beaten. Lambs just fallen, geese and turkeys big with egg all massacred without distinction! I fancied I heard the complaints of Moelibeus for the hope of his flock.[127] When the pashas travel 'tis yet worse. Those oppressors are not content with eating all that is to be eaten belonging to the peasants; after they have crammed themselves and their numerous retinue they have the impudence to exact what they call teeth money, a contribution for the use of their teeth, worn with doing them the honour of devouring their meat. This is a literal, known truth, however extravagant it seems; and such is the natural corruption of a military government, their religion not allowing of this barbarity any more than our does.

I had the advantage of lodging three weeks at Belgrade, with a principal *effendi*, that is to say a scholar. This set of men are equally capable of preferments in the law or the church, those two sciences being cast into one, and a lawyer and a priest being the same word. They are the only men really considerable in the empire; all the profitable employments and church revenues are in their hands. The Grand Signor, though general heir to his people, never presumes to touch their lands or money, which go in an uninterrupted succession to their children. 'Tis true they lose this privilege by accepting a place at court, or the title of pasha, but there are few examples of such fools among them. You may easily judge of the power of these men who have engrossed all the learning and almost all the wealth of the empire. 'Tis they that are the real authors, though the soldiers are the actors of revolutions. They deposed the late Sultan Mustafa;[128] and their power is so well known 'tis the emperor's interest to flatter them.

This is a long digression. I was going to tell you that an intimate daily conversation with the effendi Achmed Bey gave me opportunity of knowing their religion and morals in a

more particular manner than perhaps any Christian ever did. I
explained to him the difference between the religion of England
and Rome, and he was pleased to hear there were Christians
that did not worship images or adore the Virgin Mary. The
ridicule of transubstantiation appeared very strong to him.
Upon comparing our creeds together I am convinced that if our
friend Dr Clarke[129] had free liberty of preaching here it would
be very easy to persuade the generality to Christianity, whose
notions are already little different from his. Mr Whiston[130]
would make a very good apostle here. I don't doubt but his zeal
will be much fired if you communicate this account to him, but
tell him, he must first have the gift of tongues before he can
possibly be of any use.

Mohammedism is divided into as many sects as Christianity,
and the first institution as much neglected and obscured by
interpretations. I cannot here forbear reflecting on the natural
inclination of mankind, to make mysteries and novelties. The
Zeidi, Kudi, Jabari[131] etc. put me in mind of the Catholic,
Lutheran, Calvinist, etc., and are equally zealous against one
another. But the most prevailing opinion if you search into the
secret of the effendis is plain deism but this is kept from the
people who are amused with a thousand different notions,
according to the different interest of their preachers. There are
very few amongst them (Achmed Bey denied there were any) so
absurd as to set up for wit by declaring they believe no God at
all. And Sir Paul Rycaut[132] is mistaken, as he commonly is, in
calling the sect *muserin* (i.e. the secret with us) atheists, they
being deists, whose impiety consists in making a jest of their
prophet. Achmed Bey did not own to me that he was of this
opinion but made no scruple of deviating from some part of
Mohammed's law by drinking wine with the same freedom we
did. When I asked him how he came to allow himself that
liberty he made answer that all the creatures of God were good
and designed for the use of man; however, that the prohibition
of wine was a very wise maxim and meant for the common
people, being the source of all disorders amongst them, but that
the prophet never designed to confine those that knew how to

use it with moderation. However, scandal ought to be avoided and that he never drank it in public. This is the general way of thinking amongst them, and very few forbear drinking wine that are able to afford it.

He assured me that if I understood Arabic I should be very well pleased with reading the Alcoran, which is so far from the nonsense we charge it with that 'tis the purest morality delivered in the very best language. I have since heard impartial Christians speak of it in the same manner, and I don't doubt but that all our translations are from copies got from the Greek priests who would not fail to falsify it with the extremity of malice. No body of men ever were more ignorant or more corrupt. Yet they differ so little from the Romish Church that I confess there is nothing gives me a greater abhorrence of the cruelty of your clergy than the barbarous persecutions of them, whenever they have been their masters for no other reason than not acknowledging the Pope. The dissenting in that one article has got them the titles of heretics, schismatics, and, what is worse, the same treatment.

I found at Philippopolis a sect of Christians that call themselves Paulines.[133] They show an old church where, they say, St Paul preached, and he is their favourite saint, after the same manner as St Peter is at Rome; neither do they forget to give him the same preference over the rest of the apostles.

But of all the religions I have seen the Arnounts seem to me the most particular. They are natives of Arnawutluk,[134] the ancient Macedonia, and still retain the courage and hardiness, though they have lost the name of Macedonians, being the best militia in the Turkish empire, and the only check upon the janissaries. They are foot soldiers; we had a guard of them relieved in every considerable town we passed. They are all clothed and armed at their own expense, generally lusty young fellows dressed in clean white coarse cloth, carrying guns of a prodigious length, which they run with upon their shoulders, as if they did not feel the weight of them, the leader singing a sort of rude tune, not unpleasant, and the rest making up the chorus. These people living between Christians and Mohammedans, and not being skilled in controversy, declare that they are utterly unable to judge which religion is best, but to be certain of not entirely rejecting the truth they very prudently follow both and go to the mosque on Fridays and to the church on Sundays, saying for their excuse that at the day of judgement they are sure of protection from the true prophet; but which that is, they are not able to determine in this world. I believe there is no other race of mankind who have so modest an opinion of their own capacity. These are the remarks I have made on the diversity of religions I have seen. I don't ask your pardon for the liberty I have taken in speaking of the Roman. I know you equally condemn the quackery of all churches as much as you revere the sacred truths, in which we both agree.

You will expect I should say something to you of the antiquities of this country, but there are few remains of ancient Greece. We passed near the piece of an arch which is commonly called Trajan's Gate,[135] as supposing he made it to shut up the passage over the mountains between Sofia and Philippopolis, but I rather believe it the remains of some triumphal arch (though I could not see any inscription), for if that passage had been shut up there are many others that would serve for the march of an army. And notwithstanding the story of Baldwin, Earl of Flanders, being overthrown in these straits[136] after he had won Constantinople, I don't fancy the Germans would find themselves stopped by them. 'Tis true the road is now made, with great industry, as commodious as possible for the march of the Turkish army. There is not one ditch or puddle between this place and Belgrade that has not a large strong bridge of planks built over it; but the precipices are not so terrible as I had heard them represented. At the foot of these mountains we lay at the little village of Kiskoi, wholly inhabited by Christians, as all the peasants of Bulgaria are. Their houses are nothing but little huts, raised of dirt baked in the sun and they leave them and fly into the mountains some months before the march of the Turkish army, who would else entirely ruin them by driving away their whole flocks. This precaution secures them in a sort of plenty, for vast tracts of land lying in common they have liberty of sowing what they please, and are generally very industrious husbandmen. I drank here several sorts of delicious wine. The women dress themselves in a great variety of coloured glass beads and are not ugly, but of tawny complexions. I have now told you all that is worth telling you, and perhaps more, relating to my journey. When I am at Constantinople I'll try to pick up some curiosities and then you shall hear again from etc.

LETTER XXIX

To Lady Bristol,   *Adrianople, 1 April 1717*

As I never can forget the smallest of your ladyship's commands, my first business here has been to enquire after the stuffs you ordered me to look for, without being able to find what you would like. The difference of the dress here and at London is so great, the same sort of things are not proper for caftans and manteaus.[137] However, I will not give over my search but renew it again at Constantinople, though I have reason to believe there is nothing finer than what is to be found here, being at present the residence of the court.

The Grand Signor's eldest daughter was married some few days before I came and upon that occasion the Turkish ladies display all their magnificence. The bride was conducted to her husband's house in very great splendour. She is widow of the late Vizier, who was killed at Peterwardein,[138] though that ought rather to be called a contract than a marriage, not ever having lived with him. However, the greatest part of his wealth is hers. He had the permission of visiting her in the seraglio, and, being one of the handsomest men in the Empire, had very much engaged her affections. When she saw this second husband, who is at least fifty, she could not forbear bursting into tears. He is a man of merit, and the declared favourite of the Sultan (which they call *musahib*)[139] but that is not enough to make him pleasing in the eyes of a girl of thirteen.

The government here is entirely in the hands of the army and the Grand Signor with all his absolute power as much a slave as any of his subjects, and trembles at a janissary's frown. Here is indeed a much greater appearance of subjection than amongst us. A minister of state is not spoke to but upon the knee; should a reflection on his conduct be dropped in a coffee house (for they have spies everywhere) the house would be razed to the ground, and perhaps the whole company put to the torture. No huzzaing mobs, senseless pamphlets and tavern disputes about politics

> A consequential ill that freedom draws;
> A bad effect, but from a noble cause.[140]

None of our harmless calling names! But when a minister here displeases the people in three hours time he is dragged even from his master's arms. They cut off his hands, head and feet, and throw them before the palace gate with all the respect in the world, while the Sultan (to whom they all profess an unlimited adoration) sits trembling in his apartment, and dare neither defend nor revenge his favourite. This is the blessed condition of the most absolute monarch upon earth, who owns no law but his will.

I cannot help wishing, in the loyalty of my heart, that the parliament would send hither a ship load of your passive obedient men,[141] that they might see arbitrary government in its clearest, strongest light, where 'tis hard to judge whether the prince, people or ministers are most miserable. I could make many reflections on this subject but I know, madam, your own good sense has already furnished you with better than I am capable of.

I went yesterday with the French Ambassadress[142] to see the Grand Signor in his passage to the mosque. He was preceded by a numerous guard of janissaries with vast white feathers on their heads, as also by the *sipahis* and *bostcis* (these are foot and horse guards) and the royal gardeners, which are a very considerable body of men, dressed in different habits of fine lively colours so that, at a distance, they appeared like a parterre of tulips.[143] After them the Aga of the janissaries in a robe of purple velvet lined with silver tissue, his horse led by two slaves richly dressed. Next him the Kilar Aga (your ladyship knows this is the chief guardian of the seraglio ladies) in a deep yellow cloth (which suited very well to his black face) lined with sables and last his sublimity himself, in green lined with the fur of a black muscovite fox, which is supposed worth a thousand pounds sterling, mounted on a fine horse with furniture embroidered with jewels. Six more horses richly furnished were led after him and two of his principal courtiers bore one his gold and the other his silver coffee pot, on a staff. Another carried a silver stool on his head for him to sit on. It would be too tedious to tell your ladyship the various dresses and turbans by which their rank is distinguished, but they were all extremely rich and gay to the number of some thousands that, perhaps there cannot be seen a more beautiful procession. The Sultan appeared to us a handsome man of about forty, with a very graceful air but with something severe in his countenance, his eyes very full and black. He happened to stop under the window where we stood, and, I suppose being told who we were, looked upon us very attentively, that we had full leisure to consider him and the French Ambassadress agreed with me as to his good mein.

I see that lady very often; she is young and her conversation would be a great relief to me if I could persuade her to live without those forms and ceremonies that make life formal and tiresome. But she is so delighted with her guards, her twenty four footmen, gentlemen ushers, etc., that she would rather die than make me a visit without them, not to reckon a coachful of attending damsels y'cleped[144] maids of honour. What vexes me is that as long as she will visit with this troublesome equipage I am obliged to do the same. However, our mutual interest makes us much together. I went with her the other day all round the town in an open gilt chariot, with our joint train of attendants, preceded by our guards, who might have summoned the people to see what they had never seen, nor ever would see again; two young Christian ambassadresses never yet having been in this country at the same time, nor I believe ever will again. Your ladyship may easily imagine that we drew a vast crowd of spectators, but all silent as death. If any of them had taken the liberties of our mob upon any strange sight our janissaries had made no scruple of falling on them with their scimitars, without danger for so doing, being above the law. Yet these people have some good qualities; they are very zealous and faithful where they serve, and look upon it as their business to fight for you on all occasions, of which I had a very pleasant instance in a village on this side Philippopolis, where we were met by our domestic guard. I happened to bespeak pigeons for my supper, upon which one of my janissaries went immediately to the cadi (the chief civil officer of the town) and ordered him to send in some dozens. The poor man answered that he had already sent about but could get none. My janissary, in the height of his zeal for my service immediately locked him up prisoner in his room, telling him he deserved death for his impudence in offering to excuse his not obeying my command but out of respect to me he would not punish him but by my order and accordingly came very gravely to me to ask what should be done to him adding, by way of compliment, that if I pleased he would bring me his head. This may give some idea of the unlimited power of these fellows, who are all sworn brothers, and bound to revenge the injuries done to one another, whether at Cairo, Aleppo or any part of the world and this inviolable league makes them so powerful the greatest man at court never speaks to them but in a flattering tone, and in Asia any man that is rich is forced to enrol himself a janissary to secure his estate. But I have already said enough and I dare swear, dear madam, that by this time, 'tis a very comfortable reflection to you that there is no possibility of your receiving such a tedious letter but once in six months. 'Tis that consideration has given me the assurance to entertain you so long and will, I hope, plead the excuse of, dear madam, etc.

LETTER XXX

To Lady Mar, *Adrianople, 1 April 1717*

I wish to God, dear sister, that you were as regular in letting me have the pleasure of knowing what passes on your side of the globe as I am careful in endeavouring to amuse you by the account of all I see that I think you care to hear of. You content yourself with telling me over and over that the town is very dull. It may possibly be dull to you when every day does not present you with something new, but for me that am in arrear at least two months news, all that seems very stale with you would be fresh and sweet here. Pray let me into more particulars. I will try to awaken your gratitude by giving you a full and true relation of the novelties of this place, none of which would surprise you more than a sight of my person, as I am now in my Turkish habit, though I believe you would be of my opinion that 'tis admirably becoming. I intend to send you my picture. In the meantime accept of it here.

The first piece of my dress is a pair of drawers, very full, that reach to my shoes, and conceal the legs more modestly than your petticoats. They are of a thin rose colour damask, brocaded with silver flowers, my shoes of white kid leather embroidered with gold. Over this hangs my smock of a fine white silk gauze, edged with embroidery. This smock has wide sleeves hanging half way down the arm and is closed at the neck with a diamond button; but the shape and colour of the bosom is very well to be distinguished through it. The *entari* is a waistcoat made close to the shape, of white and gold damask with very long sleeves falling back and fringed with deep gold fringe, and should have diamond or pearl buttons. My caftan of the same stuff with my drawers, is a robe exactly fitted to my shape and reaching to my feet, with very long straight-falling sleeves. Over this is the girdle of about four fingers broad which all that can afford have entirely of diamonds or other precious stones; those that will not be at that expense have it of exquisite embroidery on satin, but it must be fastened before with a clasp of diamonds. The cüppe is a loose robe they throw off, or put on, according to the weather, being of a rich brocade (mine is green and gold) either lined with ermine or sables. The sleeves reach very little below the shoulders. The headdress is composed of a cap, called kalpak which is in winter of fine velvet embroidered with pearls or diamonds and in summer of a light shining silver stuff. This is fixed on one side of the head, hanging a little way down with a gold tassel, and bound on either with a circle of diamonds (as I have seen several) or a rich embroidered handkerchief. On the other side of the head the hair is laid flat and here the ladies are at liberty to show their fancies, some putting flowers, others a plume of heron's feathers and, in short, what they please; but the most general fashion is a large bouquet of jewels made like natural flowers; that is, the buds of pearl, the roses of different coloured rubies, the jessamines of diamonds, the jonquils of topazes, etc, so well set and enamelled 'tis hard to imagine anything of that kind so beautiful. The hair hangs at its full length behind, divided into tresses braided with pearl or ribbon, which is always in great quantity.

I never saw in my life so many fine heads of hair. I have counted a hundred and ten of these tresses of one lady, all natural. But, it must be owned that every beauty is more common here than with us. 'Tis surprising to see a young woman that is not very handsome. They have naturally the most beautiful complexions in the world and generally large black eyes. I can assure you with great truth that the court of England, though I believe it the fairest in Christendom, cannot show so many beauties as are under our protection here. They generally shape their eyebrows and both Greeks and Turks have a custom of putting round their eyes on the inside a black tincture that, at a distance, or by candlelight, adds very much to the blackness of them. I fancy many of our ladies would be overjoyed to know this secret, but 'tis too visible by day. They dye their nails rose colour; I own I cannot enough accustom myself to this fashion to find any beauty in it.

As to their morality or good conduct, I can say, like Harlequin, that 'tis just as 'tis with you,[145] and the Turkish ladies don't commit one sin the less for not being Christians. Now that I am a little acquainted with their ways I cannot forbear admiring either the exemplary discretion or extreme stupidity of all the writers that have given accounts of them. 'Tis very easy to see they have more liberty than we have, no woman, of what rank so ever being permitted to go in the streets without two muslins, one that covers her face all but her eyes and another that hides the whole dress of her head, and hangs half way down her back and their shapes are also wholly concealed by a thing they call a *ferace* which no woman of any sort appears without. This has straight sleeves that reaches to their fingers ends and it laps all round them, not unlike a riding hood. In winter 'tis of cloth and in summer plain stuff or silk. You may guess then how effectually this disguises them, that there is no distinguishing the great lady from her slave and 'tis impossible for the most jealous husband to know his wife when he meets her, and no man dare either touch or follow a woman in the street.

This perpetual masquerade gives them entire liberty of following their inclinations without danger of discovery. The most usual method of intrigue is to send an appointment to the lover to meet the lady at a Jew's shop, which are as notoriously convenient as our Indian houses, and yet, even those that don't make use of them do not scruple to go to buy pennyworths and tumble over rich goods, which are chiefly to be found amongst that sort of people. The great ladies seldom let their gallants know who they are, and 'tis so difficult to find it out that they can very seldom guess at her name they have corresponded with above half a year together. You may easily imagine the number of faithful wives very small in a country where they have nothing to fear from their lovers' indiscretion, since we see so many that have the courage to expose themselves to that in this world, and all the threatened punishment of the next, which is never preached to the Turkish damsels. Neither have they much to apprehend from the resentment of their husbands, those ladies that are rich having all their money in their own hands, which they take with them upon a divorce with an addition which he is obliged to give them. Upon the whole, I look upon the Turkish women as the only free people in the empire. The very Divan[146] pays respect to them and the Grand Signor himself, when a pasha is executed, never violates the privileges of the harem (or women's apartment) which remains unsearched entire to the widow. They are queens of their slaves, which the husband has no permission so much as to look upon, except it be an old woman or two that his lady chooses. 'Tis true, their law permits them four wives, but there is no instance of a man of quality that makes use of this liberty, or of a woman of rank that would suffer it. When a husband happens to be inconstant, as those things will happen, he keeps his mistress in a house apart and visits her as privately as he can, just as 'tis with you. Amongst all the great men here, I only know the *tefterdar* (ie treasurer) that keeps a number of she-slaves for his own use (that is, on his own side of the house, for a slave once given to serve a lady is entirely at her disposal) and he is spoke of as a libertine, or what we should call a rake, and his wife won't see him, though she continues to live in his house.

Thus you see, dear sister, the manners of mankind do not differ so widely as our voyage writers would make us believe. Perhaps it would be more entertaining to add a few surprising customs of my own invention, but nothing seems to me so agreeable as truth, and I believe nothing so acceptable to you. I conclude with repeating the great truth of my being, dear sister etc.

LETTER XXXI

To Alexander Pope,   *Adrianople, 1 April 1717*

I dare say you expect at least something very new in this letter, after I have gone a journey not undertaken by any Christian for some hundred years. The most remarkable accident that happened to me was my being very near overturned into the Hebrus;[147] and, if I had much regard for the glories that one's name enjoys after death I should certainly be sorry for having missed the romantic conclusion of swimming down the same river in which the musical head of Orpheus repeated verses so many ages since:[148]

> Caput a cervice revulsum,
> Gurgite cum medio, portans Oeagrius Hebrus
> Volveret, Euridicen, vox ipsa, et frigida lingua,
> Ah! Miseram Euridicen! anima fugiente vocabat,
> Euridicen toto referebant flumine ripae[149]

Who knows but some of your bright wits might have found it a subject affording many poetical turns and have told the world, in an heroic elegy that:

> As equal were our souls, so equal were our fates?

I despair of ever hearing so many fine things said of me, as so extraordinary a death would have given occasion for.

I am at this present moment writing in a house situated on the banks of the Hebrus, which runs under my chamber window. My garden is full of tall cypress trees upon the branches of which several couple of true turtles[150] are saying soft things to one another from morning till night. How naturally do boughs and vows come into my head at this minute! And must not you confess, to my praise, that 'tis more than an ordinary discretion that can resist the wicked suggestions of poetry in a place where truth for once furnishes all the ideas of pastoral? The summer is already far advanced in this part of the world and for some miles round Adrianople the whole ground is laid out in gardens, and the banks of the rivers set with rows of fruit trees, under which all the most considerable Turks divert themselves every evening, not with walking, that is not one of their pleasures, but a set party of them choose out a green spot where the shade is very thick and there they spread a carpet on which they sit drinking their coffee and generally attended by some slave with a fine voice, or that plays on some instrument. Every twenty paces you may see one of these little companies listening to the dashing of

the river, and this taste is so universal that the very gardeners
are not without it. I have often seen them and their children
sitting on the banks of the river and playing on a rural instrument, perfectly answering the description of the ancient
fistula,[151] being composed of unequal reeds with a simple but
agreeable softness in the sound. Mr Addison[152] might here make
the experiment he speaks of in his travels, there not being one
instrument of music among the Greek or Roman statues that is
not to be found in the hands of the people of this country. The
young lads generally divert themselves with making garlands for
their favourite lambs, which I have often seen painted and
adorned with flowers, lying at their feet, while they sung or
played. It is not that they ever read romances, but these are the
ancient amusements here, and as natural to them as cudgel
playing and football to our British swains; the softness and
warmth of the climate forbidding all rough exercises, which
were never so much as heard of amongst them, and naturally
inspiring a laziness and aversion to labour which the great plenty
indulges. These gardeners are the only happy race of country
people in Turkey. They furnish all the city with fruit and herbs,
and seem to live very easily. They are most of them Greeks and
have little houses in the midst of their gardens, where their
wives and daughters take a liberty not permitted in the town; I
mean to go unveiled. These wenches are very neat and handsome, and pass their time at their looms, under the shade of
their trees.

I no longer look upon Theocritus[153] as a romantic writer; he
has only given a plain image of the way of life amongst the
peasants of his country, which before oppression had reduced
them to want were, I suppose, all employed as the better sort of
them are now. I don't doubt had he been born a Briton his
Idylliums had been filled with descriptions of threshing and
churning, both which are unknown here, the corn being all
trode out by oxen and butter (I speak it with sorrow) unheard
of.

I read over your Homer[154] here with an infinite pleasure, and
find several little passages explained that I did not before

entirely comprehend the beauty of, many of the customs and much of the dress then in fashion being yet retained and I don't wonder to find more remains here of an age so distant than it is to be found in any other country, the Turks not taking that pains to introduce their own manners as has been generally practised by other nations that imagine themselves more polite.[155] It would be too tedious to you to point out all the passages that relate to the present customs, but I can assure you that the princesses and great ladies pass their time at their looms embroidering veils and robes, surrounded by their maids, which are always very numerous, in the same manner as we find Andromache[156] and Helen described. The description of the belt of Menelaus[157] exactly resembles those that are now worn by the great men, fastened before with broad golden clasps, and embroidered round with rich work. The snowy veil that Helen throws over her face is still fashionable, and I never see half a dozen of old bashaws[158] (as I do very often) with their reverend beards sitting basking in the sun but I recollect good King Priam and his counsellors.[159] Their manner of dancing is certainly the same that Diana is sung to have danced on the banks by Eurotas.[160] The great lady still leads the dance and is followed by a troop of young girls who imitate her steps and, if she sings, make up the chorus. The tunes are extreme gay and lively, yet with something in them wonderfull soft. The steps are varied according to the pleasure of her that leads the dance, but always in exact time, and infinitely more agreeable than any of our dances, at least in my opinion. I sometimes make one in the train but am not skilful enough to lead. These are Grecian dances, the Turkish being very different.

I should have told you in the first place that the Eastern manners give a great light into many scripture passages that appear odd to us, their phrases being commonly what we should call scripture language. The vulgar Turk is very different from what is spoke at court, or amongst the people of figure, who always mix so much Arabic and Persian in their discourse that it may very well be called another language. And 'tis as ridiculous to make use of the expressions commonly used in speaking to a great man or lady, as it would be to talk broad Yorkshire or Somersetshire in the drawing room. Besides this distinction they have what they call the sublime, that is, a style proper for poetry, and which is exact scripture style. I believe you would be pleased to see a genuine example of this, and I am very glad I have it in my power to satisfy your curiosity by sending you a faithful copy of the verses that Ibrahim Pasha, the reigning favourite, has made for the young princess his contracted wife, whom he is not yet permitted to visit without witnesses, though she is gone home to his house. He is a man of wit and learning and whether or no he is capable of writing good verse himself you may be sure that, on such an occasion, he would not want the assistance of the best poets in the empire. Thus the verses may be looked upon as a sample of their finest poetry, and I don't doubt you'll be of my mind that it is most wonderfully resembling The Song of Solomon,[161] which was also addressed to a royal bride.

Turkish verses addressed to the Sultana, eldest daughter of Sultan Achmed III[162]

Stanza I

The nightingale now wanders in the vines;
Her passion is to seek roses.
I went down to admire the beauty of the vines;
The sweetness of your charms has ravished my soul.
Your eyes are black and lovely,
But wild and disdainful as those of a stag.

Stanza II

The wished possession is delayed from day to day;
The cruel Sultan Achmed will not permit me to see those
    cheeks, more vermilion than roses.
I dare not snatch one of your kisses;
The sweetness of your charms has ravish'd my soul.
Your eyes are black and lovely,
But wild and disdainful as those of a stag.

Stanza III

The wretched Pasha Ibrahim sighs in these verses;
One dart from your eyes has pierc'd thro' my heart.
Ah! when will the hour of possession arrive?
Must I yet wait a long time?
The sweetness of your charms has ravished my soul.
Ah! Sultana! stag-eyed, an angel amongst angels!
I desire and, my desire remains unsatisfied.
Can you take delight to prey upon my heart?

Stanza IV

My cries pierce the heavens,
My eyes are without sleep,
Turn to me, Sultana, let me gaze on thy beauty.
Adieu, I go down to the grave.
If you call me, I return.
My heart is hot as sulphur; sigh, and it will flame.
Crown of my life! fair light of my eyes, my Sultana, my
     princess.
I rub my face against the earth: I am drown'd in scalding tears,
     I rave!
Have you no compassion? Will you not turn to look upon
     me?

I have taken abundance of pains to get these verses in a literal translation, and if you were acquainted with my interpreters, I might spare myself the trouble of assuring you that they have received no poetical touches from their hands. In my opinion, allowing for the inevitable faults of a prose translation into a language so very different, there is a good deal of beauty in them. The epithet of stag-eyed, though the sound is not very agreeable in English, pleases me extremely and is, I think, a very lively image of the fire and indifference in his mistress' eyes. Monsieur Boileau[163] has very justly observed we are never to judge of the elevation of an expression in an ancient author by the sound it carries with us, which may be extremely fine with them, at the same time it looks low or uncouth to us. You are so well acquainted with

Homer, you cannot but have observed the same thing, and you must have the same indulgence for all Oriental poetry. The repetitions at the end of the two first stanzas are meant for a sort of chorus, and agreeable to the ancient manner of writing, The music of the verses apparently changes in the third stanza where the burden is altered, and I think he very artfully seems more passionate at the conclusion, as 'tis natural for people to warm themselves by their own discourse, especially on a subject in which one is deeply concerned and is far more touching than our modern custom of concluding a song of passion with a turn which is inconsistent with it. The first verse is a description of the season of the year, all the country being now full of nightingales, whose amours with roses is an Arabian fable,[164] as well know here as any part of Ovid amongst us, and is much the same as if an English poem should begin by saying: 'Now Philomela sings'. Or what if I turned the whole into the style of English poetry to see how it would look?

Stanza I

Now Philomel renews her tender strain,
Indulging all the night her pleasing pain;
I sought the groves to hear the wanton sing,
There saw a face more beauteous than the spring.
Your large stag's eyes, where thousand glories play,
As bright, as lively, but as wild as they.

Stanza II

In vain I'm promis'd such a heav'nly prize,
Ah! cruel Sultan who delays my joys!
While piercing charms transfix my amorous heart,
I dare not snatch one kiss to ease the smart.
Those eyes like, etc.

Stanza III

Your wretched lover in these lines complains,
From those dear beauties rise his killing pains.

When will the hour of wished-for bliss arrive?
Must I wait longer? Can I wait and live?
Ah! bright Sultana! Maid divinely fair!
Can you unpitying see the pain I bear?

Stanza IV

The heavens relenting hear my piercing cries,
I loathe the light and sleep forsakes my eyes;
Turn thee, Sultana, ere thy lover dies.
Sinking to earth, I sigh the last adieu,
Call me, my goddess, and my life renew.
My queen! my angel! my fond heart's desire,
I rave, my bosom burns with heav'nly fire,
Pity that passion which thy charms inspire.

I have taken the liberty in the second verse of following what I suppose is the true sense of the author, though not literally expressed. By saying he went down to admire the beauty of the vines and her charms ravished his soul, I understand a poetical fiction, of having first seen her in a garden, where he was admiring the beauty of the spring; but I could not forbear retaining the comparison of her eyes with those of a stag, though perhaps the novelty of it may give it a burlesque sound in our language. I cannot determine, upon the whole, how well I have succeeded in the translation, neither do I think our English proper to express such violence of passion, which is very seldom felt amongst us and we want also those compound words which are very frequent and strong in the Turkish language.

You see I am pretty far gone in oriental learning, and to say truth I study very hard. I wish my studies may give me occasion of entertaining your curiosity, which will be the utmost advantage hoped from it, by etc.

LETTER XXXII

To Sarah Chiswell,   *Adrianople, 1 April 1718*

In my opinion, dear Sarah I ought rather to quarrel with you for
not answering my Nijmegen letter of August until December,
than to excuse my not writing again till now. I am sure there is
on my side a very good excuse for silence, having gone such
tiresome land journeys, though I don't find the conclusion of
them so bad as you seem to imagine. I am very easy here, and
not in the solitude you fancy me. The great quantity of Greek,
French, English and Italians that are under our protection, make
their court to me from morning till night, and I'll assure you, are
many of them very fine ladies, for there is no possibility for a
Christian to live easily under this government but by the
protection of an ambassador, and the richer they are, the greater
the danger.

Those dreadful stories you have heard of the plague have very
little foundation in truth. I own I have much ado to reconcile
myself to the sound of a word which has always given me such
terrible ideas, though I am convinced there is little more in it
than in a fever, as a proof of which we passed through two or
three towns most violently infected. In the very next house
where we lay, in one of them, two persons died of it. Luckily for
me I was so well deceived that I knew nothing of the matter and
I was made believe that our second cook, who fell ill there had
only a great cold. However, we left our doctor to take care of
him, and yesterday they both arrived here in good health, and I
am now let into the secret that he has had the plague. There are
many that escape of it, neither is the air ever infected. I am
persuaded it would be as easy to root it out here as out of Italy
and France, but it does so little mischief they are not very
solicitous about it, and are content to suffer this distemper,
instead of our variety, which they are utterly unacquainted with.

A propos of distempers I am going to tell you a thing that I am sure will make you wish yourself here. The smallpox, so fatal and so general amongst us, is here entirely harmless by the invention of engrafting, which is the term they give it. There is a set of old women who make it their business to perform the operation. Every autumn in the month of September when the great heat is abated, people send one another to know if any of their family has a mind to have the smallpox. They make parties for this purpose and when they are met (commonly fifteen or sixteen together) the old woman comes with a nutshell full of the matter of the best sort of smallpox, and asks what veins you please to have opened. She immediately rips open that you offer to her with a large needle (which gives you no more pain than a common scratch) and puts into the vein as much venom as can lie upon the head of her needle, and after binds up the little wound with a hollow bit of shell, and in this manner opens four or five veins. The Grecians have commonly the superstition of opening one in the middle of the forehead, in each arm and on the breast to mark the sign of the cross, but this has a very ill effect, all these wounds leaving little scars, and is not done by those that are not superstitious, who choose to have them in the legs or that part of the arm that is concealed. The children or young patients play together all the rest of the day, and are in perfect health until the eighth. Then the fever begins to seize them and they keep their beds two days, very seldom three. They have very rarely above twenty or thirty in their faces, which never mark, and in eight days time they are as well as before their illness. Where they are wounded there remains running sores during the distemper which I don't doubt is a great relief to it. Every year thousands undergo this operation, and the French Ambassador says pleasantly that they take the smallpox here by way of diversion, as they take the waters in other countries. There is no example of any one that has died in it, and you may believe I am well satisfied of the safety of the experiment, since I intend to try it on my dear little son. I am patriot enough to take pains to bring this useful invention into fashion in England and I should not fail to write to some of our

doctors very particulary about it if I knew anyone of them that I
thought had virtue enough to destroy such a considerable
branch of their revenue for the good of mankind. But that
distemper is too beneficial to them not to expose to all their
resentment the hardy wight[165] that should undertake to put an
end to it. Perhaps, if I live to return, I may, however, have
courage to war with them. Upon this occasion admire the
heroism in the heart of your friend, etc.

LETTER XXXIII

To Anne Thistlethwayte,   *Adrianople, 1 April 1718*

I can now tell dear Mrs Thistelthwayte that I am safely arrived
at the end of my very long journey. I will not tire you with the
account of the many fatigues I have suffered. You would rather
hear something of what I see here and a letter out of Turkey
that has nothing extraordinary in it would be as great a disappointment as my visitors will receive at London, if I return
thither without any rarities to show them. What shall I tell you
of? You never saw camels in your life, and perhaps the description of them will appear new to you. I can assure you, the first
sight of them was very much so to me, and though I have seen
hundreds of pictures of those animals I never saw any that was
resembling enough to give me a true idea of them. I am going to
make a bold observation and possibly a false one, because
nobody has ever made it before me, but I do take them to be of
the stag kind; their legs, bodies and necks are exactly shaped like
them, and their colour very near the same. 'Tis true they are
much larger, being a great deal higher than a horse, and so swift
that, after the defeat of Peterwardein, they far out-ran the
swiftest horses and brought the first news of the loss of the
battle to Belgrade. They are never thoroughly tamed; the drivers
take care to tie them one to another with strong ropes, fifty in a
string, led by an ass on which the driver rides. I have seen three

hundred in one caravan. They carry the third part more than any horse but 'tis a particular art to load them because of the bunch on their backs. They seem to me very ugly creatures, their heads being ill-formed and disproportioned to their bodies. They carry all the burdens, and the beasts destined to the plough are buffaloes, an animal you are also unacquainted with. They are larger and more clumsy than an ox. They have short black horns close to their heads, which grow turning backwards. They say this horn looks very beautiful when 'tis well polished. They are all black, with very short hair on their hides, and have extreme little white eyes that make them look like devils. The country people dye their tails and the hair of their foreheads red by way of ornament. Horses are not put here to any laborious work, nor are they at all fit for it. They are beautiful and full of spirit but generally little and not so strong as the breed of colder countries; very gentle, however, with all their vivacity, swift and sure-footed. I have a little white favourite that I would not part with on any terms. He prances under me with so much fire you would think that I had a great deal of courage to dare mount him. Yet I'll assure you I never rid a horse so much at my command. My side saddle is the first was ever seen in this part of the world and is gazed at with as much wonder as the ship of Columbus was in America. Here are some birds held in a sort of religious reverence and for that reason, multiply prodigiously: turtles on the account of their innocence and storks because they are supposed to make every winter the pilgrimage to Mecca. To say truth they are the happiest subjects under the Turkish government, and are so sensible of their privileges they walk the streets without fear and generally build in the low parts of houses. Happy are those that are so distinguished. The vulgar Turks are perfectly persuaded that they will not be that year attacked either by fire or pestilence. I have the happiness of one of their sacred nests under my chamber window.

Now I am talking of my chamber I remember the description of the houses here will be as new to you as any of the birds or beasts. I suppose you have read in most of our accounts of Turkey that their houses are the most miserable pieces of building in the world. I can speak very learnedly on that subject, having been in so many of them and I assure you 'tis no such thing. We are now lodged in a palace belonging to the Grand Signor. I really think the manner of building here very agreeable and proper for the country. 'Tis true, they are not at all solicitous to beautify the outsides of their houses and they are generally built of wood, which I own is the cause of many inconveniences, but this is not to be charged on the ill taste of the people, but on the oppression of the government. Every house, upon the death of its master, is at the Grand Signor's disposal and therefore no man cares to make a great expense which he is not sure his family will be the better for. All their design is to build a house commodious and that will last their lives, and they are very indifferent if it falls down the year after. Every house, great and small, is divided into two distinct parts, which only join together by a narrow passage. The first house has a large court before it, and open galleries all round it, which is to me a thing very agreeable. This gallery leads to all the chambers which are commonly large, and with two rows of windows, the first being of painted glass. They seldom build above two storeys, each of which has such galleries. The stairs are broad and not often above thirty steps. This is the house belonging to the lord, and the adjoining one is called the harem, that is, the ladies' apartment (for the name of seraglio is peculiar to the Grand Signor's). It has also a gallery running round it towards the garden to which all the windows are turned, and the same number of chambers as the other, but more gay and splendid, both in painting and furniture. The second row of windows are very low, with grates like those of convents.

The rooms are all spread with Persian carpets and raised at one end of them (my chamber is raised at both ends) about two feet. This is the sofa, and is laid with a richer sort of carpet, and all round it a sort of couch raised half a foot, covered with rich silk, according to the fancy or magnificence of the owner. Mine is of scarlet cloth with a gold fringe. Round about this are placed, standing against the wall, two rows of cushions, the first very large and the next little ones, and here the Turks display their greatest magnificence. They are generally brocade or embroidery of gold wire upon satin. Nothing can look more gay and splendid. These seats are so convenient and easy that I believe I shall never endure chairs as long as I live. The rooms are low, which I think no fault, the ceiling always of wood generally inlaid or painted and gilded. They use no hangings, the rooms being all wainscoted with cedar set off with silver nails or painted with flowers, which open in many places with folding doors and serve for cabinets, I think more conveniently than ours. Between the windows are little arches to set pots of perfume or baskets of flowers. But what pleases me best is the fashion of having marble fountains in the lower part of the room, which throws up several spouts of water giving, at the same time, an agreeable coolness and a pleasant dashing sound, falling from one basin to another. Some of these fountains are very magnificent. Each house has a bagnio, which consists generally in two or three little rooms, leaded on the top, paved with marble with basins, cocks of water, and all conveniences for either hot or cold baths.

You will perhaps be surprised at an account so different from what you have been entertained with by the common voyage writers, who are very fond of speaking of what they don't know. It must be under a very particular character, or on some extraordinary occasion when a Christian is admitted into the house of a man of quality, and their harems are always forbidden ground. Thus they can only speak of the outside, which makes no great appearance, and the women's apartments are always built backward, removed from sight, and have no other prospect than the gardens, which are enclosed with very high walls. There is none of our parterres in them, but they are planted with high trees which give an agreeable shade, and, to my fancy, a pleasing view. In the midst of the garden is the kiosk, that is, a large room commonly beautified with a fine fountain in the midst of it. It is raised nine or ten steps and enclosed with gilded lattices round which vines, jessamines and honeysuckles twining make a sort of green wall. Large trees are planted round this place, which is the scene of their greatest pleasures, and where the ladies spend most of their hours, employed by their music or embroidery. In the public gardens there are public kiosks where people go that are not so well accommodated at home, and drink their coffee, sherbet etc. Neither are they ignorant of a more durable manner of building. Their mosques are all of free stone, and the public hans or inns extremely magnificent, many of them taking up a large square built round with shops under stone arches, where poor artificers are lodged gratis. They have always a mosque joining to them, and the body of the han is a most noble hall, capable of holding three or four hundred persons, the court extreme spacious and cloisters round it that give it the air of our colleges. I own I think these foundations a more reasonable piece of charity than the founding of convents. I think I have now told you a great deal for once. If you don't like my choice of subjects, tell me what you would have me write upon. There is nobody more desirous to entertain you than, dear Mrs Thistelthwayte, etc.

LETTER XXXIV

To Lady Mar,   *Adrianople, 18 April 1718*

I writ to you, dear sister, and to all my other English correspondents, by the last ship and only heaven can tell when I shall have another opportunity of sending to you; but I cannot forbear writing though perhaps my letter may lie upon my hands this two months. To confess the truth my head is so full of my entertainment yesterday that 'tis absolutely necessary for my own repose to give it some vent. Without farther preface, I will then begin my story.

I was invited to dine with the Grand Vizier's lady,[166] and it was with a great deal of pleasure I prepared myself for an entertainment which was never given before to any Christian. I thought I should very little satisfy her curiosity, which I did not doubt was a considerable motive to the invitation, by going in a dress she was used to see, and therefore dressed myself in the court habit of Vienna, which is much more magnificent than ours. However, I chose to go incognito to avoid any disputes about ceremony, and went in a Turkish coach, only attended by my woman that held up my train and the Greek lady who was my interpretress. I was met at the court door by her black eunuch, who helped me out of the coach with great respect, and conducted me through several rooms, where her she-slaves, finely dressed, were ranged on each side. In the innermost I found the lady sitting on her sofa, in a sable vest. She advanced to meet me, and presented me half a dozen of her friends with great civility. She seemed a very good woman, near fifty years old. I was surprised to observe so little magnificence in her house, the furniture being all very moderate and, except the habits and number of her slaves, nothing about her that appeared expensive. She guessed at my thoughts and told me that she was no longer of an age to spend either her time or money in superfluities; that her whole expense was in charity, and her employment praying to God. There was no affectation in this speech; both she and her husband are entirely given up to devotion. He never looks upon any other woman and, what is much more extraordinary, touches no bribes, notwithstanding the example of all his predecessors. He is so scrupulous on this point, he would not accept Mr Wortley's present till he had been assured over and over that 'twas a settled perquisite of his place, at the entrance of every ambassador.

She entertained me with all kind of civility, till dinner came in, which was served, one dish at a time, to a vast number, all finely dressed after their manner, which I do not think so bad as you have perhaps heard it represented. I am a very good judge of their eating, having lived three weeks in the house of an *effendi*[167] at Belgrade, who gave us very magnificent dinners, dressed by his own cooks which the first week pleased me extremely but, I own I then began to grow weary of it and desired our own cook might add a dish or two after our manner. But I attribute this to custom. I am very much inclined to believe an Indian that had never tasted of either, would prefer

their cookery to ours. Their sauces are very high,[168] all the
roast very much done. They use a great deal of rich spice. The
soup is served for the last dish and they have at least as great
variety of ragouts as we have. I was very sorry I could not eat
of as many as the good lady would have had me, who was very
earnest in serving me of everything. The treat concluded with
coffee and perfumes, which is a high mark of respect; two
slaves kneeling censed[169] my hair, clothes and handkerchief.
After this ceremony she commanded her slaves to play and
dance, which they did with their guitars in their hands, and she
excused to me their want of skill, saying she took no care to
accomplish them in that art. I returned her thanks and, soon
after took my leave.

I was conducted back in the same manner I entered and
would have gone straight to my own house but the Greek lady
with me earnestly solicited me to visit the Kabya's lady, saying
he was the second officer in the empire and ought indeed to be
looked upon as the first, the Grand Vizier having only the name,
while he exercised the authority. I had found so little diversion
in this harem that I had no mind to go into another. But her
importunity prevailed with me and I am extremely glad I was so
complaisant. All things here were with quite another air than at
the Grand Vizier's and the very house confessed the difference
between an old devote and a young beauty. It was nicely clean
and magnificent. I was met at the door by two black eunuchs
who led me through a long gallery between two ranks of
beautiful young girls, with their hair finely plaited almost hanging to their feet, all dressed in fine light damasks brocaded with
silver. I was sorry that decency did not permit me to stop to
consider them nearer. But that thought was lost upon my
entrance into a large room or rather pavilion built round with
gilded sashes, which were most of them thrown up and the trees
planted near them gave an agreeable shade which hindered the
sun from being troublesome, the jessamines and honeysuckles
that twisted round their trunks shedding a soft perfume,
increased by a white marble fountain playing sweet water in the
lower part of the room, which fell into three or four basins with

a pleasing sound. The roof was painted with all sorts of flowers falling out to gilded baskets, that seemed tumbling down.

On a sofa raised three steps and covered with fine Persian carpets, sat the Kabya's lady, leaning on cushions of white satin, embroidered, and at her feet sat two young girls, the eldest about twelve year old, lovely as angels, dressed perfectly rich, and almost covered with jewels. But they were hardly seen near the fair Fatima (for that is her name) so much her beauty effaced everything I have seen all that has been called lovely either in England or Germany and must own that I never saw anything so gloriously beautiful, nor can I recollect a face that would have been taken notice of near hers. She stood up to receive me, saluting me after their fashion putting her hand upon her heart with a sweetness full of majesty that no court breeding could ever give. She ordered cushions to be given me and took care to place me in the corner, which is the place of honour. I confess, though, the Greek lady had before given me a great opinion of her beauty I was so struck with admiration that I could not for some time speak to her, being wholly taken up in gazing. That surprising harmony of features! That charming result of the whole! That exact proportion of body! That lovely bloom of complexion, unsullied by art! The unutterable enchantment of her smile! But her eyes! Large and black, with all the soft languishment of the blue! Every turn of her face discovering some new charm! After my first surprise was over I endeavoured, by nicely examining her face, to find out some imperfection, without any fruit of my search, but my being clearly convinced of the error of that vulgar notion, that a face perfectly regular would not be agreeable; nature having done for her, with more success, what Apelles[170] is said to have essayed, by a collection of the most exact features, to form a perfect face. And to that a behaviour so full of grace and sweetness, such easy motions, with an air so majestic, yet free from stiffness or affectation that I am persuaded, could she be suddenly transported upon the most polite throne of Europe nobody would think her other than born and bred to be a queen, though educated in a country we call barbarous. To say all in a word, our most celebrated English beauties would vanish near her.

She was dressed in a caftan of gold brocade, flowered with silver, very well fitted to her shape, and showing to advantage the beauty of her bosom, only shaded by the thin gauze of her shift. Her drawers were pale pink, her waistcoat green and silver, her slippers white, finely embroidered, her lovely arms adorned with bracelets of diamonds and her broad girdle set round with diamonds; upon her head a rich Turkish handkerchief of pink and silver, her own fine black hair hanging a great length in various tresses, and on one side of her head some bodkins of jewels. I am afraid you will accuse me of extravagance in this description. I think I have read somewhere that women always speak in rapture when they speak of beauty, but I can't imagine why they should not be allowed to do so. I rather think it virtue to be able to admire without any mixture of desire or envy. The gravest writers have spoken with great warmth of some celebrated pictures and statues. The workmanship of Heaven certainly excels all our weak imitations, and I think has a much better claim to our praise. For my part I am not ashamed to own I took more pleasure in looking on the beauteous Fatima than the finest piece of sculpture could have given me. She told me the two girls at her feet were her daughters, though she appeared too young to be their mother.

Her fair maids were ranged below the sofa, to the number of twenty, and put me in mind of the pictures of the ancient nymphs. I did not think all nature could have furnished such a scene of beauty. She made them a sign to play and dance. Four of them immediately begun to play some soft airs on instruments, between a lute and a guitar, which they accompanied with their voices, while the others danced by turns. This dance was very different from what I had seen before. Nothing could be more artful or more proper to raise certain ideas; the tunes so soft, the motions so languishing, accompanied with pauses and dying eyes, half falling back and then recovering themselves in so artful a manner that I am very positive the coldest and most rigid prude upon earth could not have looked upon them without thinking of something not to be spoke of. I suppose you may have read that the Turks have no music but what is shocking to the ears, but this account is from those who never heard any but what is played in the streets, and is just as reasonable as if a foreigner should take his ideas of English music from the bladder and string or the marrow-bones and cleavers.[171] I can assure you that the music is extremely pathetic; 'tis true, I am inclined to prefer the Italian, but perhaps I am partial. I am acquainted with a Greek lady who sings better than Mrs Robinson[172] and is very well skilled in both, who gives the preference to the Turkish. 'Tis certain they have very fine natural voices; these were very agreeable.

When the dance was over, four fair slaves came into the room with silver censers in their hands and perfumed the air with amber, aloes wood and other scents. After this they served me coffee upon their knees in the finest japan china, with soucoups[173] of silver gilt. The lovely Fatima entertained me all this while, in the most polite agreeable manner, calling me often güzel Sultanum, or the beautiful Sultana, and desiring my friendship with the best grace in the world, lamenting that she could not entertain me in my own language.

When I took my leave, two maids brought in a fine silver basket of embroidered handkerchiefs. She begged I would wear the richest for her sake and gave the others to my woman and interpretress. I retired through the same ceremonies as before, and could not help fancying I had been some time in Mohammed's paradise, so much was I charmed with what I had seen. I know not how the relation of it appears to you. I wish it may give you part of my pleasure for I would have my dear sister share in all the diversions of etc.

LETTER XXXV

To Abbé Conti,   *Adrianople, 17 May 1718*

I am going to leave Adrianople and I would not do it without giving some account of all that is curious in it, which I have taken a great deal of pains to see. I will not trouble you with wise dissertations, whether or no this is the same city that was anciently called Orestesit or Oreste, which you know better than I do. It is now called from the Emperor Adrian[174] and was the first European seat of the Turkish empire, and has been the favourite residence of many sultans. Mehmed IV the father, and Mustafa,[175] the brother of the reigning emperor were so fond of it that they wholly abandoned Constantinople, which humour so far exasperated the janissaries that it was a considerable motive to the rebellions which deposed them. Yet this man seems to love to keep his court here. I can give no reason for this partiality. 'Tis true, the situation is fine and the country all round very beautiful, but the air is extreme bad and the seraglio itself is not free from the ill effect of it. The town is said to be eight miles in compass; I suppose they reckon in the gardens. There are some good houses in it, I mean large ones, for the architecture of their palaces never makes any great show. It is now very full of people, but they are most of them such as follow the court or camp, and when they are removed, I am told, 'tis no populous city. The river Maritza (anciently the Hebrus) on which it is situated is dried up every summer, which contributes very much to make it unwholesome. It is now a very pleasant stream. There are two noble bridges built over it. I had the curiosity to go to see the Exchange in my Turkish dress which is disguise sufficient, yet I own I was not very easy when I saw it crowded with janissaries; but they dare not be rude to a woman and made way for me with as much respect as if I had been in my own figure. It is half a mile in length, the roof arched and kept extremely neat. It holds 365 shops furnished with all sorts of rich goods, exposed to sale in the same manner as at the New Exchange in London, but the pavement kept much neater and the shops all so clean they seemed just new painted. Idle people of all sorts walk here for their diversion, or amuse themselves with drinking coffee or sherbet, which is cried about as oranges and sweetmeats are in our playhouses.

I observed most of the rich tradesmen were Jews. That people are in incredible power in this country. They have many privileges above the natural Turks themselves and have formed a very considerable commonwealth here, being judged by their own laws and have drawn the whole trade of the empire into their hands, partly by the firm union amongst themselves and prevailing on the idle temper and want of industry of the Turks. Every pasha has his Jew who is his homme d'affaires. He is let into all his secrets and does all his business. No bargain is made, no bribe received, no merchandise disposed of but what passes through their hands. They are the physicians, the stewards and the interpreters of all the great men. You may judge how advantageous this is to a people who never fail to make use of the smallest advantages. They have found the secret of making themselves so necessary they are certain of the protection of the court whatever ministry is in power. Even the English, French and Italian merchants, who are sensible in their artifices are however forced to trust their affairs to their negotiation, nothing of trade being managed without them and the meanest amongst them is too important to be disobliged since the whole body take care of his interests with as much vigour as they would those of the most considerable of their members. They are many of them vastly rich but take care to make little public show of it, though they live in their houses in the utmost luxury and magnificence. This copious subject has drawn me from my description of the exchange founded by Ali Pasha, whose name it bears.[176] Near it is the Shershi, a street of a mile in length, full of shops and all kind of fine merchandise but excessive dear, nothing being made here. It is covered on the top with boards to keep out the rain, that merchants may meet conveniently in all weathers. The Bedesten near it is another exchange, built upon pillars, where all sort of horse furniture is sold; glittering everywhere with gold, rich embroidery and jewels it makes a very agreeable show.

From this place I went in my Turkish coach to the camp, which is to move in a few days to the frontiers. The Sultan is already gone to his tents, and all his court. The appearance of them is indeed very magnificent. Those of the great men are rather like palaces than tents, taking up a great compass of ground and being divided into a vast number of apartments. They are all of green and the pashas of three tails have those ensigns of their power placed in a very conspicuous manner before their tents which are adorned on the top with gilded balls, more or less according to their different ranks.[177] The ladies go in their coaches to see this camp as eagerly as ours did to that of Hyde Park,[178] but 'tis easy to observe that the soldiers do not begin the campaign with any great cheerfulness. The war is a general grievance upon the people but particularly hard upon the tradesmen.

Now the Grand Signor is resolved to lead his army in person every company of them is obliged upon this occasion to make a present according to their ability. I took the pains of rising at six in the morning to see that ceremony, which did not however begin till eight. The Grand Signor was at the seraglio window to see the procession, which passed through all the principal streets. It was preceded by an *Effendi* mounted on a camel richly furnished, reading aloud the Alcoran, finely bound, laid upon a cushion. Hew was surrounded by a pracel of boys in white, singing some verses of it, followed by a man dressed in green boughs representing a clean husbandman sowing seed. After him several reapers with garlands of ears of corn, as Ceres is pictured, with scythes in their hands seeming to mow; then a little machine drawn by oxen, in which was a windmill and boys employed in grinding corn, followed by another machine drawn by buffaloes carrying an oven and two more boys, one employed in kneading the bread and another in drawing it out of the oven. These boys threw little cakes on both sides among the crowd and were followed by the whole company of bakers marching on foot, two and two, in their best clothes, with cakes, loaves, pasties and pies of all sorts on their heads; and after then two buffoons or jack puddings with their faces and clothes smeared with meal, who diverted the mob with their antick gestures. In the same manner followed all the companies of trade in their empire, the nobler sort such as jewellers, mercers etc. finely mounted and many of the pageants that represented their trades perfectly magnificent, amongst which the furriers' made one of the best figures, being a very large machine set round with the skins of ermines, foxes etc. so well stuffed the animals seemed to be alive, followed by music and dancers. I believe there were, upon the whole, at least 20,000 men, all ready to follow his highness if he commanded them.

The rear was closed by the volunteers who came to beg the honour of dying in his service. This part of the show seemed to me so barbarous I removed from the window upon the first appearance of it. They were all naked to the middle, their arms pierced through with arrows left sticking in them, others had them sticking in their heads, the blood trickling down their faces, and some slashed their arms with sharp knives, making the blood spout out upon those that stood near, and this is looked upon as an expression of their zeal for glory. I am told that some make use of it to advance their love, and when they are near the window where their mistress stands, all the women in town being veiled to see this spectacle, they stick another arrow for her sake, who gives some sign of approbation and encouragement to this gallantry. The whole show lasted near eight hours, to my great sorrow, who was heartily tired, though I was in the house of the widow of the Captain Pasha (Admiral), who refreshed me with coffee, sweetmeats, sherbet etc. with all possible civility.

I went two days after to see the mosque of Sultan Selim I,[179] which is a building very well worth the curiosity of a traveller. I was dressed in my Turkish habit and admitted without scruple, though I believe they guessed who I was by the extreme officiousness of the door keeper to show me every part of it. It is situated very advantageously in the midst of the city and in the highest part, making a very noble show. The first court has four gates and the innermost, three. They are both of them surrounded with cloisters with marble pillars of the Ionic order, finely polished and of very lively colours, the whole pavement being white marble, the roof of the cloisters being divided into several cupelos or domes, leaded, with gilt balls on the top, in the midst of each four fine fountains of white marble; before the great gate of the mosque a portico with green marble pillars.

It has five gates, the body of the mosque being one prodigious dome. I understand so little of architecture I dare not pretend to speak of the proportions; it seemed to me very regular. This I am sure of, it is vastly high, and I thought it the noblest building I ever saw. It had two rows of marble galleries on pillars with marble balustrades, the pavement marble covered with persian carpets, and in my opinion it is a great addition to its beauty that it is not divided into pews and encumbered with forms and benches like our churches, nor the pillars (which are most of them red and white marble) disfigured by the little tawdry images and pictures that give the Roman Catholic churches the air of toyshops. The walls seemed to me inlaid with such very lively colours in small flowers, I could not imagine what stones had been made use of, but, going nearer, I saw they were crusted with japan china[180] which has a very beautiful effect. In the midst hung a vast lamp of silver gilt, besides which I do verily believe there was at least 2,000 of a lesser size. This must look very glorious when they are all lighted, but that being at night no women are suffered to enter. Under the large lamp is a great pulpit of carved wood gilt and just by it a fountain to wash, which you know is an essential part of their devotion. In one corner is a little gallery enclosed with gilded lattices for the Grand Signor; at the upper end a large niche very like an altar, raised two steps, covered with gold brocade, and standing before it two silver gilt candlesticks the height of a man and in them white wax candles as thick as a man's waist. The outside of the mosque is adorned with four towers vastly high, gilt on the top, from whence the imams[181] call the people to prayers. I had the curiosity to go up one of them, which is contrived so artfully as to give surprise to all that see it. There is but one door which leads to three different staircases going to the three different storeys of the tower in such a manner that three priests may ascend rounding without ever meeting each other, a contrivance very much admired. Behind the mosque is an exchange full of shops where poor artificers are lodged gratis. I saw several dervishes[182] at their prayers here. They are dressed in a plain piece of woollen with their arms bare and a woollen cap on their heads like a high crowned hat without brims. I went to see some other mosques built much after the same manner, but not comparable in point of magnificence to this I have described, which is infinitely beyond any church in Germany or England. I won't talk of other countries I have not seen, The seraglio does not seem a very magnificent palace, but the gardens very large, plentifully supplied with water and full of trees, which is all I know of them, never having been in them.

I tell you nothing of the order of Mr Wortley's entry and his audience. Those things are always the same and have been so often described I won't trouble you with the repetition. The young prince, about eleven year old sits near his father when he gives audience. He is a handsome boy, but probably will not immediately succeed the Sultan, there being two sons of Sultan Mustafa (his eldest brother) remaining, the eldest about 20 year old, on whom the hopes of the people are fixed.[183] This reign has been bloody and avaricious. I am apt to believe they are very impatient to see the end of it. I am, sir, your etc.

I will write to you again from Constantinople.

LETTER XXXVI

To the Abbé Conti,   *Constantinople, 29 May 1717*

I have had the advantage of very fine weather all my journey and the summer being now in its beauty I enjoyed the pleasure of fine prospects; and the meadows being full of all sort of garden flowers and sweet herbs my berlin[184] perfumed the air as it pressed them. The Grand Signor furnished us with thirty covered waggons for our baggage and five coaches of the country for my women. We found the road full of the great sipahis[185] and their equipages coming out of Asia to the war. They always travel with tents, but I chose to lie in houses all the way.

I will not trouble you with the names of the villages we passed in which there was nothing remarkable, but at Ciorlu we were lodged in a conac or little seraglio, built for the use of the Grand Signor when he goes this road. I had the curiosity to view all the apartments destined for the ladies of his court. They were in the midst of a thick grove of trees made fresh by fountains, but I was surprised to see the walls almost covered with little distiches[186] of Turkish verse writ with pencils. I made my interpreter explain them to me and I found several of them very well turned, though I easily believed him that they lost much of their beauty in the translation. One runs literally thus in English:

We come into this world, we lodge, and we depart;
He never goes that's lodged within my heart.

The rest of our journey was through fine painted meadows by the side of the sea of Marmora, the ancient Propontis. We lay the next night at Selivrea, anciently a noble town. It is now a very good sea port, and neatly built enough, and has a bridge of thirty two arches. Here is a famous ancient Greek church. I had given one of my coaches to a Greek lady who desired the convenience of travelling with me. She designed to pay her devotions and I was glad of the opportunity of going with her. I found it an ill built place, set out with the same sort of ornaments but less rich than the Roman Catholic churches. They showed me a saint's body, where I threw a piece of money and a picture of the Virgin Mary drawn by the hand of St Luke, very little to the credit of his painting, but, however, the finest madonna of Italy is not more famous for her miracles. The Greeks have the most monstrous taste in their pictures, which for more finery are always drawn upon a gold ground. You may imagine what a good air this has, but they have no notion either of shade or proportion. They have a bishop here who officiated in his purple robe, and sent me a candle almost as big as myself for a present when I was at my lodging.

We lay the next night at a town called Büjük Cekmege or Great Bridge and the night following at Kujük Cekmege, Little Bridge, in a very pleasant lodging, formerly a monastery of dervishes, having before it a large court encompassed with marble cloisters with a good fountain in the middle. The prospect from this place and the gardens round it are the most agreeable I have seen, and shows that monks of all religions know how to choose their retirements. 'Tis now belonging to a *hogia* or school master, who teaches boys here, and asking him to show me his own apartment I was surprised to see him point to a tall cypress tree in the garden, on the top of which was a place for a bed for himself and a little lower one for his wife and two children who slept there every night. I was so much diverted with the fancy I resolved to examine his nest nearer but after going up fifty steps I found I had still fifty to go and then I must climb from branch to branch with some hazard of my neck. I thought it the best way to come down again.

We arrived the next evening at Constantinople, but I can yet tell you very little of it, all my time having been taken up with receiving visits, which are at least a very good entertainment to the eyes, the young women being all beauties and their beauty highly improved by the good taste of their dress. Our palace is in Pera, which is no more a suburb of Constantinople than Westminster is a suburb to London. All the Ambassadors are lodged very near each other. One part of our house shows us the port, the city and the seraglio and the distant hills of Asia, perhaps altogether the most beautiful prospect in the world. A certain French author says that Constantinople is twice as large as Paris.[187] Mr Wortley is unwilling to own 'tis bigger than London, though I confess it appears to me to be so, but I don't believe 'tis so populous. The burying fields about it are certainly much larger than the whole city. 'Tis surprising what a vast deal of land is lost this way in Turkey. Sometimes I have seen burying places of several miles belonging to very inconsiderable villages which were formerly great towns and retain no other mark of their ancient grandeur. On no occasion they remove a stone that serves for a monument. Some of them are costly enough, being of a very fine marble. They set up a pillar with a carved turban on the top of it to the memory of a man and as the turbans by their different shapes show the quality or profession, 'tis in a manner putting up the arms of the deceased; besides, the pillar commonly bears a large inscription in gold letters. The ladies have a simple pillar without other ornament, except those that die unmarried who have a rose on top of it. The sepulchres of particular families are railed in and planted round with trees. Those of the sultans and some great men have lamps constantly burning in them.

When I spoke of their religion I forgot to mention two particularities, one of which I had read of, but it seemed so odd to me I could not believe it. Yet 'tis certainly true that when a man has divorced his wife in the most solemn manner he can take her again upon no other terms than permitting another man to pass a night with her, and there are some examples of those that have submitted to this law rather than not have back their beloved. The other point of doctrine is very extraordinary; any woman that dies unmarried is looked upon to die in a state of reprobation. To confirm this belief they reason that the end of the creation of woman is to increase and multiply, and she is only properly employed in the works of her calling when she is bringing children or taking care of them, which are all the virtues that God expects from her; and indeed, their way of life, which shuts them out of all public commerce, does not permit them any other. Our vulgar notion that they do not own women to have any souls is a mistake. 'Tis true they say they are not of so elevated a kind and therefore must not hope to be admitted into the paradise appointed for the men, who are to be entertained by celestial beauties, but there is a place of happiness destined for souls of the inferior order where all good women are to be in eternal bliss. Many of them are very superstitious and will not remain widows ten days for fear of dying in the reprobate state of a useless creature.[188] But those that like their liberty and are not slaves to their religion content themselves with marrying when they are afraid of dying. This is a piece of theology very different from that which teaches nothing to be more acceptable to God than a vow of perpetual virginity. Which divinity is most rational I leave you to determine.

I have already made some progress in a collection of Greek

medals. Here are several professed antiquaries who are ready to serve anybody that desires them, but you can't imagine how they stare in my face when I enquire about them, as if nobody was permitted to seek after medals till they were grown a piece of antiquity themselves. I have got some very valuable of the Macedonian kings, particularly one of Perseus,[189] so lively I fancy I can see all his ill qualities in his face. I have a porphyry head finely cut of the true Greek sculpture, but who it represents is to be guessed at by the learned when I return, for you are not to suppose these antiquaries, who are all Greeks, know anything. Their trade is only to sell. They have correspondents at Aleppo, Grand Cairo, in Arabia and Palestine, who send them all they can find, and very often great heaps that are only fit to melt into pans and kettles. They get the best price they can for any of them, without knowing those that are valuable from those that are not. Those that pretend to skill generally find out the image of some saint in the medals of the Greek cities. One of them, showing me the figure of Pallas[190] with a victory in her hand on a reverse, assured me it was the Virgin holding a crucifix. The same man offered me the head of a Socrates on a Sardonix,[191] and to enhance the value gave him the title of St Augustine.[192] I have bespoke a mummy, which I hope will come safe to my hands, notwithstanding the misfortune that befell a very fine one designed for the King of Sweden.[193] He gave a great price for it, and the Turks took it into their heads that he must certainly have some considerable project depending upon it. They fancied it the body of God knows who and that the fate of their empire mystically depended on the conservation of it. Some old prophecies were remembered upon this occasion, and the mummy committed prisoner to the seven towers,[194] where it has remained under close confinement ever since. I dare not try my interest in so considerable a point as the release of it, but I hope mine will pass without examination. I can tell you nothing more at present of this famous city. When I have looked a little about me you shall hear from me again. I am, sir, etc.

LETTER XXXVII

To Alexander Pope,   *Belgrade Village,*[195] *17 June 1717*

I hope before this time you have received two or three of my letters. I had yours but yesterday, though dated the third of February, in which you suppose me dead and buried. I have already let you know that I am still alive, but to say truth, I look upon my present circumstances to be exactly the same with those of departed spirits. The heats of Constantinople have driven me to this place, which perfectly answers the description of the Elysian fields.[196] I am in the middle of a wood, consisting chiefly of fruit trees, watered by a vast number of fountains famous for the excellency of their water, and divided into many shady walks upon short grass, that seems to me artificial but I am assured is the pure work of nature, within view of the Black Sea, from whence we perpetually enjoy the refreshment of cool breezes that makes us insensible of the heat of the summer. The village is wholly inhabited by the richest amongst the Christians, who meet every night at the fountain forty paces from my house to sing and dance, the beauty and dress of the women exactly resembling the ideas of the ancient nymphs as they are given us by the representations of the poets and painters. But what persuades me more fully of my decease is the situation of my own mind, the profound ignorance I am in of what passes amongst the living, which only comes to me by chance, and the great calmness with which I receive it. Yet I have still a hankering after my friends and acquaintance left in the world, according to the authority of that admirable author:

> That spirits departed are wondrous kind
> To friends and relations left behind,
> Which nobody can deny.

of which solemn truth I am a dead instance. I think Virgil is of the same opinion, that in human souls there will still be some remains of human passions.

Curae non ipsa in morte relinquunt[197]

and 'tis very necessary to make a perfect Elysium that there should be a river Lethe,[198] which I am not so happy to find. To say truth I am sometimes very weary of this singing and dancing and sunshine, and wish for the smoke and impertinencies in which you toil, though I endeavour to persuade myself that I live in a more agreeable variety than you do, and that Monday setting of partridges, Tuesday reading English, Wednesday studying the Turkish language (in which, by the way, I am already very learned), Thursday classical authors, Friday spent in writing, Saturday at my needle and Sunday admitting of visits and hearing music, is a better way of disposing the week than Monday at the Drawing Room,[199] Tuesday Lady Mohun's,[200] Wednesday the opera, Thursday the play, Friday Mrs Chetwynd's,[201] etc.; a perpetual round of hearing the same scandal and seeing the same follies acted over and over, which here affect me no more than they do other dead people. I can now hear of displeasing things with pity and without indignation. The reflection on the great gulf between you and me cools all news that comes hither. I can neither be sensibly touched with joy or grief when I consider that possibly the cause of either is removed before the letter comes to my hands; but, as I said before, this indolence does not extend to my few friendships. I am still warmly sensible of yours and Mr Congreve's and desire to live in your remembrance, though dead to all the world beside.

LETTER XXXVIII

To Lady—,[202]   *Belgrade Village, 17 June 1717*

I heartily beg your ladyship's pardon, but I really could not forbear laughing heartily at your letter and the commissions you are pleased to honour me with. You desire me to buy you a Greek slave who is to be mistress of a thousand good qualities. The Greeks are subjects and not slaves. Those who are to be bought in that manner are either such as are taken in war or stole by the Tartars from Russia, Circassia or Georgia, and are such miserable, awkward, poor wretches you would not think any of them worthy to be your housemaid. 'Tis true that many thousands were taken in the Morea, but they have been most of them redeemed by the charitable contributions of the Christians or ransomed by their own relations at Venice. The fine slaves that wait upon the great ladies or serve the pleasures of the great men are all bought at the age of eight or nine year old and educated with great care to accomplish them in singing, dancing, embroidery, etc. They are commonly Circassians and their patron never sells them except it is as a punishment for some very great fault. If ever they grow weary of them, they either present them to a friend or give them their freedoms. Those that are exposed to sale at the markets are always either guilty of some crime or so entirely worthless that they are of no use at all. I am afraid you'll doubt the truth of this account, which I own is very different from our common notions in England, but it is not less truth for all that.

Your whole letter is full of mistakes from one end to the other. I see you have taken your ideas of Turkey from that worthy author Dumont, who has writ with equal ignorance and confidence.[203] 'Tis a particular pleasure to me here to read the voyages to the Levant, which are generally so far removed from truth and so full of absurdities I am very well diverted with them. They never fail to give you an account of the women, which 'tis certain they never saw, and talking very wisely of the genius of men, into whose company they are never admitted, and very often describe mosques which they dare not peep into. The Turks are very proud and will not converse with a stranger they are not assured is considerable in his own country. I speak of the men of distinction, for as to the ordinary fellows, you may imagine what ideas their conversation can give of the general genius of the people.

As to the Balm of Mecca,[204] I will certainly send you some, but it is not so easily got as you suppose it and I cannot in conscience advise you to make use of it. I know not how it comes to have such universal applause. All the ladies of my acquaintance at London and Vienna have begged me to send pots of it to them. I have had a present of a small quantity (which I'll assure you is very valuable) of the best sort, and with great joy applied it to my face, expecting some wonderful effect to my advantage. The next morning the change indeed was wonderful; my face was swelled to a very extraordinary size and all over as red as my Lady—'s. It remained in this lamentable state three days, during which you may be sure I passed my time very ill. I believed it would never be otherwise and to add to my mortification Mr Wortley reproached my indiscretion without ceasing. However, my face is since in statu quo. Nay, I am told by the ladies here that 'tis much mended by the operation, which I confess I cannot perceive in my looking glass. Indeed, if one was to form an opinion of this balm from their faces, one should think very well of it. They all make use of it and have the loveliest bloom in the world. For my part, I never intend to endure the pain of it again. Let my complexion take its natural course and decay in its own due time. I have very little esteem for medicines of this nature; but you do as you please, madam, only remember before you use it that your face will not be such as you'll care to show in the drawing room for some days after.

If one was to believe the women in this country, there is a surer way of making oneself beloved than by becoming handsome, though you know that's our method. But they pretend to the knowledge of secrets that by way of enchantment gives them the entire empire over whom they please. For me, that am not very apt to believe in wonders, I cannot find faith for this. I disputed the point last night with a lady who really talks very sensibly on any other subject, but she was downright angry with me that she did not perceive she had persuaded me of the truth of forty stories she told me of this kind, and at last mentioned several ridiculous marriages that there could be no other reason assigned for. I assured her that in England, where we were entirely ignorant of all magic, where the climate is not half so warm nor the women half so handsome, we were not without our ridiculous marriages, and that we did not look upon it as anything supernatural when a man played the fool for the sake of a woman. But my arguments could not convince her against, as she said, her certain knowledge, though she added that she scrupled making use of charms herself, but that she could do it whenever she pleased and, staring in my face said, with a very learned air, that no enchantments would have their effect upon me, and that there were some people exempt from their power, but very few. You may imagine how I laughed at this discourse, but all the women here are of the same opinion. They don't pretend to any commerce with the devil, but that there are certain compositions to inspire love. If one could send over a shipload of them I fancy it would be a very quick way of raising an estate. What would not some ladies of our acquaintance give for such merchandise?

Adieu my dear Lady—. I cannot conclude my letter with a subject that affords more delightful scenes to imagination. I leave you to figure to yourself the extreme court that will be made to me at my return if my travels should furnish me with such a useful piece of learning. I am, dear madam, etc.

LETTER XXXIX

To Anne Thistlethwayte,   *Pera, Constantinople, 4 January 1718*

I am infinitely obliged to you, dear Mrs Thistlethwayte, for your entertaining letter. You are the only one of my correspondents that have judged right enough to think I would gladly be informed of the news amongst you. All the rest of them tell me, almost in the same words, that they suppose I know everything. Why they are pleased to suppose in this manner I can guess no reason except they are persuaded that the breed of Mohammed's pigeon[205] still subsists in this country and that I receive supernatural intelligence. I wish I could return your goodness with some diverting accounts from hence, but I know not what part of the scenes here would gratify your curiosity or whether you have any curiosity at all for things so far distant. To say the truth I am at this present writing not very much turned for the recollection of what is diverting, my head being wholly filled with the preparations necessary for the increase of my family, which I expect every day.[206] You may easily guess at my uneasy situation, but I am, however, in some degree comforted by the glory that accrues to me from it, and a reflection on the contempt I should otherwise fall under.

You won't know what to make of this speech, but in this country it is more despicable to be married and not fruitful than it is with us to be fruitful before marriage. They have a notion that whenever a woman leaves off bringing children, 'tis because she is too old for that business, whatever her face says to the contrary, and this opinion makes the ladies here so ready to make proofs of their youth (which is as necessary in order to be a received beauty as it is to show the roof of nobility to be admitted Knight of Malta)[207] that they do not content themselves with using the natural means, but fly to all sort of quackeries to avoid the scandal of being past child bearing and often kill themselves by them. Without any exaggeration, all the women of my acquaintance that have been married ten year have twelve or thirteen children, and the old ones boast of having had five-and-twenty or thirty a-piece, and are respected according to the number they have produced. When they are with child 'tis their common expression to say they hope God will be so merciful to them to send two this time, and when I have asked them sometimes how they expected to provide for such a flock as they desire, they answer that the plague will certainly kill half of them, which, indeed, generally happens without much concern to the parents, who are satisfied with the vanity of having brought forth so plentifully. The French Ambassadress[208] is forced to comply with this fashion as well as myself. She has not been here much above a year and has lain in once and is big again. What is most wonderful is the exemption they seem to enjoy from the curse entailed on the sex.

They see all company the day of their delivery and at the fornight's end return visits, set out in their jewels and new clothes. I wish I may find the influence of the climate in this particular, but I fear I shall continue an English woman in that affair as well as I do in my dread of fire and plague, which are two things very little feared here, most families having had their houses burnt down once or twice, occasioned by their extraordinary way of warming themselves, which is neither by chimneys nor stoves but a certain machine called a *tandir*, the height of two foot, in the form of a table covered with a fine carpet or embroidery. This is made only of wood, and they put into it a small quantity of hot ashes and sit with their legs under the carpet. At this table they work, read and very often sleep, and if they chance to dream, kick down the *tandir* and the hot ashes commonly sets the house on fire. There was five hundred houses burnt in this manner about a fortnight ago, and I have seen several of the owners since who seem not at all moved at so common a misfortune. They put their goods into a bark[209] and see their houses burn with great philosophy, their persons being very seldom endangered, having no stairs to descend.

But having entertained you with things I don't like, 'tis but just I should tell you something that pleases me. The climate is delightful in the extremist degree. I am now sitting, this present 4th of January, with the windows open, enjoying the warm shine of the sun, while you are freezing over a sad sea-coal fire, and my chamber is set out with carnations, roses and jonquils fresh from my garden. I am also charmed with many points of the Turkish law, to our shame be it spoken, better designed and better executed than ours, particularly the punishment of convicted liars (triumphant criminals in our country, God knows). They are burnt in the forehead with a hot iron, being proved the authors of any notorious falsehood. How many white foreheads should we see disfigured? How many fine gentlemen would be forced to wear their wigs as low as their eyebrows were this law in practice with us? I should go on to tell you many other parts of justice, but I must send for my midwife.

LETTER XL

To the Abbé Conti,   *February 1718*

I am charmed, sir, with your obliging letter; and you may perceive by the largeness of my paper that I intend to give punctual answers to all your questions, at least if my french will permit me, for it is a language I do not understand to perfection, so I much fear that, for want of expressions I shall be quickly obliged to finish. Keep in mind, therefore, that I am writing in a foreign language[210] and be sure to attribute all the impertinences and triflings dropping from my pen to the want of proper words for declaring my thoughts, but by no means to any dullness or natural levity.

These conditions being thus agreed and settled, I begin with telling you that you have a true notion of the Alcoran, concerning which the Greek priests (who are the greatest scoundrels in the universe) have invented out of their own heads a thousand ridiculous stories in order to decry the law of Mohammed; to run it down, I say, without any examination, or as much as letting the people read it, being afraid that if once they begun to sift the defects of the Alcoran they might not stop there but proceed to make use of their judgement about their own legends and fictions. In effect there's nothing so like as the fables of the Greeks and of the Mahommedans. And the last have multitudes of saints at whose tombs miracles are by them said to be daily performed, nor are the accounts of the lives of those blessed *musulmans* much less stuffed with extravagancies than the spiritual romances of the Greek papas.

As to your next enquiry, I assure you 'tis certainly false, though commonly believed in our parts of the world, that Mohammed excludes women from any share in a future happy state. He was too much a gentleman and loved the fair sex too well to use them so barbarously. On the contrary he promises a

very fine paradise to the Turkish women. He says indeed that
this paradise will be a separate place from that of their husbands. But I fancy the most part of them won't like it the worse
for that, and that the regret of this separation will not render
their paradise the less agreeable. It remains to tell you that the
virtues which Mahommed requires of women to merit the
enjoyment of future happiness are: not to live in such a manner
as to become useless to the world, but to employ themselves as
much as possible in making little *musulmans*. The virgins who die
virgins and the widows who marry not again, dying in mortal
sin, are excluded out of paradise. For women, says he, not being
capable to manage affairs of state, nor to support the fatigues of
war, God has not ordered them to govern or reform the world
but he has entrusted them with an office which is not less
honourable, even that of multiplying the human race. And such
as, out of malice or laziness do not make it their business to bear
or to breed children fulfil not the duty of their vocation and
rebel against the commands of God. Here are maxims for you,
prodigiously contrary to those of your convents. What will
become of your saint Catherines, your saint Theresas, your saint
Claras and the whole bead roll of your holy virgins and widows,
who, if they are to be judged by this system of virtue will be
found to have been infamous creatures that passed their whole
lives in a most abominable libertinism.

I know not what your thoughts may be concerning a doctrine
so extraordinary with respect to us, but I can truly inform you,
sir, that the Turks are not so ignorant as we fancy them to be in
matters of politics or philosophy, or even of gallantry. 'Tis true
that military discipline such as now practiced in Christendom
does not mightily suit them. A long peace has plunged them into
an universal sloth. Content with their condition and accustomed
to boundless luxury they are become great enemies to all
manner of fatigues. But to make amends, the sciences flourish
amongst them. The *effendis* (which is to say, the learned) do very
well deserve this name. They have no more faith in the inspiration of Mohammed than in the infallibility of the pope. They
make a frank profession of deism amongst themselves or to

those they can trust, and never speak of their law but as of a politic institution, fit now to be observed by wise men, however at first introduced by politicians and enthusiasts.

If I remember right I think I have told you in some former letter that at Belgrade we lodged with a great and rich *effendi*, a man of wit and learning, and of a very agreeable humour. We were in his house about a month and he did constantly eat with us, drinking wine without any scruple. As I rallied him a little on this subject he answered me, smiling, that all the creatures in the world were made for the pleasure of man and that God would not have let the vine grow were it a sin to taste of its juice. But that nevertheless the law, which forbids the use of it to the vulgar, was very wise because such sort of folks have not sense enough to take it with moderation. This *effendi* appeared no stranger to the parties that prevail among us. Nay, he seemed to have some knowledge of our religious disputes and even of our writers, and I was surprised to hear him ask, amongst other things, how Mr Toland did.[211]

My paper, large as it is, draws towards an end. That I may not go beyond its limits I must leap from religions to tulips, concerning which you also ask me news. Their mixture produces surprising effects. But what is to be observed most surprising is the experiment of which you speak concerning animals and which is tried here every day. The suburbs of Pera, Jtophana and Galata are collections of strangers from all countries of the universe. They have so often intermarried that this forms several races of people the oddest imaginable. There's not one single family of natives that can value itself on being unmixed. You frequently see a person whose father was born a Grecian, the mother an Italian, the grandfather a Frenchman, the grandmother an Armenian and their ancestors English, Muscovites, Asiatics, etc.

This mixture produces creatures more extraordinary than you can imagine. Nor could I ever doubt but there were several different species of men, since the whites, the woolly and the long-haired blacks, the small-eyed Tartars and Chinese, the beardless Brazilians, and, to name no more, the oily-skinned yellow Nova-Zemblians[212] have as specific differences under the same general kind as greyhounds, mastiffs, spaniels, bulldogs or the race of my little Diana, if nobody is offended at the comparison. Now as the various intermixing of these latter animals causes mongrels, so mankind have their mongrels too, divided and subdivided into endless sorts. We have daily proofs of it here, as I told you before. In the same animal is not seldom remarked the Greek perfidiousness, the Italian diffidence, the Spanish arrogance, the French loquacity and all of a sudden he's seized with a fit of English thoughtfulness bordering a little upon dulness, which many of us have inherited from the stupidity of our saxon progenitors.

But the family which charms me most is that which proceeds from the fantastical conjunction of a Dutch male with a Greek female. As these are natures opposite in extremes 'tis a pleasure to observe how the differing atoms are perpetually jarring together in the children, even so as to produce effects visible in their external form. They have the large black eyes of the country with the fat, white, fishy flesh of Holland and a lively air streaked with dulness. At one and the same time they show that love of expensiveness so universal among the Greeks and an inclination to the Dutch frugality. To give an example of this, young women ruin themselves to purchase jewels for adorning their heads while they have not the heart to buy new shoes, or rather slippers, for their feet, which are commonly in a tattered condition; a thing so contrary to the taste of our English women that it is for showing how neatly their feet are dressed, and for showing this only, they are so passionately enamoured with their hoop petticoats. I have abundance of other singularities to communicate to you, but I am at the end both of my French and my paper.

LETTER XLI

To Lady Mar, *Pera, Constantinople, 10 March 1718*

I have not writ to you, dear sister, these many months; a great piece of self-denial, but I know not where to direct or what part of the world you were in.[213] I have received no letter from you since your short note of April last in which you tell me that you are on the point of leaving England and promise me a direction for the place you stay in, but I have in vain expected it till now, and now I only learn from the Gazette that you are returned, which induces me to venture this letter to your house at London. I had rather ten of my letters should be lost than you imagine I don't write and I think 'tis hard fortune if one in ten don't reach you. However, I am resolved to keep the copies as testimonies of my inclination to give you, to the utmost of my power, all the diverting part of my travels while you are exempt from all the fatigues and inconveniencies.

In the first place I wish you joy of your niece, for I was brought to bed of a daughter five weeks ago. I don't mention this as one of my diverting adventures, though I must own that it is not half so mortifying here as in England, there being as much difference as there is between a little cold in the head, which sometimes happens here, and the consumptive coughs so common in London. Nobody keeps their house a month for lying in, and I am not so fond of any of our customs to retain them when they are not necessary. I returned my visits at three weeks end, and about four days ago crossed the sea which divides this place from Constantinople to make a new one, where I had the good fortune to pick up many curiosities.

I went to see the Sultana Hafise,[214] favourite of the last Emperor Mustafa,[215] who, you know (or perhaps you don't know) was deposed by his brother the reigning Sultan, and died a few weeks after, being poisoned, as it was generally believed.

This lady was immediately after his death saluted with an absolute order to leave the seraglio and choose herself a husband from the great men at the Port. I suppose you imagine her overjoyed at this proposal. Quite contrary. These women, who are called and esteem themselves queens, look upon this liberty as the greatest disgrace and affront that can happen to them. She threw herself at the Sultan's feet and begged him to poniard[216] her rather than use his brother's widow with that contempt. She represented to him in agonies of sorrow that she was privileged from this misfortune by having brought five princes into the Ottoman family, but all the boys being dead and only one girl surviving this excuse was not received and she compelled to make her choice. She chose Bekir Effendi, then Secretary of State[217] and above fourscore year old, to convince the world that she firmly intended to keep the vow she had made of never suffering a second husband to approach her bed, and since she must honour some subject so far as to be called his wife she would choose him as a mark of her gratitude, since it was he that had presented her at the age of ten year old to her lost lord. But she has never permitted him to pay her one visit, though it is now fifteen year she has been in his house, where she passes her time in uninterrupted mourning with a constancy very little known in Christendom, especially in a widow of twenty-one, for she is now but thirty-six. She has no black eunuchs for her guard, her husband being obliged to respect her as a queen and not enquire at all into what is done in her apartment, where I was led into a large room, with a sofa the whole length of it, adorned with white marble pillars like a ruelle,[218] covered with a pale blue figured velvet on a silver ground, with cushions of the same, where I was desired to repose till the Sultana appeared, who had contrived this manner of reception to avoid rising up at my entrance, though she made me an inclination of her head when I rose up to her. I was very glad to observe a lady that had been distinguished by the favour of an emperor to whom beauties were every day presented from all parts of the world. But she did not seem to me to have ever been half so beautiful as the fair Fatima I saw at Adrianople, though she had the remains of a fine face more decayed by sorrow than time.

But her dress was something so surprisingly rich I cannot forbear describing it to you. She wore a vest called *dolaman*, and which differs from a caftan by longer sleeves and folding over at the bottom. It was of purple cloth straight to her shape and thick set, on each side down to her feet and round the sleeves, with pearls of the best water, of the same size as their buttons commonly are. You must not suppose I mean as large as those of my Lord— but about the bigness of a pea; and to these buttons large loops of diamonds in the form of those gold loops so common upon birthday coats.[219] This habit was tied at the waist with two large tassels of smaller pearl and round the arms embroidered with large diamonds; her shift fastened at the bosom with a great diamond shaped like a lozenge, her girdle as broad as the broadest English riband entirely covered with diamonds. Round her neck she wore three chains which reached to her knees, one of large pearl at the bottom of which hung a fine coloured emerald as big as a turkey egg, another consisting of two hundred emeralds close joined together, of the most lively green, perfectly matched, every one as large as a half crown piece and as thick as three crown pieces, and another of emeralds perfectly round. But her earrings eclipsed all the rest. They were two diamonds shaped exactly like pears, as large as a big hazelnut. Round her talpack[220] she had four strings of pearl, the whitest and most perfect in the world, at least enough to make four necklaces every one as large as the Duchess of Marlborough's,[221] and of the same size, fastened with two roses consisting of a large ruby for the middle stone and round them twenty drops of clean diamonds to each. Besides this, her headdress was covered with bodkins of emeralds and diamonds. She wore large diamond bracelets and had five rings on her fingers, all single diamonds, except Mr Pitt's[222] the largest I ever saw in my life. 'Tis for the jewellers to compute the value of these things, but according to the common estimation of jewels in our part of the world, her whole dress must be worth above £100,000 sterling. This I am very sure of, that no European queen has half the quantity and the Empress's jewels, though very fine, would look very mean near hers.

She gave me a dinner of fifty dishes of meat, which, after their fashion, was placed on the table but one at a time, and was extremely tedious, but the magnificence of her table answered very well to that of her dress. The knives were of gold, the hafts set with diamonds, but the piece of luxury that grieved my eyes was the table cloth and napkins, which were all tiffany,[223] embroidered with silks and gold in the finest manner in natural flowers. It was with the utmost regret that I made use of these costly napkins, as finely wrought as the finest handkerchiefs that ever came out of this country. You may be sure that they were entirely spoilt before dinner was over. The sherbet, which is the liquor they drink at meals, was served in china bowls, but the covers and salvers massy gold. After dinner water was brought in a gold basin and towels of the same kind of the napkins, which I very unwillingly wiped my hands upon, and coffee was served in china with gold soûcoupes.[224]

The Sultana seemed in very good humour and talked to me with the utmost civility. I did not omit this opportunity of learning all that I possibly could of the seraglio, which is so entirely unknown amongst us. She assured me that the story of the Sultan's throwing a handkerchief is altogether fabulous and the manner upon that occasion no other but that he send the Kuslir Aga to signify to the lady the honour he intends her.[225] She is immediately complimented upon it by the others and led to the bath where she is perfumed and dressed in the most magnificent and becoming manner. The Emperor precedes his visit by a royal present and then comes into her apartment. Neither is there any such thing as her creeping in at the bed's feet. She said that the first he make choice of was always after the first in rank and not the mother of the eldest son, as other writers would make us believe. Sometimes the Sultan diverts himself in the company of all his ladies, who stand in a circle round him, and she confessed that they were ready to die with jealousy and envy of the happy she that he distinguished by any appearance of preference. But this seemed to me neither better nor worse than the circles in most courts where the glance of the monarch is watched and every smile waited for with impatience and envied by those that cannot obtain it.

She never mentioned the Sultan without tears in her eyes, yet she seemed very fond of the discourse. My past happiness (said she) appears a dream to me, yet I cannot forget that I was beloved by the greatest and most lovely of mankind. I was chose from all the rest to make all his campaigns with him. I would not survive him if I was not passionately fond of the princess, my daughter, yet all my tenderness for her was hardly enough to make me preserve my life when I lost him. I passed a whole twelvemonth without seeing the light. Time has softened my despair, yet I now pass some days every week in tears devoted to the memory of my Sultan. There was no affectation in these words. It was easy to see she was in a deep melancholy, though her good humour made her willing to divert me.

She asked me to walk in her garden, and one of her slaves immediately brought her a pelisse[226] of rich brocade lined with sables. I waited on her into the garden, which had nothing in it remarkable but the fountains, and from thence she showed me all her apartments. In her bedchamber her toilet was displayed, consisting of two looking glasses, the frames covered with pearls, and her night *talpak* set with bodkins of jewels, and near it three vests of fine sables, every one of which is at least worth 1000 dollars, £200 English money. I don't doubt these rich habits were purposely placed in sight, but they seemed negligently thrown on the sofa. When I took my leave of her I was complimented with perfumes as at the Grand Vizier's and presented with a very fine embroidered handkerchief. Her slaves were to the number of thirty, besides ten little ones, the eldest not above seven year old. These were the most beautiful girls I ever saw, all richly dressed, and I observed that the Sultana took a great deal of pleasure in these lovely children, which is a vast expense, for there is not a handsome girl of that age to be bought under £100 sterling. They wore little garlands of flowers, and their own hair braided, which was all their headdress, but their habits all of gold stuffs. These served her coffee kneeling, brought water when she washed, etc. 'Tis a great part of the business of the older slaves to take care of these girls, to learn them to embroider and serve them as carefully as if they were children of the family.

Now do I fancy that you imagine I have entertained you all this while with a relation that has, at least, received many embellishments from my hand. This is but too like, says you, the Arabian tales;[227] these embroidered napkins, and a jewel as large as a turkey's egg! You forget, dear sister, those very tales were writ by an author of this country and, excepting the enchantments, are a real representation of the manners here. We travellers are in very hard circumstances. If we say nothing but what has been said before us we are dull and we have observed nothing. If we tell anything new, we are laughed at as fabulous and romantic, not allowing for the difference of ranks, which afford difference of company, more curiosity, or the changes of customs that happen every twenty year in every country. But people judge of travellers exactly with the same candour, good nature and impartiality they judge of their neighbours upon all occasions. For my part, if I live to return amongst you I am so well acquainted with the morals of all my dear friends and acquaintance that I am resolved to tell them nothing at all, to avoid the imputation, which their charity would certainly incline them to, of my telling too much. But I depend upon your knowing me enough to believe whatever I seriously assert for truth, though I give you leave to be surprised at an account so new to you. But what would you say if I told you that I have been in a harem where the winter apartment was wainscoted with inlaid work of mother of pearl, ivory of different colours and olive wood, exactly like the little boxes you have seen brought out of this country; and those rooms designed for summer, the walls all crusted with japan china, the roofs gilt and the floors spread with the finest Persian carpets. Yet there is nothing more true, such is the palace of my lovely friend, the fair Fatima, who I was acquainted with at Adrianople. I went to visit her yesterday and, if possible, she appeared to me handsomer than before. She met me at the door of her chamber and, giving me her hand with the best grace in the world: 'You Christian ladies,' said she with a smile that made her as handsome as an angel, 'have the reputation of inconstancy, and I did not expect, whatever goodness you expressed for me at Adrianople, that I should ever see you again; but I am now convinced that I have really the happiness of pleasing you, and if you knew how I speak of you amongst our ladies you would be assured that you do me justice if you think me your friend.' She placed me in the corner of the sofa and I spent the afternoon in her conversation with the greatest pleasure in the world.

The Sultana Hafise is what one would naturally expect to find a Turkish lady; willing to oblige, but not knowing how to go about it, and 'tis easy to see in her manner that she has lived excluded from the world. But Fatima has all the politeness and good breeding of a court, with an air that inspires at once respect and tenderness; and now I understand her language I find her wit as engaging as her beauty. She is very curious after the manners of other countries and has not that partiality for her own so common to little minds. A Greek that I carried with me who had never seen her before (nor could have been admitted now if she had not been in my train) showed that surprise at her beauty and manner which is unavoidable at the first sight, and said to me in Italian: 'This is no Turkish lady; she is certainly some Christian.' Fatima guessed she spoke of her and asked what she said. I would not have told, thinking she would have been no better pleased with the compliment than one of our court beauties to be told she had the air of a Turk. But the Greek lady told it her and she smiled, saying: 'It is not the first time I have heard so. My mother was a Poloneze taken at the Siege of Camieniec,[228] and my father used to rally me, saying he believed his Christian wife had found some Christian gallant, for I had not the air of a Turkish girl.' I assured her that if all the Turkish ladies were like her, it was absolutely necessary to confine them from public view for the repose of mankind, and proceeded to tell her what a noise such a face as hers would make in London or Paris. 'I can't believe you', replied she agreeably; 'if beauty was so much valued in your country as you say they would never have suffered you to leave it.'

Perhaps, dear sister, you laugh at my vanity in repeating this compliment, but I only do it as I think it very well turned and give it you as an instance of the spirit of her conversation. Her house was magnificently furnished and very well fancied, her winter rooms being furnished with figured velvet on gold grounds, and those for summer with fine Indian quilting embroidered with gold. The houses of the great Turkish lades are kept clean with as much nicety as those in Holland. This was situated in a high part of the town, and from the windows of her summer apartment we had the prospect of the sea and the islands and the Asian mountains. My letter is insensibly grown so long, I am ashamed of it. This is a very bad symptom. 'Tis well if I don't degenerate into a downright story teller. It may be our proverb that knowledge is no burden may be true to oneself, but knowing too much is very apt to make us troublesome to other people.

LETTER XLII

To Lady—,[229]   *Pera, Constantinople, 16 March 1718*

I am extremely pleased, my dear lady, that you have at length found a commission for me that I can answer without disappointing your expectation, though I must tell you that it is not so easy as perhaps you think it, and that if my curiosity had not been more diligent than any other stranger's has ever yet been I must have answered you with an excuse, as I was forced to do when you desired me to buy you a Greek slave. I have got for you, as you desire, a Turkish love letter, which I have put in a little box, and ordered the Captain of the Smyrniote to deliver it to you with this letter.[230] The translation of it is literally as follows. The first piece you should pull out of the purse is a little pearl, which is in Turkish called ingi and should be understood in this manner:

| Pearl | Sensin Uzellerin gingi |
| Ingi | Fairest of the young. |

Caremfil	Caremfilsen cararen Yok
a clove	conge gulsun timarin yok
	Benseny chok tan severim
	Senin benden haberin Yok
	You are as slender as this clove;
	You are an unblown Rose;
	I have long lov'd you, and you have not known it.
Pul	derdime derman bul
a jonquil	Have pity on my passion.
Kihat	Biîlerum sahat sahat
paper	I faint every hour.
ermut	ver bize bir umut
pear	Give me some hope.
sabun	Derdinden oldum Zabun
soap	I am sick with love.
chemur	ben oliyim size umur
coal	May I die, and all my years be yours!
Gul	ben aglarum sen gul
a rose	May you be pleased, and all your sorrows mine!
hazir	Oliïm sana Yazir
a straw	Suffer me to be your slave.
Jo ha	ustune bulunmaz Paha
cloth	Your price is not to be found.
tartsin	sen ghel ben checkeim senin hargin
cinamon	But my Fortune is yours.
Gira	esking-ilen oldum Ghira
a match	I burn, I burn, my flame consumes me.
Sirma	uzunu benden ayirma
gold thread	Don't turn away your face.
Satch	Bazmazun tatch
hair	Crown of my head.
Uzum	Benim iki Guzum
grape	my eyes.
tel	uluyorum tez ghel
gold wire	I die—come quickly.

And by way of postscript:

biber	Bize bir dogru haber
pepper	Send me an answer.[231]

You see this letter is all verses, and I can assure you there is as much fancy shown in the choice of them as in the most studied expressions of our letters, there being, I believe, a million of verses designed for this use. There is no colour, no flower, no weed, no fruit, herb, pebble or feather that has not a verse belonging to it; and you may quarrel, reproach or send letters of passion, friendship or civility, or even of news, without ever inking your fingers.

I fancy you are now wondering at my profound learning but, alas, dear madam, I am almost fallen into the misfortune so common to the ambitious: while they are employed on distant, insignificant conquests abroad a rebellion starts up at home. I am in great danger of losing my English. I find it is not half so easy to me to write in it as it was a twelve month ago. I am forced to study for expressions, and must leave off all other languages and try to learn my mother tongue. Human understanding is as much limited as human power or human strength. The memory can retain but a certain number of images, and 'tis as impossible for one human creature to be perfect master of ten different languages as to have in perfect subjection ten different kingdoms, or to fight against ten men at a time. I am afraid I shall at last know none as I should do. I live in a place that very well represents the Tower of Babel; in Pera they speak Turkish, Greek, Hebrew, Armenian, Arabic, Persian, Russian, Slavonian, Walachian, German, Dutch, French, English, Italian, Hungarian; and, what is worse, there is ten of these languages spoke in my own family. My grooms are Arabs, my footmen French, English and Germans, my nurse an Armenian, my housemaids Russians, half a dozen other servants Greeks, my steward an Italian, my janissaries Turks, that I live in the perpetual hearing of this medley of sounds, which produces a very extraordinary effect upon the people that are born here. They learn all these languages at the same time and without knowing any of them well enough to write or read in it. There is very few men, women or children here that have not the same compass of words in five or six of them. I know myself several infants of three or four year old that speak Italian, French,

Greek, Turkish and Russian, which last they learn of their nurses, who are generally of that country. This seems almost incredible to you and is, in my mind, one of the most curious things in this country, and takes off very much from the merit of our ladies who set up for such extraordinary geniuses upon the credit of some superficial knowledge of French and Italian. As I prefer English to all the rest I am extremely mortified at the daily decay of it in my head, where I'll assure you, with grief of heart, it is reduced to such a small number of words I cannot recollect any tolerable phrase to conclude my letter, and am forced to tell your ladyship very bluntly that I am your faithful, humble servant.

LETTER XLIII

To Wortley,[232]   *Constantinople, 23 March 1718*

This day news is come of the *Greyhound*'s safe arrival at Smyrna. It has brought the minister for this place, and my money that was in my uncle's hands.[233] The Captain has writ that he met the *Preston* man-of-war at Cadiz having orders for Barbary and did not propose for this part of the world till July at soonest. The Dutch madam[234] is a perfect mad woman. I sent a jeweller to her to offer her the money for her pearls and she would not take it, which she is very much in the right, for they are worth more, but 'tis very strange she should get a good bargain and complain of it. But she cheats the Ambassador. Her own vanity caused the discovery of her secret, which I kept very faithfully, and now he is, I suppose, angry at her laying her money out in ornaments. She would make him believe she did it to oblige me, and would seem glad to get rid of them, at the same time she won't part with them.

The boy was engrafted last Tuesday, and is at this time singing and playing and very impatient for his supper.[235] I pray God my next may give as good an account of him. I suppose you know the allowance the King has made the Company on this occasion.[236] I think you may with more justice insist on your extraordinaries which has never yet been refused neither Sir R Sutton nor no other ambassador.[237]

I cannot engraft the girl; her nurse has not had the smallpox.

LETTER XLIV

To Wortley,   *Constantinople, 1 April 1718*

Your son is as well as can be expected, and I hope past all manner of danger. The ship that has brought my pieces of eight is safe arrived in the port. 'Tis directed to Mr Lethieullier[238] and therefore I thought him the properest person to apply to to take care of my money that is on board, and sent for him and desired him to keep it in his warehouse, giving me a note for the receipt of it. He tells me that they are now lower than ever, this place being overstocked with them and that he has himself 16000 lying dead upon his hands, but I know all that he says is not to be literally depended on. However, having received at the same time a letter from Sir John Williams[239] in which he offers to pay me back my 1600 livres in England, I don't know whether I had not best accept of it, and should be glad to have your advice who understand business better than I do. You have made me no answer to my question whether you can carry goods from hence custom free. In that case I could turn every dollar into four shillings. I beg you would write particularly on this subject as soon as possible because Sir John Williams desires a speedy answer to his offer.

P.S. Pray send me my letters.

LETTER XLV

To Wortley, *Constantinople, 9 April 1718*

I have Mr Barker's note[240] for the 2000 dollars. I have not mentioned to anybody whatever your design of going sooner than by the man-of-war, but it has been writ to several people from Adrianople. I was asked and made answer, as I always do upon your affairs, that I know nothing of it. I perceive by my father's letter that he is desirous to be well with us, and am very clearly of opinion, if my opinion is of any weight with you, that you should write him a civil letter. The birth of your daughter is a proper occasion, and you may date your letter as if writ during my lying in. I know him perfectly well, and am sure such a trifling respect would make a great impression upon him. You need not apprehend my expressing any great joy for our return. I hope 'tis less shocking to you than to me, who have really suffered in my health by the uneasiness it has given me, though I take care to conceal it here as much as I can. Your son is very well; I cannot forbear telling you so, though you do not so much as ask after him.

Pray send me my other letters.

I hear the French Ambassador's business at Adrianople is to buy the Holy Land, and that there is a thousand purses offered for it, which is to pass through his hands. I believe he neglects no opportunity.

I sent for Mr Lethieullier two days ago to speak to him concerning my pieces of eight, and he made me abundance of compliments and offers of service, saying that if you would leave your money consigned to him and have patience to wait for it, he would engage to send it home at four shillings or four shillings six pence a dollar. I told him I would write word to you of it. I suppose you'll thank him, but 'tis very proper to think more than once of accepting it. You bid me prepare for our journey without saying in what manner. If you mean anything of money matters, pray be particular in your orders about them.

Here is some table gilt plate offered to me for the weight. It is not fine silver but makes the same show. If you think you shall want anything of that kind, it may be a pennyworth.

LETTER XLVI

To Lady Bristol,   *Constantinople, 10 April 1718*

At length I have heard, for the first time from my dear Lady Bristol, this present 10th of April 1718. Yet I am persuaded you have had the goodness to write before, but I have had the ill fortune to lose your letters. Since my last I have stayed quietly at Constantinople, a city that I ought in conscience to give your ladyship a right notion of, since I know you can have none but what is partial and mistaken from the writings of travellers. 'Tis certain there are many people that pass years here in Pera without having ever seen it, and yet they all pretend to describe it.

Pera, Tophana and Galata, wholly inhabited by Frank Christians,[241] and which together make the appearance of a very fine town, are divided from it by the sea, which is not above half so broad as the broadest part of the Thames, but the Christian men are loathe to hazard the adventures they sometimes meet with amongst the levents or seamen (worse monsters than our watermen) and the women must cover their faces to go there, which they have a perfect aversion to do. 'Tis true they wear veils in Pera, but they are such as only serve to show their beauty to more advantage, and which would not be permitted in Constantinople. Those reasons deter almost every creature from seeing it, and the French Ambassadress will return to France, I believe, without ever having been there. You'll wonder, madam, to hear me add that I have been there very often. The yasmak, or Turkish veil, is become not only very easy but agreeable to me, and if it was not, I would be content to endure some inconvenience to content a passion so powerful with me as curiosity; and indeed the pleasure of going in a barge to Chelsea is not comparable to that of rowing upon the canal of the sea here, where for twenty miles together down the Bosphorus the most beautiful variety of prospects present themselves. The Asian side is covered with fruit trees, villages and the most delightful landscapes in nature. On the European stands Constantinople, situated on seven hills. The unequal heights make it seem as large again as it is (though one of the largest cities in the world), showing an agreeable mixture of gardens, pine and cyprus trees, palaces, mosques and public buildings, raised one above another with as much beauty and appearance of symmetry as your ladyship ever saw in a cabinet adorned by the most skilful hands, jars showing themselves above jars, mixed with canisters, babies[242] and candlesticks. This is a very odd comparison, but it gives me an exact image of the thing.

I have taken care to see as much of the seraglio as is to be seen. It is on a point of land running into the sea; a palace of prodigious extent, but very irregular, the gardens a large compass of ground full of high cypress trees, which is all I know of them, the buildings all of white stone, leaded on top, with gilded turrets and spires, which look very magnificent, and indeed I believe there is no Christian king's palace half so large. There are six large courts in it all built round and set with trees, having galleries of stone; one of these for the guard, another for the slaves, another for the officers of the kitchen, another for the stables, the fifth for the divan, the sixth for the apartment destined for audiences. On the ladies' side there is at least as many more, with distinct courts belonging to their eunuchs and attendants, their kitchens, etc.

The next remarkable structure is that of St Sophia, which it is very difficult to see. I was forced to send three times to the *Kaymakam* (the governor of the town), and he assembled the chief *effendis* or heads of the law and enquired of the *mufti* whether it was lawful to permit it. They passed some days in this important debate, but I insisting on my request, permission was granted. I can't be informed why the Turks are more delicate on the subject of this mosque than any of the others, where what Christian pleases may enter without scruple. I fancy they imagine that having been once consecrated, people on pretence of curiosity might profane it with prayers, particularly to those saints who are still very visible in mosaic work, and no other way defaced but by the decays of time, for 'tis absolutely false what is so universally asserted, that the Turks defaced all the images that they found in the city. The dome of St Sophia is said to be 113 foot diameter, built upon arches, sustained by vast pillars of marble, the pavement and staircase marble. There is two rows of galleries supported with pillars of particoloured marble, and the whole roof mosaic work, part of which decays very fast and drops down. They presented me a handful of it. The composition seems to me a sort of glass or that paste with which they make counterfeit jewels. They show here the tomb of the Emperor Constantine, for which they have a great veneration. This is a dull, imperfect description of this celebrated building, but I understand architecture so little that I am afraid of talking nonsense in endeavouring to speak of it particularly.[243]

Perhaps I am in the wrong, but some Turkish mosques please me better. That of Sultan Suleiman is in an exact square with four fine towers on the angles, in the midst of a noble cupola supported with beautiful marble pillars, two lesser at the ends supported in the same manner, the pavement and gallery round the mosque of marble.[244] Under the great cupola is a fountain adorned with such fine coloured pillars I can hardly think them natural marble. On one side is the pulpit of white marble, and on the other the little gallery for the Grand Signor. A fine staircase leads to it and it is built up with gilded lattices. At the upper end is a sort of altar where the name of God is written, and before it stands two candlesticks as high as a man, with wax candles as thick as three flambeaux. The pavement is spread with fine carpets and the mosque illuminated with a vast number of lamps. The court leading to it is very spacious, with galleries of marble with green fountains covered with twenty-eight leaded cupolas on two sides, a fine fountain of three basins in the midst of it. The description may serve for all the mosques in Constantinople; the model is exactly the same, and they only differ in largeness and richness of materials. That of the Validé is the largest of all, built entirely of marble, the most prodigious and, I think, the most beautiful structure I ever saw, be it spoke to the honour of our sex, for it was founded by the mother of Mohammed IV.[245] Between friends, St Paul's Church would make a pitiful figure near it, as any of our squares would do near the Atmeydan, or Place of Horses, 'at' signifying horse in Turkish.

This was the Hippodrome[246] in the reign of the Greek emperors. In the midst of it is a brazen column of three serpents twisted together with their mouths gaping. 'Tis impossible to learn why so odd a pillar was erected; the Greeks can tell nothing but fabulous legends when they are asked the meaning of it, and there is no sign of its having ever had any inscription. At the upper end is an obelisk of porphyry, probably brought from Egypt, the hieroglyphics all very entire, which I look upon as mere ancient puns. It is placed on four little brazen pillars upon a pedestal of square free stone full of figures in bas relief on two sides, one square representing a battle, another an assembly. The others have inscriptions in Greek and Latin. The last I took in my pocket book and is literally:

Difficilis quondam Dominis parere serenis
Iussus et extinctis palmam portare Tyrannis
Omnia Theodosio cedunt, sobolique perreni.[247]

Your lord will interpret these lines. Don't fancy they are a love letter to him. All the figures have their heads on, and I cannot forbear reflecting again on the impudence of authors who all say they have not, but I dare swear the greatest part of them never saw them, but took the report from the Greeks, who resist with incredible fortitude the conviction of their own eyes whenever they have invented lies to the dishonour of their enemies. Were you to ask them, there is nothing worth seeing in Constantinople but St Sophia, though there are several larger mosques.

That of Sultan Achmed has that of particular, its gates are of brass.[248] In all these mosques there are little chapels where are the tombs of the founders and their families, with vast candles burning before them.

The exchanges are all noble buildings, full of fine alleys, the greatest part supported with pillars, and kept wonderfully neat. Every trade has their distinct alley, the merchandise disposed in the same order as in the New Exchange at London.[249] The Bedesten, or jewellers' quarter shows so much riches, such a vast quantity of diamonds and all kind of precious stones, that they dazzle the sight. The embroiderers' is also very glittering, and people walk here as much for diversion as business. The markets are most of them handsome squares, and admirably well provided, perhaps better than in any other part of the world. I know you'll expect I should say something particular of that of the slaves, and you will imagine me half a Turk when I don't speak of it with the same horror other Christians have done before me, but I cannot forbear applauding the humanity of the Turks to those creatures. They are never ill used and their slavery is in my opinion no worse than servitude all over the world. 'Tis true they have no wages, but they give them yearly clothes to a higher value than our salaries to any ordinary servant. But you'll object men buy women with an eye to evil. In my opinion they are bought and sold as publicly and more infamously in all our Christian great cities. I must add to the description of Constantinople that the Historical Pillar is no more, dropped down about two year before I came.[250] I have seen no other footsteps of antiquity, except the aqueducts, which are so vast that I am apt to believe they are yet ancienter than the Greek Empire, though the Turks have clapped in some stones with Turkish inscription to give their nation the honour of so great a work, but the deceit is easily discovered.

The other public buildings are the hans and monasteries, the first very large and numerous, the second few in number and not at all magnificent. I had the curiosity to visit one of them and observe the devotions of the dervishes, which are as whimsical as any in Rome. These fellows have permission to marry, but are confined to an odd habit, which is only a piece of coarse white cloth wrapped about them, with their legs and arms naked. Their order has few other rules, except that of performing their fantastic rites every Tuesday and Friday, which is in this manner. They meet together in a large hall, where they all stand, with their eyes fixed on the ground and their arms across, while the imam or preacher reads part of the Alcoran from a pulpit placed in the midst; and when he has done, eight or ten of them make a melancholy consort with their pipes, which are no unmusical instruments. Then he reads again and makes a short exposition on what he has read, after which they sing and play till their superior (the only one of them dressed in green) rises and begins a sort of solemn dance. They all stand about him in a regular figure, and while some play the others tie their robe, which is very wide, fast round their waists and begin to turn round with an amazing swiftness and yet with great regard to the music, moving slower or faster as the tune is played. This lasts above an hour without any of them showing the least appearance of giddiness, which is not to be wondered at when it is considered they are all used to it from infancy, most of them being devoted to this way of life from their birth, and sons of dervishes. There turned amongst them some little dervishes of six or seven years old who seem no more disordered by that exercise than the others. At the end of the ceremony they shout out; 'there is no other god but God, and Mohammed is his prophet', after which they kiss the superior's hand and retire. The whole is performed with the most solemn gravity. Nothing can be more austere than the form of these people. They never raise their eyes and seem devoted to contemplation, and as ridiculous as this is in description there is something touching in the air of submission and mortification they assume.

This letter is of a horrible length but you may burn it when you have read enough.

Mr Wortley is not yet here, but I may assure your ladyship in his name of the respect he has for you. I give humble service to my Lord Bristol and Mr Hervey.[251]

LETTER XLVII

To Madame—,[252]   *April 1718*

I am so glad to find you again, my dear madam, that I cannot complain any more of having lost you, and the pleasure given me by that letter which I have just received today makes me forget completely the uneasiness of the past ten months.

Idleness is the mother of vices, as you know, and having nothing better to do, I have produced a daughter. I know you will tell me that I have done very badly, but if you had been in my place I believe, God forgive me, that you would have produced two or three. In this country it is just as necessary to show proofs of youth to be recognised among beauties as it is to show proofs of nobility to be admitted among the Knights of Malta. I was very angry at this necessity, but, noticing that people looked at me with a great air of contempt I finally complied with the fashion and I lay in like the others. For that reason, among innumerable others, I wish with all my heart to hasten my return, because I am absolutely obliged to lie in every year as long as I remain here. The French Ambassadress has complied to her heart's content; she has lain and is big again. The ladies of the country respect women only for the number of their offspring. I can hardly convince them that I have a legitimate excuse for being three months without pregnancy because my husband is a hundred leagues away from me.

I pray every day to see my king, my country and my friends again. I take great pains to see everything. I speak the language passably and I have had the advantage of forming friendships with Turkish ladies and of their liking me, and I can boast of being the first foreigner ever to have had that pleasure. I have visited a Sultana, widow of the late Emperor and by this means I have learned all about the intrigue of the seraglio. She assured me that the story of the handkerchief, so firmly believed among us, has not a syllable of truth.

I have got hold of a Turkish love letter which I will bring you, and which is so truly curious that I cannot sufficiently marvel at the stupidity of travellers in not having brought back to Europe before. My dear madam, may God give you (in the Turkish phrase) whatever pleasure would make you happy, and to me that of seeing you again.

LETTER XLVIII

To the Countess of—,[253]   *Pera, Constantinople, May 1718*

Your ladyship may be assured I received yours with very great pleasure. I am very glad to hear that our friends are in good health, particularly Mr Congreve, who I heard was ill of the gout. I am now preparing to leave Constantinople, and perhaps you will accuse me of hypocrisy when I tell you 'tis with regret, but I am used to the air and have learnt the language. I am easy here, and as much as I love travelling, I tremble at the inconveniences attending so great a journey with a numerous family and a little infant hanging at the breast. However, I endeavour upon this occasion to do as I have hitherto done in all the odd turns of my life; turn them, if I can, to my diversion. In order to this, I ramble every day, wrapped up in my ferace and yasmak[254] about Constantinople and amuse myself with seeing all that is curious in it. I know you'll expect this declaration should be followed with some account of what I have seen, but I am in no humour to copy what has been writ so often over. To what purpose should I tell you that Constantinople was the ancient Byzantium, that 'tis at present the conquest of a race of people supposed Scythians, that there is five or six thousand mosques in it, that St Sophia was founded by Justinian etc? I'll assure you 'tis not want of learning that I forbear writing all these bright things. I could also, with little trouble, turn over Knolles and Sir Paul Rycaut to give you a list of Turkish emperors, but I will not tell you what you may find in every author that has writ of this country.[255]

I am more inclined, out of a true female spirit of contradiction, to tell you the falsehood of a great part of what you find in authors; as, for example, the admirable Mr Hill,[256] who so gravely asserts that he saw in St Sophia a sweating pillar very balsamic for disordered heads. There is not the least tradition of any such matter, and I suppose it was revealed to him in vision during his wonderful stay in the Egyptian catacombs, for I am sure he never heard of any such miracle here. 'Tis also very pleasant to observe how tenderly he and all his brethren voyage-writers lament on the miserable confinement of the Turkish ladies, who are, perhaps, freer than any ladies in the universe, and are the only women in the world that lead a life of uninterrupted pleasure, exempt from cares, their whole time being spent in visiting, bathing or the agreeable amusement of spending money and inventing new fashions. A husband would be thought mad that exacted any degree of economy from his wife, whose expenses are no way limited but by her own fancy. 'Tis his business to get money and hers to spend it, and this noble prerogative extends itself to the very meanest of the sex. Here is a fellow that carries embroidered handkerchiefs upon his back to sell, as miserable a figure as you may suppose such a mean dealer, yet I'll assure you his wife scorns to wear anything less than cloth of gold, has her ermine furs and a very handsome set of jewels for her head. They go abroad when and where they please. 'Tis true they have no public places but the bagnios,[257] and there can only be seen by their own sex. However, that is a diversion they take great pleasure in.

I was three days ago at one of the finest in the town and had the opportunity of seeing a Turkish bride received there and all the ceremonies used on that occasion, which made me recollect the epithalamium of Helen by Theocritus,[258] and it seems to me that the same customs have continued ever since. All the she-friends, relations and acquaintance of the two families newly allied meet at the bagnio. Several others go out of curiosity and I believe there was that day at least 200 women. Those that were or had been married placed themselves round the room on the marble sofas, but the virgins very hastily threw off their clothes and appeared without other ornament or covering than their own long hair braided with pearl or ribbon. Two of them met the bride at the door, conducted by her mother and another grave relation. She was a beautiful maid of about seventeen, richly dressed and shining with jewels, but was presently reduced by them to the state of nature. Two others filled silver gilt pots with perfume and begun the procession, the rest following in pairs to the number of thirty. The leaders sung an epithalamium answered by the others in chorus, and the two last led the fair bride, her eyes fixed on the ground with a charming affectation of modesty. In this order they marched round the three large rooms of the bagnio. 'Tis not easy to represent to you the beauty of this sight, most of them being well proportioned and white skinned, all of them perfectly smooth and polished by the frequent use of bathing. After having made their tour, the bride was again led to every matron round the rooms, who saluted her with a compliment and a present, some of jewels, others pieces of stuff, handkerchiefs, or little gallantries of that nature, which she thanked them for by kissing their hands.

I was very well pleased with having seen this ceremony and you may believe me that the Turkish ladies have at least as much wit and civility, nay, liberty, as ladies amongst us. 'Tis true the same customs that give them so many opportunities of gratifying their evil inclinations (if they have any) also puts it very fully in the power of their husbands to revenge them if they are discovered, and I don't doubt but they suffer sometimes for their indiscretions in a very severe manner. About two months ago there was found at daybreak not very far from my house the bleeding body of a young woman, naked, only wrapped in a course sheet, with two wounds with a knife, one in her side and another in her breast. She was not yet quite cold, and so surprisingly beautiful that there were very few men in Pera that did not go to look upon her, but it was not possible for anybody to know her, no woman's face being known. She was supposed to be brought in dead of night from the Constantinople side and laid there. Very little enquiry was made about the murderer and the corpse privately buried without noise. Murder is never pursued by the king's officers as with us. 'Tis the business of the

next relations to revenge the dead person, and if they like better
to compound the matter for money, as they generally do, there
is no more said of it. One would imagine this defect in their
government should make such tragedies very frequent, yet they
are extremely rare, which is enough to prove the people not
naturally cruel, neither do I think in many other particulars they
deserve the barbarous character we give them.

I am well acquainted with a Christian woman of quality who
made it her choice to live with a Turkish husband, and is a very
agreeable sensible lady. Her story is so extraordinary I cannot
forbear relating it, but I promise you it shall be in as few words
as I can possibly express it. She is a Spaniard, and was at Naples
with her family when that Kingdom was part of the Spanish
dominion.[259] Coming from thence in a felucca, accompanied
by her brother they were attacked by the Turkish Admiral,
boarded and taken; and now how shall I modestly tell you the
rest of her adventure? The same accident happened to her that
happened to the fair Lucretia[260] so many years before her, but
she was too good a Christian to kill herself as that heathenish
Roman did. The admiral was so much charmed with the beauty
and long suffering of the fair captive that as his first compliment
he gave immediate liberty to her brother and attendants, who
made haste to Spain and in a few months sent the sum of £4000
sterling as a ransom for his sister. The Turk took the money,
which he presented to her, and told her she was at liberty, but
the lady very discreetly weighted the different treatment she
was likely to find in her native country. Her Catholics relations,
as the kindest thing they could do for her in her present
circumstances, would certainly confine her to a nunnery for the
rest of her days. Her infidel lover was very handsome, very
tender, fond of her and lavished at her feet all the Turkish
magnificence. She answered him very resolutely that her liberty
was not so precious to her as her honour, that he could no way
restore that but by marrying her. She desired him to accept the
ransom as her portion and give her the satisfaction of knowing
no man could boast of her favours without being her husband.
The Admiral was transported at this kind offer and sent back the

money to her relations, saying he was too happy in her possession. He married her and never took any other wife, and (as she
says herself) she never had any reason to repent the choice she
made. He left her some years after one of the richest widows in
Constantinople, but there is no remaining honourably a single
woman, and that consideration has obliged her to marry the
present Captain Pasha (ie Admiral), his successor.[261] I am afraid
you'll think that my friend fell in love with her ravisher, but I
am willing to take her word for it that she acted wholly on
principles of honour, though I think she might be reasonably
touched at his generosity, which is very often found amongst
Turks of rank.

'Tis a degree of generosity to tell the truth, and 'tis very rare
that any Turk will assert a solemn falsehood. I don't speak of the
lowest sort, for as there is a great deal of ignorance, there is very
little virtue amongst them, and false witnesses are much cheaper
than in Christendom, those wretches not being punished (even
when they are publicly detected) with the rigour they ought to
be. Now I am speaking of their law, I don't know whether I
have ever mentioned to you one custom peculiar to this country. I mean adoption, very common amongst the Turks and yet
more amongst the Greeks and Armenians. Not having it in their
power to give their estates to a friend or distant relation to
avoid its falling into the Grand Signor's treasury, when they are
not likely to have children of their own they choose some pretty
child of either sex amongst the meanest people and carry the
child and its parents before the *cadi*, and there declare they
receive it for their heir. The parents at the same time renounce
all future claim to it, a writing is drawn and witnessed and a
child thus adopted cannot be disinherited. Yet I have seen some
common beggars that have refused to part with their children in
this manner to some of the richest amongst the Greeks, so
powerful is the instinctive fondness natural to parents! Though
the adopting fathers are generally very tender to these children
of their souls, as they call them. I own this custom pleases me
much better than our absurd following our name. Methinks 'tis
much more reasonable to make happy and rich an infant whom

I educate after my own manner, brought up, in the Turkish phrase, upon my knees, and who has learnt to look upon me with a filial respect, than to give an estate to a creature without other merit or relation to me than by a few letters. Yet this is an absurdity we see frequently practised.

Now I have mentioned the Armenians, perhaps it will be agreeable to tell you something of that nation, with which I am sure you are utterly unacquainted. I will not trouble you with the geographical account of the situation of their country, which you may see in the map, or a relation of their ancient greatness, which you may read in the Roman history. They are now subject to the Turks, and, being very industrious in trade, and increasing and multiplying, are dispersed in great numbers through all the Turkish dominions. They were, as they say, converted to the Christian religion by St Gregory,[262] and are perhaps the devoutest Christians in the whole world. The chief precepts of their priests enjoin the strict keeping of their Lents, which are at least seven months in every year, and are not to be dispensed with on the most emergent necessity. No occasion whatever can excuse them if they touch anything more than mere herbs or roots, without oil, and plain dry bread. This is their Lenten diet. Mr Wortley has one of his interpreters of this nation, and the poor fellow was brought so low with the severity of his fasts that his life was despaired of, yet neither his master's commands or the doctor's entreaties (who declared nothing else could save his life) were powerful enough to prevail with him to take two or three spoonfuls of broth. Excepting this, which may rather be called custom than an article of faith, I see very little in their religion different from ours. 'Tis true they seem to incline very much to Mr Whiston's doctrine,[263] neither do I think the Greek church very distant from it, since 'tis certain the insisting on the Holy Spirit only proceeding from the Father is making a plain subordination in the Son. But the Armenians have no notion of transubstantiation, whatever account Sir Paul Rycaut gives of them[264] (which account I am apt to believe was designed to compliment our court in 1679), and they have a great horror for those amongst them that change to the Roman religion.

What is most extraordinary in their customs is their matrimony, a ceremony I believe unparalleled all over the world. They are always promised very young, but the espoused never see one another till three days after their marriage. The bride is carried to church with a cap on her head in the fashion of a large trencher,[265] and over it a read silken veil which covers her all over to her feet. The priest asks the bridegroom whether he is contented to marry that woman, be she deaf, be she blind. These are the literal words, to which having answered yes, she is led home to his house accompanied with all the friends and relations on both sides, singing and dancing, and is placed on a cushion in the corner of the sofa, but her veil never lifted up, not even by her husband, till she has been three days married. There is something so odd and monstrous in these ways that I could not believe them till I had enquired of several Armenians myself who all assured me of the truth of them, particularly one young fellow who wept when he spoke of it, being promised by his mother to a girl that he must marry in this manner, though he protested to me he had rather die than submit to this slavery, having already figured his bride to himself with all the deformities in nature.

I fancy I see you bless yourself at this terrible relation. I cannot conclude my letter with a more surprising story, yet 'tis as seriously true as that I am, dear sister, your etc.

LETTER XLIX

To the Abbé Conti,   *Pera, Constantinople, 19 May 1718*

I am extremely pleased with hearing from you, and my vanity (the darling frailty of humankind)[266] not a little flattered by the uncommon questions you ask me, though I am utterly incapable of answering them, and indeed were I as good a mathematician as Euclid himself, it requires an age's stay to make just observations on the air and vapours.

I have not been yet a full year here and am on the point of removing; such is my rambling destiny. This will surprise you, and can surprise nobody so much as myself. Perhaps you will accuse me of laziness of dulness, or both together, that can leave this place without giving you some account of the Turkish court. I can only tell you that if you please to read Sir Paul Rycaut you will there find a full and true account of the viziers, the Berglerbleys,[267] the civil and spiritual government, the officers of the seraglio, etc., things that 'tis very easy to procure lists of and therefore may be depended on, though other stories, God knows – I say no more – everybody is at liberty to write their own remarks. The manners of people may change or some of them escaped the observation of travellers, but 'tis not the same of the government, and for that reason, since I can tell you nothing new I will tell nothing of it. In the same silence shall be passed over the arsenal and seven towers, and for the mosques, I have already described one of the noblest to you very particularly; but I cannot forbear taking notice to you of a mistake of Gemelli[268] (though I honour him in a much higher degree than any other voyage-writer). He says that there is no remains of Calcedon. This is certainly a mistake. I was there yesterday and went cross the canal in my galley, the sea being very narrow between that city and Constantinople, 'Tis still a large town and has several mosques in it. The Christians still call it Calcedonia, and the Turks give it a name I forgot, but which is only a corruption of the same word.[269] I suppose this an error of his guide, which his short stay hindered him from rectifying, for I have, in other matters, a very just esteem for his veracity.

Nothing can be pleasanter than the canal, and the Turks are so well acquainted with its beauties, all their pleasure seats are built on its banks, where they have at the same time the most beautiful prospects in Europe and Asia. There are near one another some hundreds of magnificent palaces. Human grandeur being here yet more unstable than anywhere else, 'tis common for the heirs of a great three-tailed pasha not to be rich enough to keep in repair the house he built; thus in a few years they all fall to ruin. I was yesterday to see that of the late Grand

Vizier who was killed at Peterwardein. It was built to receive his
royal bride, daughter of the present Sultan, but he did not live
to see her there. I have a great mind to describe it to you, but I
check that inclination, knowing very well that I cannot give you,
with my best description, such an idea of it as I ought. It is
situated on one of the most delightful parts of the canal, with a
fine wood on the side of a hill behind it. The extent of it is
prodigious; the guardian assured me there is 800 rooms in it. I
will not answer for that number since I did not count them, but
'tis certain the number is very large and the whole adorned with
a profusion of marble, gilding and the most exquisite painting of
fruit and flowers. The windows are all sashed with the finest
crystalline glass brought from England, and all the expensive
magnificence that you can suppose in a palace founded by a vain
young luxurious man with the wealth of a vast empire at his
command. But no part of it pleased me better than the apartments destined for the bagnios. There are two exactly built in
the same manner, answering to one another; the baths, fountains and pavements all of white marble, the roofs gilt and the
walls covered with japan china; but adjoining to them two
rooms, the upper part of which is divided into a sofa; in the four
corners falls of water from the very roof, from shell to shell of
white marble to the lower end of the room, where it falls into a
large basin surrounded with pipes that throw up the water as
high as the room. The walls are in the nature of lattices and on
the outside of them vines and woodbines planted that form a
sort of green tapestry and give an agreeable obscurity to these
delightful chambers. I should go on and let you into some of the
other apartments, all worthy your curiosity, but 'tis yet harder
to describe a Turkish palace than any other, being built entirely
irregular. There is nothing can be properly called front or wings,
and though such a confusion is, I think, pleasing to the sight, yet
it would be very unintelligible in a letter. I shall only add that
the chamber destined for the Sultan, when he visits his daughter, is wainscotted with mother of pearl fastened with emeralds
like nails; there are others of mother of pearl and olive wood
inlaid, and several of japan china. The galleries, which are

numerous and very large, are adorned with jars of flowers and porcelain dishes of frit of all sorts, so well done in plaster and coloured in so lively a manner that it has an enchanting effect. The garden is suitable to the house, where arbours, fountains and walks are thrown together in an agreeable confusion. There is no ornament wanting except that of statues.

Thus you see, sir, these people are not so unpolished as we represent them. 'Tis true their magnificence is of a different taste from ours, and perhaps of a better. I am almost of opinion they have a right notion of life; while they consume it in music, gardens, wine and delicate eating, while we are tormenting our brains with some scheme of politics or studying some science to which we can never attain, or if we do, cannot persuade people to set that value upon it we do ourselves, 'Tis certain what we fell and see is properly (if anything is properly) our won, but the good of fame, the folly of praise, hardly purchased, and when obtained, poor recompense for loss of time and health! We die, or grow old and decrepit before we can reap the fruit of our labours. Considering what short lived, weak animals men are, is there any study so beneficial as the study of present pleasure? I dare not pursue this then; perhaps I have already said too much, but I depend upon the true knowledge you have of my heart. I don't expect from you the insipid railleries I should suffer from another in answer to this letter. You know how to divide the idea of pleasure from that of vice, and they are only mingled in the heads of fools – but I allow you to laugh at me for the sensual declaration that I had rather be a rich effendi with all his ignorance than Sir Isaac Newton with all his knowledge. I am, sir, etc.

LETTER L

To the Abbé Conti,   *Tunis, 31 July 1718*

I left Constantinople the sixth of last month, and this is the first port from whence I could send a letter, though I have often wished for the opportunity that I might impart some of the pleasure I have found in this voyage through the most agreeable part of the world, where every scene presents me some poetical idea.

> Warm'd with poetic transport I survey
> Th' Immortal Islands, and the well known Sea,
> For here so oft the Muse her harp has strung
> That not a Mountain rears his head unsung.[270]

I beg your pardon for this sally, and will, if I can, continue the rest of my account in plain prose. The second day after we set sail we passed Gallipolis, a fair city situate in the Bay of Chersonessus and much respected by the Turks, being the first town they took in Europe. At five the next morning we anchored in the Hellespont between the Castles of Sestos and Abydos, now called the Dardanelli. There is now two little ancient castles, but of no strength, being commanded by a rising ground behind them which, I confess, I should never have taken notice of if I had not heard it observed by our Captain and officers, my imagination being wholly employed by the tragic story that you are well acquainted with:

> The swimming lover and the nightly bride,
> How Hero lov'd, and how Leander dy'd.

Verse again! I am certainly infected by the poetical air I have passed through. That of Abydos is undoubtedly very amorous, since that soft passion betrayed the castle into the hands of the Turks in the reign of Orchanes, who besieged it.[271] The governor's daughter, imagining to have seen her future husband in a dream, though I don't find she had wither slept upon bride cake or kept St Agnes' Feast[272] fancied she afterwards saw the dear figure in the form of one of her besiegers and, being willing to obey her destiny, tossed a note to him over the wall with the offer of her person and the delivery of the castle. He showed it to his general who consented to try the sincerity of her intentions and withdrew his army, ordering the young man to return with a select body of men at midnight. She admitted him at the appointed hour; he destroyed the garrison, took her father prisoner and made her his wife. This town is in Asia, first founded by the Milesians. Sestos is in Europe and was once the principal city in Chersonessus. Since I have seen this strait I find nothing improbable in the adventure of Leander or very wonderful in the bridge of boats of Xerxes.[273] 'Tis so narrow, it is not surprising a young lover should attempt to swim it or an ambitious king try to pass his army over it. But then 'tis so subject to storms, 'tis no wonder the lover perished and the bridge was broken. From hence we had a full view of Mount Ida,

> Where Juno once carres'd her Amorous Jove
> And the World's Master lay subdu'd by Love.

Not many leagues sail from hence I saw the point of land where poor old Hecuba was buried[274] and about a league from that place is Cape Janissary, the famous promontory of Sigeum, where we anchored, and my curiosity supplied me with strength to climb to the top of it to see the place where Achilles was buried and where Alexander ran naked round his tomb in his honour,[275] which, no doubt, was a great comfort to his ghost. I saw there the ruins of a very large city and found a stone on which Mr Wortley plainly distinguished the words of Sigaeon Polin.[276] We ordered this on board the ship but were showed others much more curious by a Greek priest, though a very ignorant fellow that could give no tolerable account of anything. On each side the door of his little church lies a large stone about ten foot long each, five in breadth and three in thickness. That on the right is very fine white marble, the side of it beautifully carved in bas relief. It represents a woman who seems to be designed for some deity sitting on a chair with a footstool, and before her another woman weeping and presenting to her a young child that she has in her arms, followed by a procession of women with children in the same manner. This is certainly part of a very ancient tomb, but I dare not pretend to give the true explanation of it. On the stone on the left side is a very fair inscription, which I am sure I took off very exactly, but the

Greek is too ancient for Mr Wortley's interpretation. This is the exact copy. [In the manuscript here follow eleven double lines of Greek, apparently copied in another hand.] I am very sorry not to have the original in my possession, which might have been purchased of the poor inhabitants for a small sum of money, but our captain assured us that without having machines made on purpose, 'twas impossible to bear it to the sea side, and when it was there his long boat would not be large enough to hold it.

The ruins of this great city is now inhabited by poor Greek peasants who wear the sciote[277] habit, the women being in short petticoats fastened by straps round their shoulders and large smock sleeves of white linen, with neat shoes and stockings, and on their heads a large piece of muslin which falls in large folds on their shoulders. One of my countrymen, Mr Sandys, whose book I do not doubt you have read as one of the best of its kind,[278] speaking of these ruins supposes them to have been the foundation of a city begun by Constantine before his building at Byzantium, but I see no good reason for that imagination and am apt to believe them much more ancient. We saw very plainly form this promontory the River Simois rolling from Mount Ida and running through a very spacious valley. It is now a considerable river, and called Simores, joined in the vale by the Scamander, which appeared a small stream half choked with mud, but is perhaps large in the winter. This was Xanthus amongst the gods, as Homer tells us,[279] and 'tis by that heavenly name of Scamander, till the adventure which Monsieur de la Fontaine has told so agreeably abolished that heathenish ceremony.[280] When the stream is mingled with the Simois they run together to the sea.

All that is now left of Troy is the ground on which it stood, for I am firmly persuaded whatever pieces of antiquity may be found round it are much more modern, and I think Strabo says the same thing.[281] However, there is some pleasure in seeing the valley where I imagined the famous duel of Menelaus and Paris had been fought,[282] and where the greatest city in the world was situated, and 'tis certainly the noblest situation that can be

found for the head of a great empire, much to be preferred to that
of Constantinople, the harbour there being always convenient for
ships from all parts of the world and that of Constantinople
inaccessible almost six months in the year while the north wind
reigns. North of the promontory of Sigeum we saw that of
Rhoeteum, famed for the sepulchre of Ajax. While I viewed these
celebrated fields and rivers I admired the exact geography of
Homer, whom I had in my hand. Almost every epithet he gives to
a mountain or plain is still just for it, and I spent several hours in
as agreeable cogitations as ever Don Quixote had on Mount
Montesinos.[283] We sailed that night to the shore where 'tis
vulgarly reported Troy stood and I took the pains of rising at two
in the morning to view cooly those ruins which are commonly
showed to strangers, and which the Turks call eski-Stamboul, ie
Old Constantinople.[284] For that reason, as well as some others, I
conjecture them to be the remains of that city begun by
Constantine.[285] I hired an ass (the only voiture to be had there)
that I might go some miles into the country and take a tour round
the ancient walls, which are of a vast extent. We found the
remains of a castle on a hill and another in a valley, several broken
pillars and two pedestals from which I took these latin inscriptions. [Here follow two inscriptions of nine and twelve lines.] I do
not doubt but the remains of a temple near this place are the ruins
of one dedicated to Augustus,[286] and I know not why Mr Sandys
calls it a Christian temple, since the Romans certainly built
hereabouts. Here are many tombs of fine marble and vast pieces
of granite, which are daily lessened by the prodigious balls that
the Turks make from them for their cannon.

We passed that evening the Isle of Tenedos, once under the
patronage of Apollo, as he gave it in himself in the particular of
his estate when he courted Daphne.[287] It is but ten mile in
circuit, but in those days very rich and well peopled, still famous
for its excellent wine. I say nothing of Tenes, from whom it was
called, but naming Mytilene where we passed next I cannot
forbear mentioning Lesbos, where Sappho sung and Pittacus
reigned, famous for the birth of Alcaeus, Theophrastus and
Arion, those masters in poetry, philosophy and music.[288] This

was one of the last islands that remained in the Christian dominion after the conquest of Constantinople by the Turks.[289] But need I talk to you of Catucuseno[290] etc., princes that you are as well acquainted with as I am? 'Twas with regret I saw us sail swift from this island into the Aegean sea, now the archipelago, leaving Scio (the ancient Chios) on the left, which is the richest and most populous of these islands, fruitful in cotton, corn and silk, planted with groves of orange and lemon trees, and the Arvisian mountain, still celebrated for the nectar that Virgil mentions.[291] Here is the best manufacture of silks in all Turkey. The town is well built, the women famous for their beauty, and show their faces as in Christendom. There are many rich families, though they confine their magnificence to the inside of their houses to avoid the jealousy of the Turks, who have a pasha here. However, they enjoy a reasonable liberty and indulge the genius of their country,

> And eat and sing and dance away their time,
> Fresh as their Groves, and happy as their Clime.

Their chains hang lightly on them, though 'tis not long since they were imposed, not being under the Turk till 1566; but perhaps 'tis as easy to obey the Grand Signior as the state of Genoa, to whom they were sold by the Greek Emperor. But I forget myself in these historical touches, which are very impertinent when I write to you.

Passing the strait between the island of Andros and Achaia (now Libadia) we saw the promontory of Sunium (now called Cape Colonna), where are yet standing the vast pillars of a temple of Minerva. This venerable sight made me think with double regret on a beautiful temple of Theseus which I am assured was almost entire at Athens till the last campaign in the Morea that the Turks filled it with powder and it was accidentally blown up.[292] You may believe I had a great mind to land on the famed Peloppones, though it were only to look on the rivers of Asopus, Peneus, Inachus and Eurotas, the fields of Arcadia and other scenes of ancient mythology. But instead of demigods and heroes I was credibly informed 'tis now overrun by robbers and that I should run a great risk of falling into their hands by undertaking such a journey through a desert country, for which, however, I have so much respect I have much ado to hinder myself from troubling you with its whole history from the foundation of Mycena and Corinth[293] to their last campaign there. But I check that inclination as I did that of landing, and sailed quietly by Cape Angelo, once Malea, where I saw no remains of the famous temple of Apollo. We came that evening in sight of Candia. It is very mountainous; we easily distinguished that of Ida. We have Virgil's authority here was 100 cities,

Centum urbes habitant magnas[294]

the chief of them, Gnossus the scene of monstrous passions.[295] Metellus first conquered this birth place of his Jupiter.[296] It fell afterwards into the hands of —. I am running on to the very siege of Candia[297] and I am so angry at myself that I will pass by all the other islands with this general reflection, that 'tis impossible to imagine anything more agreeable than this journey would have been between two and three thousand years since, when, after drinking a dish of tea with Sappho I might have gone the same evening to visit the temple of Homer in Chios,[298] and have passed this voyage in taking plans of magnificent temples, delineating the miracles of statuaries and conversing with the most polite and most gay of humankind. Alas! Art is extinct here. The wonders of nature alone remain, and 'twas with vast pleasure I observed that of Mount Etna, whose flame appears very bright in the night many leagues off at sea, and fills the head with a thousand conjectures. However, I honour philosophy too much to imagine it could turn that of Empedocles and Lucian shall never make me believe such a scandal of a man of whom Lucretius says

–vix humana videatur stirpe creatus.[299]

We passed Trinacria without hearing any of the syrens that Homer describes, and being neither thrown on Scylla nor Charibdis came safe to Malta,[300] first called Melita from the abundance of honey. It is a whole rock covered with very little earth. The grand master lives here in a state of sovereign prince,[301] but his strength at sea is now very small. The fortifications are reckoned the best in the world, all cut in the solid rock with infinite expense and labour. Off of this island we were tossed by a severe storm, and very glad after eight days to be able to put into Porta Farine on the Africa shore, where our ship now rides.

We were met here by the English consul who resides at Tunis.[302] I readily accepted of the offer of his house there for some days, being very curious to see this part of the world and particularly the ruins of Carthage. I set out in his chaise at nine at night; the moon being at full, I saw the prospect of the country almost as well as I could have done by daylight, and the heat of the sun is now so intolerable 'tis impossible to travel at any other time. The soil is for the most part sandy, but everywhere fruitful in date, olive and fig trees, which grow without art, yet afford the most delicious fruit in the world. Their vineyards and melon fields are enclosed by hedges of that plant we call the Indian fig,[303] which is an admirable fence, no wild beast being able to pass it. It grows a great height, very thick and the spikes or thorns are as long and sharp as bodkins. It bears a fruit much eaten by the peasants and which has no ill taste. It being now the season of the Turkish ramadan (or lent) and all here professing at least the Mohammedan religion, they fast till the going down of the sun and spend the night in feasting. We saw under the trees in many places companies of the country people eating, singing and dancing to their wild music. They are not quite black, but all mulattoes, and the most frightful creatures that can appear in a human figure. They are almost naked, only wearing a piece of coarse serge wrapped about them, but the women have their arms to their very shoulders and their necks and faces adorned with flowers, stars and various sort of figures impressed by gunpowder; a considerable addition to their natural deformity, which is, however, esteemed very ornamental amongst them, and I believe they suffer a good deal of pain by it. About six mile from Tunis we saw the remains of that noble aqueduct which carried the water to Carthage over several high mountains the length of forty mile. There is still many arches entire. We spent two hours viewing it with great attention and Mr Wortley assured me that of Rome is very much inferior to it. The stones are of a prodigious size and yet all polished and so exactly fitted to each other, very little cement has been make use of to join them. Yet they may probably stand 1000 years longer if art is not used to pull them down.

Soon after daybreak I arrived at Tunis, a town fairly built of a very white stone, but quite without gardens, which, they say, were all destroyed and their fine groves cut down when the Turks first took it. None having been planted since, the dry sand gives a very disagreeable prospect to the eye, and the want of shade contributing to the natural heat of the climate renders it so excessive I have much ado to support it. 'Tis true here is every noon the refreshment of the sea breeze, without which it would be impossible to live, but no fresh water but what is preserved in the cisterns of the rains that fall in the month of September. The women in the town go veiled from head to foot under a black crepe and, being mixed with a breed of renegades, are said to be many of them fair and handsome. This city was besieged in 1270 by Louis, King of France,[304] who died under the walls of it of a pestilential fever. After his death, Philip, his son and our Prince Edward, son of Henry III, raised the seige on honourable conditions.[305] It remained under its natural African kings till betrayed into the hands of Barberussa, admiral of Süleiman the Magnificent. The Emperor Charles V expelled Barberussa, but it was recovered by the Turk under the conduct of Sinan Pasha in the reign of Selim II.[306] From that time till now it has remained tributary to the Grand Signor, governed by a *bey* who suffers the name of subject to the Turk, but has renounced the subjection, being absolute and very seldom paying any tribute. The great city of Baghdad is at this time in the same circumstance, and the Grand Signor connives at the loss of these dominions for fear of losing even the titles of them.

I went very early yesterday morning (after one night's repose) to see the ruins of Carthage. I was, however, half broiled in the sun and overjoyed to be led into one of the subterranean apartments which they called the stables of the elephants, but which I cannot believe were ever designed for that use. I found in many of them broken pieces of columns of fine marble and some of porphyry. I cannot think anybody would take the insignificant pains of carrying them thither, and I cannot imagine such fine pillars were designed for the ornament of a stable. I am apt to believe they were summer apartments under their palaces, which the heat of the climate rendered necessary. They are now used as granaries by the country people. While I sat here from the town of tents not far off many of the women flocked in to see me and we were equally entertained with viewing one another. Their posture in sitting, the colour of their skin, their lank black hair falling on each side their faces, their features and the shape of their limbs differ so little from their own country people, the baboons, 'tis hard to fancy them a distinct race, and I could not help thinking here had been some ancient alliances between them. When I was a little refreshed by rest and some milk and exquisite fruit they brought me, I went up the little hill where once stood the caste of Birsa, from whence I had a distinct view of the situation of the famous city of Carthage, which stood on an isthmus, the sea coming in on each side of it. 'Tis now a marshy ground on one side where there is salt ponds. Strabo calls Carthage forty mile in circuit.[307] There is now no remains of it but what I have described, and the history of it too well known to want my abridgement of it.

You see that I think you esteem obedience more than compliments. I have answered your letter by giving you the accounts you desired and have reserved my thanks to the conclusion. I intend to leave this place tomorrow and continue my journey through Italy and France. In one of those places I hope to tell you by word of mouth that I am your humble servant.

LETTER LI

To Lady Mar,   *Genoa, 28 August 1718*

I beg your pardon, my dear sister, that I did not write to you
from Tunis (the only opportunity I have had since I left Constantinople), but the heat there was so excessive and the light so
bad for the sight, I was half blind by writing one letter to the
Abbé Conti and durst not go on to write many others I had
designed, nor, indeed, could I have entertained you very well
out of that barbarous country. I am now surrounded with
objects of pleasure, and so much charmed with the beauties of
Italy, I should think it a kind of ingratitude not to offer a little
praise in return for the diversion I have had here. I am in the
house of Mrs D'avenant[308] at St Pierre l'Arene[309] and should be
very unjust not to allow her a share of that praise I speak of,
since her good humour and good company has very much
contributed to render this place agreeable to me. Genoa is
situated in a very fine bay, and being built on a rising hill,
intermixed with gardens and beautified with the most excellent
architecture, gives a very fine prospect off at sea, though it lost
much of its beauty in my eyes having been accustomed to that of
Constantinople. The Genoese were once masters of several
islands in the archipelago and all that part of Constantinople
which is now called Galata. Their betraying the Christian cause
by facilitating the taking of Constantinople by the Turk,[310]
deserved what has since happened to them, the loss of all their
conquest on that side to those infidels. They are at present far
from rich, and despised by the French since their Doge was
forced by the late King to go in person to Paris to ask pardon for
such a trifle as the arms of France over the house of the envoy
being spattered with dung in the night, I suppose by some of the
Spanish faction, which still makes up the majority here, though
they dare not openly declare it.[311]

The ladies affect the French habit and are more genteel than those they imitate. I do not doubt but the custom of *cicisbeismo* has very much improved their airs. I know not whether you have ever heard of those animals. Upon my word, nothing but my own eyes could have convinced me there were any such upon earth. The fashion begun here and is now received all over Italy, where the husbands are not such terrible creatures as we represent them. There are none amongst them such brutes to pretend to find fault with a custom so well established and so politically founded, since I am assured here that it was an expedient first found out by the senate to put an end to those family hatreds which tore their state to pieces, and to find employment for those young men who were forced to cut one another's throats *pour passer le temps*, and it has succeeded so well that since the institution of *cicisbeismo* there has been nothing but peace and good humour amongst them. These are gentlemen that devote themselves to the service of a particular lady (I mean a married one, for the virgins are all invisible, confined to convents). They are obliged to wait on her to all public places, the plays, opera and assemblies (which are called here conversations), where they wait behind her chair, take care of her fan and gloves if she plays, have the privilege of whispers, etc. When she goes out they serve her instead of lackeys, gravely trotting by her chair. 'Tis their business to present against any day of public appearance, not forgetting that of her name. In short, they are to spend all their time and money in her service who rewards them according to her inclination (for opportunity they want none), but the husband is not to have the impudence to suppose 'tis any other than a pure platonic friendship. 'Tis true they endeavour to give her a *cicisbeismo* of their own choosing, but when the lady happens not to be of the same taste (as that often happens) she never fails to bring it about to have one of her own fancy. In former times one beauty used to have eight or ten of these humble admirers, but those days of plenty and humility are no more; men grow more scarce and saucy and every lady is forced to content herself with one at a time. You see the glorious liberty of a republic, or more properly an aristocracy, the common people being here as errant slaves as the French, but the old nobles pay little respect to the Doge, who is but two years in his office, and at that very time his wife assumes no rank above another noble lady. 'Tis true the family of Andrea Doria[312] (that great man who restored them that liberty they enjoy) has some particular privileges; when the senate found it necessary to put a stop to the luxury of dress, forbidding the wear of jewels and brocades, they left them at liberty to make what expense they pleased. I looked with great pleasure on the statue of that hero which is in the court belonging to the House of Duke Doria.

This puts me in mind of their palaces, which I can never describe as I ought. Is it not enough that I say they are most of them of the design of Palladio?[313] The street called Strada Nova here is perhaps the most beautiful line of building in the world. I must particularly mention the vast palace of Durazzo, those of two Balbi joined together by a magnificent colonnade, that of the Imperiali at this village of St Pierre l'Arene, and another of the Doria. The perfection of architecture and the utmost profusion of rich furniture is to be seen here, disposed with most elegant taste and lavish magnificence, but I am charmed with nothing so much as the collection of pictures by the pencils of Raphael, Paulo Veronese, Titian, Carache, Michael Angelo, Guido and Corregio,[314] which two I mention last as my particular favourites. I own I can find no pleasure in objects of horror, and in my opinion the more naturally a crucifix is represented the more disagreeable it is. These, my beloved painters, show nature and show it in the most charming light. I was particularly pleased with a Lucretia in the house of Balbi. The expressive beauty of that face and bosom gives all the passion of pity and admiration that could be raised in the soul by the finest poem on that subject. A Cleopatra of the same hand deserves to be mentioned, and I should say more of her if Lucretia had not first engaged my eyes.[315] Here are also some inestimable ancient busts. The church of St Lawrence is all black and white marble, where is kept the famous plate of a single emerald, which is not now permitted to be handled since a plot which, they say, was discovered to throw it on the pavement and break it, a childish piece of malice which they ascribe to the King of Sicily, to be revenged for their refusing to sell it to him. The church of the Annunciata is finely lined with marble, the pillars of red and white marble, that of St Ambrose very much adorned by the Jesuits; but I confess all those churches appeared so mean to me after that of St Sophia, I can hardly do them the honour of writing down their names; but I hope you'll own I have made good use of my time in seeing so much, since 'tis not many days that we have been out of the quarantine from which nobody is exempt coming from the Levant. But ours was very much shortened and very agreeably passed in Mrs Davenant's company in the village of St Pierre l'Arene, about a mile from Genoa in a house built by Palladio, so well designed and so nobly proportioned 'twas a pleasure to walk in it. We were visited here only in the company of a noble Genoese commissioned to see we did not touch one another. I shall stay here some days longer and could almost wish it for all my life, but mine, I fear, is not destined to so much tranquillity.

LETTER LII

To Lady Mar,   *Turin, 12 September 1718*

I came in two days from Genoa through fine roads to this place. I have already seen what is showed to strangers in the town, which indeed is not worth a very particular description, and I have not respect enough for the holy handkerchief to speak long of it.[316] The church is handsome and so is the King's palace, but I did not give much of my attention to these pieces. The town itself is fairly built, situated in a fine plain on the banks of the Po. At a little distance from it we saw the palaces of La Venerie and La Valentin, both very agreeable retreats.[317] We were lodged in the Piazza Royale, which is one of the noblest squares I ever saw, with a fine portico of white stone quite round it. We were immediately visited by the Chevalier—, whom you knew in England, who with great civility begged to introduce us at court, which is now kept at Rivoli about a league from Turin. I went thither yesterday and had the honour of waiting on the Queen,[318] being presented to her by her first lady of honour. I found her majesty in a magnificent apartment, with a train of handsome ladies all dressed in gowns, amongst which it was easy to distinguish the fair Princess of Carignan.[319] The Queen entertained me with a world of sweetness and affability and seemed mistress of a great share of good sense. She did not forget to put me in mind of her English blood, and added that she always felt in herself a particular inclination to love the English. I returned her civility by giving her the title of majesty as often as I could, which perhaps she will not have the comfort of hearing many months longer.[320] The King has a great vivacity in his eyes, and the young Prince of Piedmont is a very handsome youth,[321] but the great devotion which this court is at present fallen into does not permit any of those entertainments proper for his age. Processions and masses are all the magnificences in fashion here, and gallantry so criminal that the poor Count of —, who was our acquaintance at London, is very seriously disgraced for some small overtures he presumed to make to a maid of honour. I intend to set out tomorrow to pass those dreadful Alps, so much talked of. If I come alive to the bottom you shall hear of me.

LETTER LIII

To Anne Thistlethwayte,   *Lyons, 25 September 1718*

I received at my arrival here both your obliging letters, and from many of my other friends, designed to Constantinople and sent me from Marseilles hither, our merchant there knowing we were upon our return.

I am surprised to hear my sister Mar has left England. I suppose what I writ to her from Turin will be lost, and where to direct I know not, having no account of her affairs from her own hand. For my own part, I am confined to my chamber, having kept my bed till yesterday ever since the 17th that I came to this town, where I have had so terrible a fever I believed for some time that all my journeys were ended here, and I do not at all wonder that such fatigues as I have passed should have such an effect. The first day's journey, from Turin to Novalese, is through a very fine country, beautifully planted and enriched by art and nature. The next day we begun to ascend Mont Cenis, being carried in little seats of twisted osiers[322] fixed upon poles on men's shoulders, our chaises taken to pieces and laid upon mules. The prodigious prospect of mountains covered with eternal snow, clouds hanging far below our feet, and the vast cascades tumbling down the rocks with a confused roaring, would have been solemnly entertaining to me if I had suffered less from the extreme cold that reigns here; but the misty rain which falls perpetually penetrated even the thick fur I was wrapped in and I was half dead with cold before we got to the foot of the mountain, which was not till two hours after 'twas dark. This hill has a spacious plain on the top of it, and a fine lake there, but the descent is so steep and slippery 'tis surprising to see these chairmen go so steadily as they do, yet I was not half so much afraid of breaking my neck as I was of falling sick, and the event has showed that I placed my fears in the right place. The other mountains are now all passable for a chaise, and very fruitful in vines and pastures; amongst them is a breed of the finest goats in the world. Aiguebellet is the last, and soon after we entered Point Beauvoisin, the frontier town of France, whose bridge parts this kingdom and the dominion of Savoy. The same night we arrived late at this town, where I have had nothing to do but to take care of my health. I think myself already out of any danger, and am determined that the sore throat, which still remains, shall not confine me long. I am impatient to see the antiquities of this famous city and more impatient to continue my journey to Paris from whence I hope to write you a more diverting letter than 'tis possible for me to do now, with a mind weakened by sickness, a head muddled with spleen, from a sorry inn and a chamber crammed with the mortifying objects of apothecaries' vials and bottles.

LETTER LIV

To Alexander Pope,   *Lyons, 28 September 1718*

I received yours here and should thank you for the pleasure you express for my return, but I can hardly forbear being angry at you for rejoicing at what displeases me so much. You will think this but an odd compliment on my side. I'll assure you 'tis not from insensibility of the joy of seeing my friends, but when I consider that I must at the same time see and hear a thousand disagreeable impertinents, that I must receive and pay visits, make curtsies and assist at tea tables where I shall be half killed with questions; on the other part, that I am a creature that cannot serve anybody but with insignificant good wishes, and that my presence is not a necessary good to any one member of my native country, I think I might much better have stayed where ease and quiet made up the happiness of my indolent life. I should certainly be melancholy if I pursued this theme one line farther. I will rather fill the remainder of this paper with the inscriptions on the tables of brass that are placed on each side the townhouse here.

[Thirty nine lines of Latin inscription follow.]

I cannot take the pains with the second table I have done with the first. You may easily imagine it in the same character and pointed after the same manner. These are the words.

[Forty lines of Latin inscription follow.]

I was also showed without the gate of St Justinus[323] some remains of a Roman aqueduct, and behind the monastery of St Mary's there is the ruins of the imperial palace where the Emperor Claudius was born and where Severus lived.[324] The great cathedral of St John is a good gothic building and its clock much admired by the Germans. In one of the most conspicuous parts of the town is the late King's statue set up, trampling upon mankind.[325] I can't forbear saying one word here of the French statues (for I never intend to mention any more of them) with their gilded full bottomed wigs. If their King had intended to express, in one image, ignorance, ill taste and vanity, his sculptures could have made no other figure to represent the odd mixture of an old beau who had a mind to be a hero, with a bushel of curled hair on his head and a gilt truncheon in his hand. The French have been so voluminous on the history of this town I need say nothing of it. The houses are tolerably well built and the Belle Cour[326] well planted, from whence is seen the celebrated joining of the Soane and the Rhone.

> Ubi Rhodanus ingens amne praerapido fluit,
> Araraque dubitans quo suos fluctus agat.[327]

I have had time to see everything with great leisure, having been confined several days to this town by a swelling in my throat, the remains of a fever occasioned by a cold I got in the damps of the Alps. The doctors here, who are charmed with a new customer, threaten me with all sorts of distempers if I dare to leave them till this swelling is quite vanished, but I that know the obstinacy of it think it just as possible to continue my way to Paris with it as to go about the streets of Lyons, and am determined to pursue my journey tomorrow in spite of doctors, apothecaries and sore throats. When you see Lady Rich tell her I have received her letter and will answer it from Paris, believing that the place she would most willingly hear of.

LETTER LV

To Lady Rich,   *Paris, 10 October 1718*

I cannot give my dear Lady Rich a better proof of the pleasure I
have in writing to her than choosing to do it in this seat of
various amusements, where I am *acablée*[328] with visits, and those
so full of vivacity and compliment that 'tis full employment to
harken whether one answers or not. The French Ambassadress
at Constantinople has a very considerable and numerous family
here, who all come to see me and are never weary of making
enquiries. The air of Paris has already had a good effect on me,
for I was never in better health, though I have been extreme ill
all the road from Lyons to this place. You may judge how
agreeable the journey has been to me, which did not need that
addition to make me dislike it. I think nothing so terrible as
objects of misery, except one had the god-like attribute of being
capable to redress them, and all the country villages of France
shows nothing else. While the post horses are changed the
whole town comes out to beg, with such miserable starved faces
and thin, tattered clothes, they need no other eloquence to
persuade one of the wretchedness of their condition.

This is all the French magnificence till you come to Fon-
tainebleau. There you begin to think the kingdom rich when
you are showed 1500 rooms in the King's hunting palace. The
apartments of the royal family are very large and richly gilt, but
I saw nothing in the architecture or painting worth remember-
ing. The long gallery, built by Henry IV,[329] has prospects of all
the King's houses on its walls, designed after the taste of those
times, but appears now very mean. The park is indeed finely
wooded and watered, the trees well grown and planted, and in
the fish ponds are kept tame carp, said to be some of them eighty
years of age. The late King[330] passed some months every year at
this seat, and all the rocks round it, by the pious sentences

inscribed on them, show the devotion in fashion at his court, which I believe died with him; at least, I see no exterior marks of it at Paris, where all people's thoughts seem to be on present diversion. The fair of St Lawrence is now in season. You may be sure I have been carried thither and think it much better disposed than ours of Bartholomew. The shops being all set in rows so regularly well lighted they made up a very agreeable spectacle. But I was not at all satisfied with the *grosseirté* of their *arlequin*,[331] no more than with their music at the opera, which was abominable grating after being used to that of Italy. Their house is a booth compared to that of the Haymarket,[332] and the playhouse not so neat as that in Lincoln's Inn Fields; but then it must be owned to their praise, their tragedians are much beyond any of ours. I should hardly allow Mrs Oldfield[333] a better place than to be confidante to La Desmares. I have seen the tragedy of *Bajazet* so well represented,[334] I think our best actors can be only said to speak, but these to feel, and 'tis certainly infinitely more moving to see a man appear unhappy than to hear him say that he is so, with a jolly face and a stupid smirk in his countenance. A propos of countenances, I must tell you something of the French ladies. I have seen all the beauties and such (I can't help making use of the coarse word) nauseous—, so fantastically absurd in their dress! So monstrously unnatural in their paint, their hair cut short and curled round their faces, loaded with powder that makes it look like white wool, and on their cheeks to their chins, unmercifully laid on, a shining red japan[335] that glistens in a most flaming manner, that they seem to have no resemblance to human faces, and I am apt to believe took the first hint of their dress from a fair sheep newly ruddled.[336] 'Tis with pleasure I recollect my dear pretty country women, and if I was writing to anybody else I should say that these grotesque daubers give me still a higher esteem of the natural charms of dear Lady Rich's auburn hair and the lively colours of her unsullied complexion.

I have met the Abbé Conti[337] here, who desires me to make his compliments to you.

LETTER LVI

To Anne Thistlethwayte,   *Paris, 16 October 1718*

You see I am just to my word in writing to you from Paris,
where I was very much surprised to meet my sister Mar; I need
not add, very much pleased. She as little expected to see me as I
her, having not received my late letters, and this meeting would
shine under the hand of Mr de Scudery,[338] but I shall not
imitate his style so far as to tell you how often we embraced,
how she enquired by what odd chance I returned from Constantinople. And I answered her by asking what adventure brought
her to Paris.[339] To shorten the story, all questions and answers
and exclamations and compliments being over, we agreed upon
running about together and have seen Versailles, Trianon, Marli
and St Cloûd. We had an order for the waters to play for our
diversion, and I was followed thither by all the English at Paris. I
own Versailles appeared to me rather vast than beautiful, and
after having seen the exact proportions of the Italian buildings, I
thought the irregularity of it shocking. The King's cabinet of
antiques and medals is indeed very richly furnished, Amongst
that collection none pleased me so well as the Apotheosis of
Germanicus[340] on a large agate, which is one of the most
delicate pieces of the kind that I remember to have seen. I
observed some ancient statues of great value, but the nauseous
flattery and tawdry pencil of Le Brun[341] are equally disgusting in
the gallery. I will not pretend to describe to you the great
apartment, the vast variety of fountains, the theatre, the grove
of Aesop's fables,[342] etc., all of which you may read very amply
particularised in some of the French authors that have been paid
for those descriptions. Trianon in its littleness pleased me better
than Versailles, Marli better than either of them, and St Cloûd
best of all, having the advantage of the Seine running at the
bottom of the gardens. The great cascade etc. you may find in

the foresaid books if you have any curiosity to know the exact number of the statues and how many foot they cast up the water. We saw the King's pictures in the magnificent house of the Duc D'Antin,[343] who has the care of preserving them till his majesty is of age. There is not many, but of the best hands. I looked with great pleasure on the archangel of Raphael, where the sentiments of superior beings are as well expressed as in Milton.[344] You won't forgive me if I say nothing of the Tuilleries, much finer than our Mall, and the Cour[345] more agreeable than our Hyde Park, the high trees giving shade in the hottest season. At the Louvre I had the opportunity of seeing the King, accompanied by the Duke Regent. He is tall and well shaped, but has not the air of holding the crown so many years as his grandfather.[346] And now I am speaking of the court, I must say I saw nothing in France that delighted me so much as to see an Englishman (at least a Briton) absolute at Paris. I mean Mr Law,[347] who treats their dukes and peers extremely *de haut en bas*, and is treated by them with the utmost submission and respect. Poor souls! This reflection on their abject slavery puts me in mind of the Place des Victoires,[348] but I will not take up your time and my own with such descriptions, which are too numerous. In general I think Paris has the advantage of London in the neat pavement of the streets, and the regular lighting of them at nights, the proportion of the streets, the houses being all built of stone, and most of those belonging to people of quality beautified by gardens; but we certainly may boast of a town very near twice as large, and when I have said that, I know nothing else we surpass it in. I shall not continue here long. If you have anything to command me during my short stay write soon, and I shall take pleasure in obeying you.

LETTER LVII

To the Abbé Conti,   *Dover, 31 October 1718*

I am willing to take your word for it that I shall really oblige you
by letting you know as soon as possible my safe passage over the
water. I arrived this morning at Dover after being tossed a
whole night in the packet boat in so violent a manner that the
master, considering the weakness of his vessel, thought it prudent to remove the mail, and gave us notice of the danger. We
called a little fisher boat, which could hardly make up to us,
while all the people on board us were crying to heaven, and 'tis
hard to imagine oneself in a scene of greater horror than on such
an occasion; and yet, shall I own it to you, though I was not at
all willing to be drowned, I could not forbear being entertained
at the double distress of a fellow passenger? She was an English
lady that I had met at Calais, who desired me to let her go over
with me in my cabin. She had bought a fine point head[349] which
she was contriving to conceal from the custom house officers.
When the wind grew high and our little vessel cracked, she fell
very heartily to her payers and thought wholly of her soul.
When it seemed to abate she returned to the worldly care of her
headdress, and addressed herself to me. 'Dear madam, will you
take care of this point? If it should be lost...ah Lord! We shall
all be lost! Lord have mercy on my soul. Pray, madam, take
care of this headdress'. This easy transition from her soul to
her headdress, and the alternate agonies that both gave her,
made it hard to determine which she thought of greatest value.
But, however, the scene was not so diverting but I was glad to
get rid of it and be thrown into the little boat, though with
some hazard of breaking my neck. It brought me safe hither
and I cannot help looking with partial eyes on my native land.
That partiality was certainly given us by nature to prevent
rambling, the effect of an ambitious thirst after knowledge

which we are not formed to enjoy. All we get by it is fruitless desire of mixing the different pleasures and conveniences which are given to different parts of the world and cannot meet in any one of them. After having read all that is to be found in the languages I am mistress of, and having decayed my sight by midnight studies, I envy the easy peace of mind of a ruddy milk maid who, undisturbed by doubt, hears the sermon with humility every Sunday, having not confused the sentiments of natural duty in her head by the vain enquiries of the schools, who may be more learned, yet after all must remain as ignorant. And, after having seen part of Asia and Africa and almost made the tour of Europe, I think the honest English squire more happy who verily believes the Greek wines less delicious than March beer,[350] that the African fruits have not so fine a flavour as golden pippins,[351] and the becáfiguas[352] of Italy are not so well tasted as a rump of beef, and that, in short, there is no perfect enjoyment of this life out of Old England. I pray God I may think so for the rest of my life, and since I must be contented with our scanty allowance of daylight, that I may forget the enlivening sun of Constantinople.

LETTER LVIII

To Alexander Pope,   *Dover, 1 November 1718*

I have this minute received a letter of yours sent me from Paris. I believe and hope I shall very soon see both you and Mr Congreve, but as I am here in an inn where we stay to regulate our march to London, bag and baggage, I shall employ some of my leisure time in answering that part of yours that seems to require an answer.

I must applaud your good nature in supposing that your pastoral lovers (vulgarly called haymakers) would have lived in everlasting joy and harmony if the lightening had not interrupted their scheme of happiness.[353] I see no reason to imagine

that John Hughs and Sarah Drew were either wiser or more
virtuous than their neighbours. That a well set man of twenty-
five should have a fancy to marry a brown woman of eighteen is
nothing marvellous, and I cannot help thinking that had they
married, their lives would have passed in the common tract with
their fellow parishioners. His endeavouring to shield her from
the storm was a natural action and what he would have certainly
done for his horse if he had been in the same situation. Neither
am I of opinion that their sudden death was a reward to their
mutual virtue. You know the Jews were reproved for thinking a
village destroyed by fire more wicked than those that had
escaped the thunder. Time and chance happen to all men. Since
you desire me to try my skill in an epitaph, I think the following
lines perhaps more just, though not so poetical as yours:

> Here lies John Hughs and Sarah Drew;
> Perhaps you'll say, what's that to you?
> Believe me, friend, much may be said
> On this poor couple that are dead.
> On Sunday next they should have marr'd,
> But see how oddly things are carr'd.
> On Thursday last it rained and lightened;
> These tender lovers sadly frightened
> Sheltered beneath the cocking hay
> In hopes to pass the storm away.
> But bold thunder found them out
> (Commissioned for that end no doubt)
> And seizing on their trembling breath,
> Consign'd them to the shades of death.
> Who knows if 'twas not kindly done?
> For had they seen the next year's sun
> A beaten wife and cuckold swain
> had jointly curs'd the marriage chain.
> Now they are happy in their doom
> For Pope has wrote upon their tomb.

I confess these sentiments are not altogether so heroic as
yours, but I hope you will forgive them in favour of the two last
lines. You see how much I esteem the honour you have done

them, though I am not very impatient to have the same and had rather continue to be your stupid living humble servant than be celebrated by all the pens in Europe.

I would write to Mr Congreve but suppose you will read this to him if he enquires after me.

NOTES

In these notes *Wharncliffe* refers to the first edition of *The Letters and Works of Lady Mary Wortley Montagu*, by Lord Wharncliffe, 3 Vols. London, 1837. By the W. Moy Thomas's third edition of Wharncliffe, 2 Vols. London, 1861, a number of the ascriptions had been removed. Halsband *Letters* are R. Halsband *The Complete Letters of Lady Mary Wortley Montagu*, 3 Vols. Oxford, 1965-7.

[1] The Turkish Embassy Letters derive from two principal sources – the letters that Lady Mary wrote to her friends and relations in England while she was abroad; and a journal which she kept during her travels in 1716. Halsband identified only two passages as deriving from the journal which was destroyed by Lady Mary's daughter See Halsband, *Letters.* 1: XV.

[2] Frances Pierrepont (1690–1761) younger sister of Lady Mary who married John Erskine, Earl of Mar. Like her sister she spent many years abroad, residing chiefly in Paris.

[3] Carriages.

[4] Holland was often the first country English visitors went to on the Grand Tour in the eighteenth century. Most of them had a favourable impression of it but for a mockingly critical view, see William Beckford's *Dreams, Waking Thoughts & Incidents* (1777) in *Vathek & Other Stories* ed. Malcolm Jack, (London, Pickering & Chatto, 1993).

[5] Jane Smith (d.1730) Childhood friend of Lady Mary who became a maid of honour to the Princess of Wales.

[6] Central square in the Hague.

[7] Sarah Chiswell (d.1726). Another childhood friend whom Lady Mary failed to persuade to accompany her to Constantinople. She died of smallpox, a disease that also afflicted Lady Mary.

[8] River Maas.

[9] Ben Jonson's comedy, *Bartholomew Fair* was published in 1631, already having been performed as early as 1614. The fair is set in Smithfield and the play ends with a puppet performance.

[10] Either Sarah Chiswell's brother or perhaps her brother-in-law, Humphrey Perkins (c.1646–c.1717) Rector of Holme Pierrepont, near Thoresby from 1680–1717.

[11] Wharncliffe identifies the addressee as Lady Rich i.e. Elisabeth Griffin, Lady Rich (1692–1773) wife of Sir Robert Rich, Lady-in-Waiting to Queen Caroline. See *Wharncliffe* I:7 but Halsband leaves the letter unaddressed. *Letters* 1:252.

[12] Cases with glass sides so that the remains of saints and holy men could be seen by the faithful.

[13] According to legend, the British Princess Ursula went to Rome on a pilgrimage with 11,000 virgins in the ninth century. On their way home, they were martyred by Huns at Cologne for refusing to renounce their Christian faith.

[14] Plate on which toilet accessories are laid out.

[15] St Christopher was a legendary figure whose original task of transporting people across a river led to his adoption as the patron saint of travellers.

[16] Ornamental bowl.

[17] Elizabeth Felton (1676–1741) second wife of John Hervey, 1st Earl of Bristol, a close friend of Lady Mary. The Countess of Bristol, who was notoriously addicted to card playing, served as a Lady of the Bedchamber to the Queen. Also see below, n.251.

[18] Laws designed to regulate personal expenditure; in this case by prescribing styles of dress for persons of different status. A contemporary of Lady Mary, Bernard Mandeville, attacked sumptuary laws in *The Fable of the Bees* (1714 & 1728), beginning a debate about luxury and its moral effects that continued throughout the century.

[19] François de Salignac de la Mothe Fénelon (1651–1715) French cleric and eminent man of letters who wrote widely on religious, educational and political themes.

[20] Anne Thistlethwayte (b.1669) a friend of Lady Mary who lived near West Dean in Wiltshire.

[21] Seat of the German Imperial Diet.

[22] Rudolf Johann Freherron Wrisberg, envoy to St James's, 1714–16.

[23] Mrs Blackacre is the litigious widow in William Wycherley's play, *The Plain Dealer* (1677). In Act III she scorns the idea that a dispute should be settled by a Master in Chancery.

[24] Wortley had been sent to Vienna in 1716 to offer British mediation in the war between Austria and Turkey. He arrived a month after Prince Eugene, leading the Imperial army, had routed the Turks at Peterwardein.

[25] The second siege of Vienna by the Turks was in 1683.

[26] Charles VI (1685–1740) Holy Roman Emperor.

[27] Friederich Karl, Count von Schönborn (1674–1746) Viennese statesman and society figure.

[28] Imperial complex of palaces and houses of courtiers.

[29] Elisabeth Christine (1691–1750) daughter of Ludwig Rudolf, Duke of Brunswick-Wolfenbüttel. She married Charles VI in 1708.

[30] Alexander Pope (1688–1744) poet, satirist, translator of Homer, met Lady Mary in 1715 and was captivated by her charm and learning. While she was abroad, they engaged in a correspondence which from his side was in the epistolatory gallant style, with touches of humour. Their emotional relationship later came to grief and ungallantly, Pope described Lady Mary as a

'pox'd Sappho' in his 'Imitations of Horace' *Poetical Works* ed. H. Davis (Oxford, 1966), p.343.

[31] Angelica Vincitrice di Alcina, an opera of Johann Josef Fux (1660–1741) Court Composer and Cappellmeister who was a prolific composer of masses and operas.

[32] Titus Maccus Plautus (254–184 BC) Roman comic playwright whose theme of Amphitryon was taken up by Molière in 1688 and John Dryden in 1690.

[33] Trickster.

[34] Jeremy Collier (1650–1726) a non-juring bishop who attacked the restoration playwrights for lax morality in his *Short View of the Immorality and Profaneness of the English Stage* (1698).

[35] Ornamental collar covering the throat and shoulders.

[36] Hairpins.

[37] In Greek mythology the three graces, daughters of Zeus, represented beauty or loveliness. They were often shown in attendance upon other, more important goddesses.

[38] The Medici were Florentine bankers and great patrons of the arts from the fifteenth century.

[39] Card game.

[40] Joseph I (1678–1711) Holy Roman Emperor. His wife, now the dowager, was Wilhelmine Amalie (1673–1742) whom he married in 1699.

[41] Eleonore Magdelene (1655–1720), the Dowager Empress, a severe, ascetic character.

[42] Shoulder cape with hanging ends.

[43] Publius Vergilius Maro (70–19 BC) *Aeneid*, V. 490–546. trans. James Rhoades (Oxford, 1921) p.112 ff.

[44] Mrs Henrietta Howard (c.1688–1763) later Countess of Suffolk. Onetime mistress of the Prince of Wales, she was a friend and neighbour of Pope at Twickenham. Henrietta Cavendish Holles (1694–1755) Countess of Oxford and childhood friend of Lady Mary, was the daughter of the Duke of Newcastle.

[45] Cordial or liquor, flavoured with almonds, apricot peach of cherry kernels.

[46] Making things known.

[47] Wharncliffe identifies the addressee as Mrs Thistlethwaite (see above, n.20) see *Wharncliffe* 1:296 but this is disputed by Halsband, see *Letters*, 1:272 n.3.and 1:273 n.1.

[48] Dorothea Elisabeth (1645–1725) daughter of the Duke of Holstein and wife of Count von Rabutin.

[49] Card games.

[50] Michael Johann III (1679–1722) Count von Althann, Privy councillor and Grand Master of the Horse.

[51] St Laurence was popular because his intercession is believed to have

resulted in Christian victory at the battle of Lechfeld against the Magyars in 955.

[52] A son of Franz Wilhelm (1672–1734) Count von Salm.

[53] Johann Adam, Prince von Liechtenstein (1656–1712), Austrian Field Marshal.

[54] Antonio Allegri known as Corregio (c.1494–1534) Italian painter; Tiziano Vecelli (c.1487–1576) leading Venetian painter of the sixteenth century.

[55] Black iron that has been magnetized.

[56] A story in the *Tatler*, No. 18 (21 May, 1709).

[57] Wortley had been ordered to travel to Hanover to attend upon the King for instructions.

[58] Sir Richard Vernon (1678–1725); Madame de Lorme, wife of Charles Pierre de Lorme, the representative of Saxony in London from 1710 to 1714.

[59] Simperers.

[60] Anna Constanze von Brockdorf (1680–1765) who became Countess of Cosel in 1706.

[61] Triangular fortification between bastions.

[62] Wharncliffe identifies the addressee as the Countess of Mar see *Wharncliffe* 1:312 but this is disputed by Halsband, *Letters* 1: 285 n.1.

[63] August Wilhelm (1662–1731) Duke of Brunswick-Wolfenbüttel.

[64] King George I who reigned from 1714 to 1727.

[65] Local beer.

[66] Frederick Louis (1707–51), eldest son of the Prince of Wales.

[67] A large entourage followed the King when he returned to Hanover.

[68] Dom Luis da Cunha (1662–1740), Portuguese Ambassador in London 1697–1710 and 1715–18.

[69] Mrs Salmon's waxwork exhibition in Fleet Street.

[70] Sledges.

[71] The infant archduke, Leopold, who died aged seven months on 4 November, 1716.

[72] Christine Luise (1671–1747).

[73] Card game.

[74] The opera house was built in 1688–9 by Ernst August I (1629–98). It was located within the royal palace.

[75] A baroque manor built around 1660.

[76] Pineapples. These fruit were still a rarity. A few years later Mandeville mentions the first pineapple being cultivated in England by Sir Matthew Decker at his house in Richmond. See B. Mandeville, *The Fable of the Bees* ed. F.B. Kaye (Oxford, 1924) 2:195.

[77] Wharncliffe claims that this letter was addressed to Lady Rich. See *Wharncliffe* 1:320 but it is unascribed by Halsband, *Letters* 1:291. Also see above, n.11.

[78] Marie Catherine Le Jumel de Barneville, comtesse d'Aulnoy (c.1650–1705), author of fairy stories and travel writing about Spain.

[79] Frederick IV (1671–1730).

[80] Prince Eugene of Savoy (1663–1736), Austrian general and victor of the battle of Peterwardein. See above n. 24.

[81] According to Greek mythology, the Delphic Oracle ordered Hercules to sell himself as a slave to Omphale, Queen of Lydia to expiate the murder of Iphitus.

[82] Dom Manuel of Bragança (1697–1736) Portuguese prince who fought at the battle of Peterwardein against the order of his brother, Joao V, King of Portugal.

[83] Nicholas Rowe (1674–1718) *Tamerlane* (1702) Act I 1. l.265.

[84] Lady Rich. See previous Letter, number XXI.

[85] Cannibals.

[86] A gap in fortifications.

[87] The Montagus were escorted by a considerable contigent of Imperial troops.

[88] William Congreve (1670–1729), Restoration playwright, friend of Lady Mary and of Pope. He was one of the writers attacked by Collier, see above, n. 34.

[89] Petrovaradin in Serbia. Halsband suggests that this letter may be from Lady Mary's journal.

[90] Ladislaus, Count Nádasdy (d.1730) Bishop of Banad. Temeswar is now Timisoara in Romania.

[91] Among the illustrious Nádasky family was the patriot Count Ferencz Nadasky, who tried to gain Hungary independence but was executed for treason by the Imperial army.

[92] Kodja Sinan Pasha (d.1596) and Murad III (1546–95), Ottoman Emperor from 1574–95.

[93] Adolf Count von Schwarzenberg (1547–1600); Nikolaus II, Count Palffy (1552–1600).

[94] Turkish soldiers disguised as peasants dragged carts of hay, in which other soldiers were hidden, into the town.

[95] Leopold I acted against Protestants following a conspiracy of Hungarian nobles who had tried to seize independence.

[96] Maximilian Ludwig Regal (d.1717) Count von Kranichsfeld; Eleonore Christiana, Countess von Metternich.

[97] Buda is on the West bank of the Danube; its inhabitants were Serbs.

[98] Suleiman (1494–1566), most famous of the Ottoman emperors whose rule was from 1520–66. He was a military strategist, lawgiver, builder and patron of the arts.

[99] Ferdinand I (1503–64) King of Bohemia and Hungary from 1526; Holy Roman Emperor from 1558; John I Zapolya (1487–1540), King of Hungary;

Joachim II (1505–71), Elector of Brandenburg; Hermann Christof, Count von Russworn (1565–1605); Charles IV, Duke of Lorraine (1643–90); Abdul al-Rahman Pasha.

[100] Mehmed IV (1642–92) Ottoman Emperor from 1648–87.

[101] Mohacs, on the Danube, is the site of two major battles which marked the beginning and end of Turkish dominion in Hungary. The first was on 29 August, 1526 when Suleiman the Magnificent defeated the Hungarian King, Louis II. The second was on 12 August, 1687, when the Austrians under Charles of Lorraine decisively defeated the Turks.

[102] Wildfowl.

[103] Julius Franz, Count Veterani (1666–1736).

[104] Heroes in the conflicts between the Holy Roman Emperor and the Turks who retained control of a part of Hungary.

[105] Sir Paul Rycaut's *History of the Turks* (1700).

[106] Greek Orthodox Church from which the Serbian Church gained independence in 1557.

[107] By the Treaty of Karlowitz, 1699, the Austrians gained control of Peterwardein from the Turks.

[108] Thomas Hobbes, *Leviathan*, Chapter XIII. ed. W.G. Pogson Smith (Oxford, 1909) pp. 94–8. Hobbes's state of nature was designed to show how unpleasant life in a pre-civil condition would be. Admitting to being a Hobbist, even in this one matter, was daring of Lady Mary since Hobbes was associated with materialism and even atheism.

[109] The aga was the commander of the elite corps of Turkish troops, the janissaries, who had first been recruited by forced levy from Christian children.

[110] Belgrade was first captured by the Turks in 1521 and passed from Turkish to Austrian hands and back several times over the next two centuries.

[111] Ahmed III (1673–1736) Ottoman Emperor from 1703–20, famous for his love of tulips. See below n.143.

[112] Cadi a civil magistrate; mufti a lawyer expert in Muslim law.

[113] Ahmed Bey Effendi. Effendi was a term of respect given to a scholar, teacher or man of letters.

[114] Central office of state of Ottoman government.

[115] Halsband located a copy of François Pétis de la Croix's *Les Mille et un Jours, Contes Persanes* (1710–12) in Lady Mary's library. See *Letters* 1: 308 n.i. These tales may not, in fact, be oriental originals. In 1705 Antoine Galland had started to produce a French version of *Arabian Nights Entertainments* which greatly influenced the vogue for oriental tales in France and in England throughout the eighteenth century.

[116] This letter is not part of the Embassy series. Frances Hewet was a friend of Lady Mary's to whom she wrote in her single days. Some of these earlier letters are collected in *Wharncliffe* 3: 203–24. Also see Halsband *Letters*, 1:308 n.4.

Adrianpolis, modern Edirne in European Turkey was the location of the Seraglio, the Sultan's personal household although Constantinople was the capital of the Ottoman Empire.

[117] Wilhelmina Caroline of Ansbach, consort to King George II. She was Queen of England from 1727 to 1738 when she died.

[118] Now Lovdivin in Bulgaria.

[119] Wharncliffe identifies the addressee as Lady Rich see *Wharncliffe* 1:351 but the letter is unaddressed in Halsband, see *Letters* 1:312.

[120] Bathing house.

[121] Eve. See John Milton *Paradise Lost* IV l.492. *The Poetical Works of John Milton*, ed. H. Darbishire, 2 Vols. (Oxford, 1952) 1:85.

[122] Guido Reni (1575–1642) Bolognese painter.

[123] Charles Jervas (?1675–1739) Irish portrait painter, disciple of Kneller; friend of Pope and well known to literary circles.

[124] Justinian (AD 527–65) Roman Emperor at Constantinople. He reorganised Roman Law, leaving an important Code summarising his system. He also had the great church of St Sophia built at Constantinople.

[125] Antonio Conti (1677–1749) Italian dramatist, savant and man of letters. He translated, among other things, Pope's poetry. He met Lady Mary in England in 1715.

[126] French Huguenot (protestant) refugees fled to England after the Revocation of the Edict of Nantes in 1685 which once again led to persecution of non-Catholics. They settled in Soho where Greek Street is located.

[127] Virgil *Eclogue* I l 8 trans James Rhoades, (Oxford 1921) p.391.

[128] Mustafa II Ottoman Emperor from 1695 until 1703 when he was deposed.

[129] Samuel Clarke (1675–1729) Metaphysician and moralist who defended a rational theology. His work, *A Discourse of Natural Religion*, based on the Boyle lectures of 1704, was widely read.

[130] William Whiston (1667–1752) disciple of Newton and his successor in the Lucasian chair of Mathematics at Cambridge. He was a friend of Samuel Clarke. See above n. 129.

[131] Al-Zaidiya, Kadariya and Djabariya, sects of Islam.

[132] See above, n.105. Rycaut had served in the British legation at Constantinople in the 1660s. He also wrote *The Present State of the Ottoman Empire* (1668).

[133] Sect of Christians who incorporated non-Christain elements into their interpretation of St Paul.

[134] Albania.

[135] Marcos Ulpius Trajanus (AD 53–117) Roman Emperor of Spanish origin who extended the Empire to the Persian Gulf.

[136] Baldwin I (d.1205) Count of Flanders, Emperor of Constantinople, 1204.

[137] Caftan is a long under-tunic tied at the waist; manteau a loose cape.

[138] Ali Pasha (c.1667–1716), Grand Vizier from 1713–16. Princess Fatima (1704–33), his wife, later married Ibrahim Pasha (c.1666–1730) who succeeded Ali Pasha as Grand Vizier, a post he held until his death.

[139] The Sultan's friend or adviser.

[140] Halsband finds the verse repeated in a poem about Robert Walpole written by Lady Mary in the 1730s. See *Letters* 1:322 n.1.

[141] The doctrine of passive obedience was espoused by Tory monarchists in defence of the Crown. It derived from the ancient theory of the divine right of Kings which made obedience to the monarch absolute and not dependent on consent. Sir Robert Filmer made a strong defence of the principle in *Patriarcha*, published in 1680.

[142] Madeleine-Françoise de Gontaut-Biron (1698–1739). Her husband, Jean Louis d'Usson Marquis of Bonac (1672–1738) had been appointed Ambassador in 1716 and they arrived in Adrianople early in 1717.

[143] The reign of Ahmed III, from 1703–20 was known as the 'Age of Tulips'. See above n. 111.

[144] Called.

[145] Harlequin, a character in Aphra Behn's *The Emperor of the Moon* (1687), reported that morality applied on the moon as on earth.

[146] Council or ministry of Sultan.

[147] River Maritza in Northern Greece.

[148] In Greek mythology, the Maenads (mad women) were votaries of Dionysius who tore Orpheus to pieces. His severed head, floating down the river, was still heard singing until it reached Lesbos where it was buried.

[149] 'Then too, even then, what time the Hebrus stream,
Oeagrian Hebrus, down mid-current rolled,
Rent from the marble neck, his drifting head,
The death-chilled tongue found yet a voice to cry
"Eurydice! ah! poor Eurydice!"
With parting breath he called her, and the banks
From the broad stream caught up "Eurydice!"'.
Virgil *Georgics* IV 521–8 trans. J Rhoades (Oxford 1921) p.385 ff.

[150] Turtle doves.

[151] Reed instrument or pipe of ancient Romans.

[152] Joseph Addison (1672–1719), classical scholar, essayist, who travelled on the Continent between 1699–1703. His contributions, with Richard Steele, to the *Tatler* and *Spectator* secured his place in English letters.

[153] (fl. c. 270 BC) His poems, the *Idylls* celebrate pastoral life.

[154] Pope's translation of Homer's *Iliad* first appeared in 1715, the second volume was published in 1716 and it was completed in 1720.

[155] Refined, advanced.

[156] In Greek mythology, Andromache was the wife of Hector and in the Illiad represents the true wife and mother.

[157] In Greek mythology Helen was the daughter of Zeus. She was reputed to

be the most beautiful woman in the world and was married to Menelaus, the younger brother of Agamemnon.

[158] Military chiefs or generals.

[159] In Greek mythology, Priam was King of Troy, slain when the city fell to the Greeks.

[160] In Greek mythology, Erymanthus was the name of a mountain and river in Arcadia which Lady Mary has changed to the Eurotas, now Iri in Laconia.

[161] Book of the Old Testament.

[162] See above, n. 111 & n.143.

[163] Boileau-Despréaux, Nicholas (1636–1711), writer and critic who founded modern French literary criticism. His *Art Poétique* (1674) was particularly influential.

[164] In Persian and Turkish poetry, the nightingale sings of his unrequited love for the rose.

[165] Fellow.

[166] Wife of Arnand Khalit Pasha (1655–1733), an Albanian, who had been in office since August 1716.

[167] See above, n. 113.

[168] Strongly flavoured.

[169] Sprinkled.

[170] Apelles (fl. 4th century BC) Court painter to Philip and Alexander of Macedon, reckoned to be one of the finest of Greek painters though none of his work survives.

[171] Primitive musical instruments.

[172] Anastasia Robinson (d.1755) a well-known London singer.

[173] Saucers.

[174] Publius Aelius Hadrianus, Roman Emperor (AD 117–138) of Spanish descent. He was a Hellenist, codifier of laws and builder who developed Adrianople (now Edirne) from its modest origins.

[175] Mehmed IV (1642–93) Ottoman Emperor from 1648–87; Mustafa II (1664–1703) Ottoman Emperor from 1695 until his death.

[176] Ali Pasha See above n.138

[177] There were three grades of Pasha who were entitled to display different numbers of horsetails outside their tents.

[178] The Jacobite cause, much associated with the Tories, was dedicated to restoring the Stuarts to the throne. There were numerous attempts to overthrow the Hanoverian dynasty after 1714 and on the occasion mentioned troops were camped in Hyde Park.

[179] Mosque of Selimiye Camiil (Selim II) is reckoned a masterpiece of Ottoman art. It was built between 1569–75 by the architect Sinan and dominates the city as Lady Mary observes.

[180] Iznik ceramics.

[181] Officiating priests of Islam.

[182] Members of an austere sect known for devotional practices which include trance enduced states and dancing of a frenzied kind.

[183] Young Prince Suleiman. The other two sons of Mustafa became Mahmud I (1696–1754), Ottoman Emperor from 1730–54 and Osman III (1699–1757), Ottoman Emperor from 1754–57. There was a third son, Hassan (1699–1733) who is not mentioned by Lady Mary.

[184] A four wheeled carriage first used in Berlin in the late seventeenth century.

[185] Turkish cavalrymen.

[186] Couplets.

[187] Jean Dumont *Nouveau Voyage au Levant* (1694) translated into English in 1696.

[188] In fact matrimony does not affect the spiritual fate of Muslim women; a widow may remarry after four months and ten nights. See Halsband, *Letters* 1: 364 n.1

[189] In Greek mythology, the son of Zeus who obtained the head of Medusa without himself being petrified, then used it to defeat rivals for Andromache.

[190] Athena, daughter of Zeus who emerged full-blown from his head. Protectress of Athens and patroness of the urban arts and crafts.

[191] Kind of onyx used as a gemstone.

[192] St Augustine of Hippo (345–430) leading Catholic theologian, philosopher and prolific writer. His work, particularly his *City of God*, has remained influential until modern times.

[193] Charles XII (1682–1718).

[194] Castle on S.E. side of Constantinople.

[195] Village outside Constantinople used as a retreat from summer heat and epidemics.

[196] In Greek mythology, the place where those favoured by the Gods enjoy a blissful existence after death.

[197] 'Their pangs even death removes not' Virgil, *Aeneid* vi 443. trans. J. Rhoades (Oxford, 1921) p.138.

[198] In Latin poets, a river in Hades whose water is drunk by souls about to be reincarnated so that they might forget their previous existences. Virgil describes Aeneas witnessing such a scene. *Aeneid* VI 703ff. trans. J. Rhoades (Oxford, 1921) p.146ff.

[199] At St James's Palace.

[200] Elisabeth Lawrence (d.1725) mother of Lady Rich.

[201] Mary Berkeley (1671–1741) whose home was a favourite rendez-vous for Society gossips.

[202] Wharncliffe identifies the addressee as Lady Rich see *Wharncliffe* 2:11 but the letter is unaddressed in Halsband, see *Letters*, 1: 367.

[203] See above, n.187.

[204] Healing ointment.

[205] A pigeon is said to have taught Mohammed to pick corn out of his ear; thought to be whisperings of the Holy Ghost.

[206] A daughter was born to Lady Mary two weeks later, on January 19th.

[207] Order of St John of Jerusalem founded during the First Crusade.

[208] Madeleine Françoise d'Usson Bonnac (1698–1739) who became a close friend of Lady Mary and accompanied her on a visit to a harem.

[209] Small boat.

[210] This letter is not in the Turkish Embassy series. It was written in French and the translation used was made by Halsband, *Letters* 1:454–7.

[211] John Toland (1670–1722) Irish freethinker whose *Christianity Not Mysterious* (1696) sparked off the deist controversy.

[212] Inhabitants of Nova Zemblya, islands stretching from the north coast of Russia into the Arctic Ocean.

[213] Lady Mar was in France in 1717. Her husband, along with other Tory politicians, was implicated in the Jacobite plots after 1714. See above, n.178

[214] Hafise (b.1683).

[215] Mustafa II was deposed in 1703.

[216] Stab. Poinard is a dagger.

[217] Ebubekir Effendi (d. 1723) Minister for Foreign Affairs.

[218] Boudoir where visitors could be received.

[219] Ornate court wear.

[220] Headdress.

[221] Sarah Jennings (1660–1744) wife of John Churchill, Duke of Marlborough and for a time the favourite of Queen Anne.

[222] Thomas Pitt (1653–1726) owner of a large diamond.

[223] Thin silk gauze.

[224] Saucers.

[225] The reference is to an incident, recorded by Rycaut, in which the the Grand Signor threw his handkerchief to one of the women in the Seraglio as a sign that she should come to his bed. P. Rycaut, *Present State of the Ottoman Empire* (1668) p. 39.

[226] Full length silk gown.

[227] See above n.115.

[228] Polish fortress taken by Mehmed IV in 1672.

[229] Wharncliffe identifies the addressee as Lady Rich see *Wharncliffe* II:30 but the letter is unaddressed in Halsband, see *Letters* 1:387.

[230] The ship Smyrnote arrived at Smyrna (modern Ismir) in February, 1718, reaching Constantinople in mid-March.

[231] For a translation of the Turkish, See Halsband *Letters* 1:464–5.

[232] Wortley was at Adrianople taking his leave of the Court as he had been recalled.

[233] Lady Mary had lent William Fielding, her uncle, £1550.

[234] Catharina de Bourg, wife of Count Jacob Colyer (1657–1725), the Dutch ambassador to Turkey.

[235] Edward Wortley Montagu had been vaccinated against smallpox on 18 March.

[236] Wortley's pro-Turkish sympathies, which it was thought would compromise his position as a negotiator, had led to his recall. The Levant Company was compensated for the loss of the Ambassador of its choice.

[237] Wortley was granted £500 to cover his return expenses, the same sum that had been granted to his predecessor, Sir Robert Sutton, who was Ambassador from 1701–16.

[238] John Lethieullier (1667–1737), Turkey merchant.

[239] Sir John Williams (d.1743) prominent figure in the Turkey trade.

[240] Edward Barker (d.1747) treasurer of the Levant Company in Constantinople.

[241] French Christians.

[242] Small cups.

[243] St Sophia, the centre of religious life in Constantinople, was begun by Constantine and consecrated in 360, the penultimate year of his son's reign. A new church was built by Justinian in 537. In 1453 St Sophia's was converted into a mosque by Mohammed II after his capture of the city. Mausoleums of Ottoman Sultans are in the church but Constantine is represented only by a mosaic.

[244] The Suleymaniye Mosque was built between 1550–57 by Sinan, architect of the mosque in Adrianople (see above n.179) and is regarded as the finest monument of Muslim art in the city.

[245] Hadice Turhan (1627–82), Valide Sultan (princess–mother) favourite of Ibrahim (1615–48), Ottoman Emperor from 1640–48.

[246] Course or circus for horse racing and chariot racing.

[247] The inscription is concluded with two further lines:
 'Ter denis sic victus ego domitusque diebus
 Iudice sub Proclo superas elatus ad auras'.
The whole has been translated as: 'Of lords serene a stubborn subject once, bidden to bear the palm to tyrants also that have met their doom – all yields to Theodosius and his undying issue – so conquered I in thrice ten days and tamed, was under Proclus' judgeship raised to the skies above'. Halsband *Letters* I: 400 n.3.

[248] The Blue Mosque, built between 1609 and 1616 for Sultan Ahmed I, Ottoman Emperor from 1603–17.

[249] The New Exchange took over business from the Royal Exchange after the fire of 1666.

[250] Arcadian column, copied after Trajan's column in Rome, came down in 1695.

[251] John Hervey (1665–1751) Vice-Chamberlain to Queen Charlotte, courtier, wit and author of *Memoirs of the Reign of George II* (published in 1848) was

a close friend of Lady Mary who joined the battle against Pope. See above, n. 17.

[252] This letter was first written in French, addressed to Madame de Bonnac and published without Lady Mary's permission. Translated by Halsband, *Letters* 1:458.

[253] Wharncliffe identifies the addressee as the Countess of Bristol, see *Wharncliffe* II:44 whereas Halsband leaves the letter unaddressed and guesses at the date. See *Letters* 1:405.

[254] Double veil concealing the face which Muslim ladies wore in public.

[255] Richard Knolles (1550–1610) *The History of the Turks* (1603); P. Rycaut *The History of the Turks* (1700) was a continuation of it.

[256] A. Hill *A Full and Just Account of the Present State of the Ottoman Empire* (1709).

[257] Public baths.

[258] See above, n.157. An Epithalamium is a celebration of nuptials.

[259] Naples was part of the Spanish Empire from 1522.

[260] According to Roman legend, she killed herself after being raped by Sextus while her husband, Tarquinius Collatinus, was away.

[261] Ibrahim Pasha, first admiral until 1718 when he was succeeded by Suleiman Koca.

[262] Gregory (240–332) converted the Armenian King, Tiridates.

[263] Whiston supported the Arian doctrine that denied that Christ's body was the same body as God's. Also see above n. 130.

[264] P. Rycaut *Present State of the Greek and Armenian Churches* (1679) p.433.

[265] Cap.

[266] Lady Mary's allusion to human frailty is very much in the tradition of seventeenth- and eighteenth-century literary psychology where man was represented as a creature of passions, one of which, the 'darling' or 'predominant' was called the 'ruling passion'.

[267] A beglerbey was governor of a province, next in rank to the Grand Vizier.

[268] Giovanni Francesco Gemelli Careri (1651–1725) Neopolitan man of letters.

[269] Kadikoy in modern Turkey.

[270] Second couplet from J. Addison, *Letters from Italy* (1703).

[271] Orhan Gazi (1288–1369) Ottoman Emperor from 1324–60.

[272] St Agnes is patron saint of the Virgins, her feast day is 21 January.

[273] Hellespont separates European Turkey from Asia Minor, north of ancient Troy. According to Greek legend, Leander swam the Hellespont to be with his lover, Hero, but was drowned when the light that guided him was extinguished in the water.

During the Persian Wars in the 480s BC, the Persian Emperor Xerxes built a bridge of ships across it.

[274] Tragic figure in a play by Euripides (c.480–406 BC) about the events after the fall of Troy.

[275] A story first related by Diodorus Siculus (c.40 BC).

[276] The marble stone lay in the precincts of the Temple of Minerva. It was brought back to England by Wortley and is today set in a wall at the entrance of Trinity College, Cambridge.

[277] Traditional form of dress.

[278] George Sandys *A Relation of a Journey containing a description of the Turkish Empire* (1615).

[279] Homer *Iliad* XXXI trans. E. V. Rieu (London, 1950), p.234 ff.

[280] Jean de la Fontaine, Le Fleuve Scamandre (Contes et Nouvelles) (1664).

[281] Strabo Geography VI 74–5 trans. Loeb Library.

[282] In the Homeric legend, a truce was called during the Greek seige of Troy while Menelaus and Paris met in single combat to obtain the hand of Helen. Although Menelaus was the better fighter, the Goddess Aprodite protected Paris and restored him to Helen.

[283] In Miguel de Cervantes Saavedra's *Don Quijote* (1605), Don Quijote, the hero, spends an hour in the cave at Montesinos in a visionary trance.

[284] Ruins at Alexandria Troas.

[285] Flavius Valerius Constantinus, Roman Emperor (285–337), founder of Constantinople.

[286] Gaius Julius Caesar Octavianus (63 BC–14 AD), known as Augustus, he was the first Roman Emperor.

[287] In Greek mythology, Daphne was beloved by Apollo. To escape his attentions, she was transformed into a laurel tree but Apollo still loved her and gave the laurel never-fading leaves.

[288] Aegean island which was the centre of literature, whose patron was Apollo. Sappho was a poetess; Pittacus democratic leader; Alcaeus lyric poet; Theophrastus, poet and philosopher and Arion composer of Corinthian chorus.

[289] Lesbos whose capital was Mytilene finally fell to the Turks in 1462.

[290] John V (1293–1383) a member of the Cantacuzene family, ruled the Eastern Roman Empire during its decline.

[291] Virgil *Eclogues* V 75 trans. James Rhoades (Oxford, 1921) p.55.

[292] The Parthenon was damaged during the siege of Athens by the Venetians in 1687.

[293] Mycenae and Corinth, cities in Argolis.

[294] Virgil *Aeneid* iii. l.106 trans. James Rhoades (Oxford, 1921) p.55.

[295] In Greek mythology the place where the Cretan minatour, half-beast, half-man, fed on Athenian youth until killed by Theseus.

[296] Crete was said to be the birthplace of Jupiter in Greek mythology. Quintus Caecilius Metellus Cretcus (fl.50 BC) Roman general who conquered Crete in 67 BC.

[297] Candia was besieged by the Turks from 1648–69.

[298] Ionian island off Asia Minor, claimed as Homer's birthplace.

[299] 'He seems hardly to have been born of human stock' Lucretius *de Rerum Natura* l: l. 733. ed. R. E. Latham (London, 1951) p.48. Empedocles was a Sicilian philosopher and scientist whom Lucretius greatly admired. He is said to have committed suicide by flinging himself into Mount Etna.

[300] According to Homeric lore, the sirens were sea nympths who lured passing vessels to the rocks.

[301] Ramon Perellos y Roccaful, Grand Master of the Order of St John 1697–1720.

[302] Richard Lawrence who had been consul from 1711.

[303] Prickly pear.

[304] Louis IX (1214–70).

[305] Phillip III (1245–85) King of France; Edward I (1293–1307) and Henry III (1207–72) Kings of England.

[306] Tunis was captured in 1534 by Barbarossa (Khair al-Din (c. 1483–1546) was taken in 1535 by Charles V and retaken in 1574 by Kodja Sinan Pasha. See above, n.92.

[307] Strabo *Geography* VIII 184–5 trans. Loeb Library.

[308] Frances Bathurst, wife of the British envoy to Genoa, Henry Davenant

[309] A fashionable suburb of Genoa.

[310] When the Turks sieged Constantinople, eventually taking it in 1453, the Genoese had supported them.

[311] Francesco Imperiale Lercaro (1628–1712), doge of Genoa, apologized to Louis XIV at Versailles.

[312] Andrea Doria (1466–1560), Genoese naval commander who expelled the French from Genoa in 1528 and re-established the Republic.

[313] Andrea Palladio (1508–80), one of the most important Italian architects and theorists of his time. He had a deep knowledge of Roman style and building, worked in the classical mode and was later imitated in England Inigo Jones (1573–1652).

[314] Sanzio Raphael (1483–1520); Paolo Veronese (1528–88); Tiziano Vecellio (1477–1576); Annibale Carracci (1560–1609) Michelangelo Buonarroti (1475–1564); Guido Reni (1575–1642); Antonio Allegri Corregio (1494–1534).

[315] Paintings by Guido Reni.

[316] The Shroud of Turin, supposed to be the sheet in which Christ's body was wound after the crucifixion.

[317] The Venaria was a hunting lodge built by Charles Emanuel II (1634–75); the Valentino a palace.

[318] Ann (1669–1766) who married Victor Amadeus II (1666–1732), Duke of Savoy and King of Sicily from 1713.

[319] Maria Anna (1690–1766), illegitimate daughter of Victor Amadeus II; granddaughter of Charles I.

[320] Sicily became part of Aragon in 1282.

[321] Charles Emmanuel III (1701–73).

[322] Willow twigs.

[323] St Justus (374–81), Bishop of Lyon.

[324] Tiberius Claudius Drusus Nero Germanicus (10 BC–AD 54), Roman Emperor from 41 AD; Lucius Septimus Severus (146–211), Roman Emperor from 193 and governor of the Gallic province whose capital was Lyon.

[325] An equestrian statue of Louis XIV (1638–1715) stood in the Place Louis le Grand.

[326] Place Bellecour, one of the largest town squares in Lyon.

[327] From Seneca *Apocolocyntosis*, trans in Halsband as:
'Hence, mighty Rhone, thy rapid torrents flow
And Arar, much in doubt which way to go'.
See *Letters* 1:437. A full text of the Latin inscriptions in this letter may be read in *Wharncliffe* 2: 84–7.

[328] Overwhelmed.

[329] Henry IV (1553–1610) first Bourbon King of France.

[330] Louis XIV (1638–1715).

[331] Coarseness of the harlequin.

[332] The Paris opera was housed in the Palais Royal. In London, the opera was in the Haymarket, designed by Vanburgh and completed in 1705. The Comédie Française was at St Germain des Près; the new theatre in Lincoln Inn Fields opened in 1714.

[333] Ann Oldfield (1683–1730) leading actress.

[334] Racine's play, *Bajazet* (1672).

[335] Black gloss.

[336] Marked as in ruddling of sheep to identify ownership.

[337] To whom Lady Mary had addressed a number of her letters.

[338] Georges de Scudery (1601–90), playwright.

[339] See above, n. 213.

[340] Germanus (c.634–733) resisted Pope Leo II's edict against the veneration of icons.

[341] Charles Le Brun (1619–90) French painter and decorator, disciple of Poussin.

[342] Lead statues depicting characters from Aesop's fables designed by Le Notre in 1673.

[343] Duc d'Antin had been superintendant of Works for the Crown since 1716.

[344] John Milton, *Paradise Lost* II 345–71. *The Poetical Works of John Milton*, ed. H. Darbishire, 2 Vols. (Oxford, 1953) 1:62.

[345] Cour de la Mayne, series of walkways running parallel with the Seine.

[346] Louis XV who succeeded to the French throne in 1715 was grandson of Louis XIV. Phillipe, Duc d'Orleans (1674–1729) acted as Regent.

[347] John Law (1671–1729) Scottish Controller General of French finance, organised the Mississippi scheme whereby Louisiana was handed over to a group of investors to establish a company on the lines of the English East India Company.

[348] Site of a statue of Louis XIV, surrounded by slaves.

[349] Lace cap.

[350] Strong bitter beer, brewed in March.

[351] Type of apple.

[352] Type of bird.

[353] Pope had sent Lady Mary a tale of the death of two country lovers struck by lightning.

APPENDIX

The original French version of the letter on p. 109 is reproduced here. The punctuation and spelling are MWM's own and have not been edited.

Je suis charmée de votre obligeante Lettre, Monsieur; et vous voyez par ce grand papier, que j'ay dessein de repondre exactement à toutes vos questions, du moins si mon François me le permet. Car comme c'est une langue que je ne sçai pas à fonds, je crains fort que je seray obligée de finir bientot, faute d'expressions. Souvenez vous donc, que j'ecris dans une langue qui m'est etrangere, et croyez bonnement que toutes les impertinences et les fadaizes, qui partiront de ma plume, ne viennent que de mon incapacité à pouvoir exprimer ce que je pense, mais nullement de stupidité ou d'une legereté naturelle.

Ces conditions ainsi faites et stipulées, je vous dirai d'abord que vous avez une idée juste de l'Alcoran, dont les prêtres Grecs (la plus grande canaille de l'univers) font des contes ridicules, qu'ils ont inventé à plaisir, pour decrier la Loy de Mahomet; pour la condamner, dis-je, sans aucun examen; car ils ne veulent pas seulement que le peuple la lise: craignant, que s'il començoit une fois à decouvrir ses defauts, il ne s'arretât pas là; mais qu'il pourroit bien encore faire usage de son discernement, à l'égard de leurs propres fictions et de leurs legendes. En effet, rien ne se ressemble mieux, que les fables des Grecs et celles des Mahometans. Ces derniers ont une multitude de Saints, aux tombeaux desquels il se fait des miracles, selon eux, tous les jours; et les relations de la vie de ces bienheureux Musulmans, ne sont gueres moins farcies d'extravagances, que les Romans spirituels des *Papas* Grecs.

Quant à votre seconde demande, je vous diray que c'est une chose certainement fausse, quoique communément crue parmi nous, que *Mahomet* exclut les femmes de toute participation à une vie future et bienheureuse. Il etoit trop galant homme et aimoit trop beau Sexe, pour le traiter d'une maniere si barbare. Au contraire, il promet un trèsbeau Paradis aux femmes Turques. Il dit, à la verité, que ce sera un Paradis separé de celuy de leurs Maris: mais je crois que la pluspart n'en seront pas moins contentes pour cela; et que le regret de cette separation, ne leur rendra pas ce Paradis moins agreable. Au reste, les vertus que *Mahomet* exige des femmes, pour leur procurer la jouïssance de la felicité future, c'est de ne pas vivre d'un maniere qui les rende inutiles sur la terre; mais de s'occuper, autant qu'il est possible, à faire des petits *Mussulmans*. Les Vierges que meurent Vierges, et les veuves qui ne se remarient point, mourant dans un peché damnable, sont exclues du Paradis. Car les femmes, dit-il, n'etant capables ni d'affaires d'Etat, ni d'essuier les fatigues de la Guerre, Dieu ne leur donne pas le soin de gouverner ni de reformer le monde; mais il les charge (employ qui n'est pas moins honorable) de multiplier la race humaine: et celles, qui, par malice ou par paresse, ne s'occupent point à porter ou à elever des enfans, ne remplissent pas le devoir de leur vocation, et sont rebelles aux ordres de Dieu. Voilà des Maximes terriblement contraires à vos Couvents. Que deviendront vos Saintes Catherines, Thereses, Claires, et toute la bande de vos pieuses *Vierges et Veuves*? lesquelles, etant jugées par ce Systeme de vertu, sont des infames, qui ont passé toute leur vie dans un libertinage effroyable.

Je ne sçai ce que vous penserez d'une doctrine si extraordinaire à notre egard: mais je puis vous assurer, Monsieur, que les Turcs no sont point si ignorants en matiere de Politique, de Philosophie, ou meme de Galanterie, que nous le croyons. Il est vrai, que la Discipline militaire, telle qu'elle est pratiquée presentement dans la Chretienté, ne les accommode point. Une longue Paix les a plongez dans une paresse universelle. Contents de leur etat, et accountumez à un luxe sans bornes, ils sont devenus grands ennemis de toute sorte de fatigues. Mais, en recompense, les Sciences fleurissent chez eux. Les *Effendis*, (ce mot veut dire les Sçavans) sont fort dignes de ce nom. Ils n'ont pas plus de foy pour l'Inspiration de *Mahomet*, que pour l'Infaillibilité du *Pape*. Ils font profession ouverte de *Deisme* entre eux, ou avec ceux en qui ils ont de la confiance; et ne parlent jamais de leur Loy, que comme d'une Institution politique, que les personnes sages doivent observer à present, quoiqu'introduite au commencement par des Politiques et des Enthousiastes.

Il me semble (si je m'en souviens bien) que je vous ay deja ecrit, que nous avons logé à Belgrade chez un grand Effendi, fort riche, homme d'esprit, de sçavoir, et d'une humeur fort agreable. Nous fumes environ un mois dans sa maison, et il mangeoit toujours avec nous, buvant du vin sans scrupule. Comme je le raillai un peu là-dessus, il me repondit en souriant, que toutes les creatures du monde ont été faites pour le plaisir de l'homme; et que Dieu n'auroit pas laissé croite la vigne, s'il y avoit du peché à en gouter le jus: mais que cependant la Loy qui en defendoit l'usage au vulgaire, etoit fort sage; parce que ces sortes de gens n'ont pas assex d'esprit, pour s'en servir avec moderation. Cet Effendi n'ignoroit pas les differens parits, qui regnenet chex nous: il paroissoit meme avoir quelque connoissance de nos disputes de Religion et de nos Ecrivains; et je fus surprise de luy entendre demander, entre autres choses, *comment se portoit Monsieur Toland*.

Mon papier, tout grand qu'il est, va finir. Pour ne pas aller plus loin que ses bornes, il faut que je saute des Religions aux *Tulipes*, dont vous me demandez des nouvelles. Leur Melange fait des Effets surprenants. Mais ce qu'on voit de plus surprenant, c'est l'experience dont vous parlez concernant les Animaux, et qu'on fait ici tous les jours. Les fauxbourgs de Pera, Jophana, et Galata, sont des collections d'Etrangers de touts les Pays de l'univers. Ils se sont si souvent entre-mariés, que cela forme des races les plus bizarres du monde. Il n'y a pas une seule famille de Natifs, qui se puisse vanter de n'estre point melée. On voit fort souvent une personne, sont le pere est né Grec, la mere Italienne, le grand-pere François, la grand'mere Armenienne, et les Ancêtres Anglois, Russiens, Asisatiques, etc.

Ce mêlange fait naitre des creatures plus extraordinaires, que vous ne sçauriez imaginer; aussi n'ay-je pu jamais douter, qu'il ne se trouvât des especes d'hommes toutes differentes: puisque les blancs, les noirs velus et à longue chevelure, les Chinois et les Tartares aux petits yeux, les Brasiliens sans barbe, et (pour n'en pas nommer d'avantage) les Nova-zembliens avec leur peau jaune et huileuse, ont des differences aussi specifiques sous le meme genre, que les levriers, les mâtins, les epagneuls, les *Bull-dogs*, ou la race de ma petite *Diane*, s'il m'est permis de me servir de cette comparaison. Or comme les differents melanges de ces derniers animaux produisent des Mêtifs: de meme les hommes ont aussi les leurs, divisés en des especes infinies. Nous en avons ici des preuves tous les jours, comme je vous l'ay dit auparavant. On remarque quelque fois dans le meme animal la fausseté Grecque, la meffiance Italienne, l'arrogance Espagnole, le caquet François; et tout d'un coup il luy vient des accès d'un serieux Anglois, tirant un peu sur l'hebeté, que plusieurs d'entre nous ont herité de la stupidité de nos ancetres Saxons.

Mais la famille qui me charme le plus, c'est celle qui provient de la bizarre conjonction d'un male Hollandois avec une femelle Grecque. Comme ce sont des Natures extremement opposées, c'est un plaisir de remarquer, comment les atomes differents se font une guerre perpetuelle dans les enfants, meme jusque dans leur figure externe. Ils ont les grands yeux noirs du païs, avec la chair grasse, blanche, poissoneuse de Hollande, et un air vif raïé de stupidité. Ils montrent en meme temps cet amour pour la depense, si universel parmi les Grecs, et un penchant vers la frugalité Hollandoise. Pour en donner un exemple, les filles se ruinent pour se parer la tête de Bijoux, mais elles n'ont pas neuves, leurs piés etant ordinairement dans un etat bien pietre. Pratique bein opposée à celle de nos Angloises, qui, pour faire voir la propreté de leur chaussure, et nullement pour montrer autre chose, sont si passionement amourachées de leurs *Hoop-pettycoats*. J'aurois bien d'autres particularités à vous communiquer, mais je suis au bout de mon Papier et de mon François. 2.

The original French of the translated letter which appears on p. 132 is reproduced here. The punctuation and spelling are MWM's own and have not been edited.

Je suis si aise de vous retrouver, Ma chere Madame, que je ne puis plus me plaindre de vous avoir perduë; et le plaisir que me donne cette lettre que je viens de recevoir aujourd'huy, me fait entierement oublier les inquietudes de dix mois passez.

L'Oisiveté est la mere des vices (comme vous sçavez) et n'ayant rien de meilleur à faire, j'ai fait une fille. Je sçai que vous m'allez dire que j'ai fort mal fait; mais, si vous aviez été à ma place, je crois (Dieu me pardonne) que vous en auriez fait deux ou trois. Dans ce paîs ci, il est tout aussi necessaire de faire voir des preuves de jeunesse, pour être reçüë parmi les beautez, que de montrer des preuves de Nobelesse pour être reçû parmi les Chevaliers de Malte. J'etois très fâchée de cette necessité; mais, remarquant qu'on me regardoit avec un grand air de mépris, je me suis mise enfin á la mode, et je suis accouchée comme les autres. Pour cette raison là, entre une infinité d'autres, je voudrois de tout mon coeur hâter mon retour, parce que je suis obligée absolument d'accoucher tous les ans, tant que je resterai ici. L'Ambassadrice de France s'en est donné à coeur joye; elle est accouchée et est encore grosse. Les Dames du païs n'estiment les femmes, que selon la quantit‹a› de leurs productions; et j'ai peine à leur persuader que c'est une excuse legitime d'être trois mois sans grossesse, parce que mon Mari est à cent lieuës de moi.

Je fais tous les jours des voeux pour revoir mon Roy, ma patrie, et mes amis. Je suis fort diligente de tout voir; je parle passablement la langue, et j'ai eu l'avantage de faire amitié avec des Dames Turques, et de leur être agreable; et je puis me vanter d'être la premiere étranger qui ait jamais eu ce plaisir. J'ai visité une Sultane veuve du feu Empereur; et par ce moyen, je suis instruite de tout le manege du Serail; elle m'a assuré que l'histoire du Mouchoir si bien cruë chez nous, n'a pas un mot de vrai.

J'ai attrapé un billet doux Turc que je vous porterai, et qui est veritablement si curieux, que je ne puis assez admirer la stupidité des Voyageurs de n'en avoir pas encore aporté en Europe. Ma chere Madame, Dieu vous donne (en phrase Turque) le plaisir qui vous contenteroit, et à moi celui de vous revoir.